DEVELOPMENT AND ASSESSMENT
OF SELF-AUTHORSHIP

DEVELOPMENT AND ASSESSMENT OF SELF-AUTHORSHIP

Exploring the Concept
Across Cultures

Edited by

*Marcia B. Baxter Magolda, Elizabeth G.
Creamer, and Peggy S. Meszaros*

STERLING, VIRGINIA

Published by Stylus Publishing, LLC
22883 Quicksilver Drive
Sterling, Virginia 20166-2102

Library of Congress Cataloging-in-Publication-Data
 Development and assessment of self-authorship : exploring the
concept across cultures / edited by Marcia B. Baxter Magolda,
Elizabeth G. Creamer, and Peggy S. Meszaros.—1st ed.
  p. cm.
 Includes index.
  ISBN 978-1-57922-367-0 (cloth : alk. paper)—
ISBN 978-1-57922-368-7 (pbk. : alk. paper)
 1. Learning, Psychology of—Cross-cultural studies—
Congresses. 2. Constructivism (Education)—Cross-cultural
studies—Congresses. 3. Cognitive styles—Cross-cultural
studies—Congresses. 4. Self-actualization—Cross-cultural
studies—Congresses. 5. Developmental psychology—
Cross-cultural studies—Congresses. I. Baxter Magolda,
Marcia B., 1951- II. Creamer, Elizabeth G. III. Meszaros,
Peggy S. (Peggy Sisk), 1938-
  LB1060D476 2010
  370.15′23—dc22

                                    2009026699

13-digit ISBN: 978-1-57922-367-0 (cloth)
13-digit ISBN: 978-1-57922-368-7(paper)

Bulk Purchases

Quantity discounts are available for use in workshops
and for staff development.
Call 1-800-232-0223

First Edition, 2010

10 9 8 7 6 5 4 3 2 1

In memory of Alex Meszaros,
whose flair for organization was crucial to the success of the Riva Conference

CONTENTS

LIST OF FIGURES AND TABLES

Figures

Tables

ACKNOWLEDGMENTS

This book is a product of a working conference, Self-Authorship Theory Development and Assessment Across the Lifespan and Across Cultures, held in Riva San Vitale, Switzerland in May 2008. A multiyear collaboration among Peggy S. Meszaros, Elizabeth Creamer, and Marcia Baxter Magolda exploring self-authorship in adolescence and college spawned the idea of bringing self-authorship scholars together to further refine the concept. The conference aimed to create the context for a small, cross-disciplinary, international group of scholars to share preliminary drafts of papers and engage in intense dialogue to advance theoretical understanding of self-authorship development and its assessment from adolescence through mature adulthood. An organizing committee including Peggy Meszaros, Elizabeth Creamer, and Anne Laughlin from Virginia Tech; Marcia Baxter Magolda from Miami University; Lisa Boes from Harvard University; and Jane Pizzolato from University of Pittsburgh (now from UCLA) conceptualized and coordinated the conference. The three editors of this volume proposed the book at the close of the conference and engaged participants in crafting a plan to refine the research papers we created for the conference.

We are indebted to Peggy Meszaros and her leadership in pursuing funding from three entities at Virginia Tech: the Institute for Society, Culture and Environment; Virginia Tech Outreach and International Affairs; and the College of Liberal Arts and Human Sciences. Their sponsorship of the conference enabled participants to attend by providing a stipend to cover lodging, meals, and some travel expenses. We are grateful for additional financial support from the Bok Center for Teaching and Learning at Harvard University. Daniela Doninelli, managing director of the Villa Maderni at the Virginia Tech Center for European Studies and Architecture, facilitated our on-site conference arrangements, providing everything from gourmet food service to medical assistance. Anne Laughlin, in her role as graduate assistant, coordinated identification of participants and on-site arrangements as well as travel, lodging, and registration. We also wish to thank Robert Kegan of Harvard University whose scholarship inspired our work. He was unable to attend the conference but graciously participated via a two-hour videotaped interview in Boston prior to the conference.

After the conference, the majority of participants refined their original conference papers for inclusion in this volume. We thank John von Knorring at Stylus press for his support of this work. We are particularly grateful for the conference participants' investment in dialogues across different perspectives and hope this book will engender similar dialogues among scholars interested in advancing the theoretical understanding of self-authorship.

PART ONE

THEORETICAL FOUNDATIONS OF SELF-AUTHORSHIP

Marcia Baxter Magolda

The three chapters in this section describe the theoretical foundations of self-authorship. Boes, Baxter Magolda, and Buckley articulate the foundational assumptions of constructive-developmental theory, subject-object relations, and holistic development as a backdrop for understanding the evolution of self-authorship. They integrate epistemological, intrapersonal, and interpersonal research strands to form a holistic perspective of self-authorship. Baxter Magolda then uses a narrative from her 22-year longitudinal study to illustrate possibilities of the evolution of self-authorship, exploring the interweaving of the three dimensions in shaping the evolution of self-authorship. Hamer and van Rossum's chapter summarizes their 25-year research program based on students in Dutch universities and higher professional education. They demonstrate similarities and differences between their learning and teaching conceptions and U.S. theories of epistemology and self-authorship. These chapters introduce the role of personal and contextual dynamics in the evolution of self-authorship, a topic that is addressed in greater depth in Part Two and Part Three of this volume.

This section raises two major theoretical questions. First, what are the possibilities and dilemmas in using a constructive-developmental theoretical approach to understanding self-authorship in multiple contexts and cultures? Second, what can be gained in refining our understanding of the evolution of self-authorship by exploring the interweaving of the three dimensions across multiple ages and cultures? These chapters offer multiple perspectives on these questions and set the stage for further exploration in the remaining sections.

I

FOUNDATIONAL ASSUMPTIONS AND CONSTRUCTIVE-DEVELOPMENTAL THEORY

Self-Authorship Narratives

Lisa M. Boes, Marcia B. Baxter Magolda, and Jennifer A. Buckley

Abstract: This chapter outlines the foundational assumptions behind self-authorship and constructive-developmental theory. The authors emphasize the multidimensional nature of self-authorship, integrating epistemology, identity, and relational theory. We use narratives from Baxter Magolda's and Boes's studies to portray the nature of self-authorship.

This chapter explores the theoretical foundations that have shaped theories of self-evolution and our understanding of the capacities of self-authorship, including constructive-developmental theory and subject-object relations. In particular, we examine three dimensions of adult development: (1) epistemological theories that concern assumptions about the nature and sources of knowledge; (2) intrapersonal theories that explore forms of identity development and self-definition; and (3) interpersonal theories that relate to how one constructs and participates in relationships. Drawing upon prior research, we offer an integrated theory and portrait of self-authorship and explore the ways this holistic perspective is relevant for adults with varying personal characteristics in different cultural contexts.

We distinguish the capacities of *self-authorship* from the broader theories of *self-evolution*. The term *self-authorship* refers to a phase of development within the lifelong process of self-evolution. Robert Kegan (1982, 1994) and Marcia Baxter Magolda (1992, 2001, 2009) define self-authorship as a holistic meaning-making capacity. Self-authorship is characterized by internally generating and coordinating one's beliefs, values, and internal loyalties, rather than depending on external values, beliefs, and interpersonal loyalties. Self-authoring individuals take internal and external responsibility for their thinking, feeling, and acting. In addition to seeing themselves as the creator of feelings, they can internally reflect on and hold conflicting or contradictory feelings rather than being subject to these changing emotions. Questions of personal integrity are important from a self-authoring perspective because individuals evaluate themselves based on internal standards.

From a self-authoring perspective, one can differentiate parts of self from parts of others and distinguish between roles and relationships. In relationships an internally generated sense of authority is a resource for setting limits, maintaining boundaries, and managing differences and different power positions that may exist within one relationship. For self-authoring individuals criticism is seen as one perspective among many, which can be evaluated based on one's own system.

To demonstrate the personal and contextual nuances in the evolution of self-authorship we use narratives of three young adults, Mike, Jane, and Dawn. Their stories illustrate the emergence of self-authorship as a developmental process and demonstrate the integration of the three developmental dimensions—epistemological, intrapersonal, and interpersonal—in the full achievement of self-authorship.

Foundational Assumptions of Constructive-Developmental Theory

The developmental concept of self-authorship builds on the work of Piaget (1952, 1965), the Swiss psychologist who studied children's reasoning and cognitive growth. Piaget identified four increasingly complex schemes that children develop through experience in order to understand the world and perform logical operations. Contemporary neo-Piagetian researchers have extended his work on abstract thought into adolescence and adulthood (Baxter Magolda, 1992, 2001; Kegan, 1982, 1994; King & Kitchener, 1994; Kohlberg 1969; Perry 1970). These theories of self-evolution are grounded in two sets of assumptions about knowledge and adult learning. The first is *constructivism*, which is based on the premise that people create knowledge through interpreting their experience, rather than knowledge being an objective truth that exists outside the individual (Lincoln & Guba, 2000; Piaget, 1952). Individuals make meaning in the space between their experiences and their reactions to them:

> The activity of being a person is the activity of meaning-making. There is no feeling, no experience, no thought, no perception, independent of a meaning-making context in which it *becomes* a feeling, an experience, a thought, a perception, because we *are* the meaning-making context. (Kegan, 1982, p. 11, italics in original)

Learning occurs as people make sense of the world through connecting new ideas with their existing understanding of the world in a process of constant revision. Constructivism provides a lens for understanding how adolescents and adults interpret and learn from their experiences because it focuses on the *meaning* that is made of the experience from an individual perspective.

The second assumption is that self-evolution has an underlying structure that is *developmental* in nature. Developmental theories provide frameworks for understanding qualitative differences between individuals and the transformative changes that occur in individuals over time. Developmental theory focuses not on *what* we know—the content of our thinking—but on the complexity, underlying structure, and pattern of meaning-making, or *how* we know. In constructivist theories the individual is an active change agent in growth and development. "These theoretical models share the conviction that individuals are consistently engaged in constructing knowledge, imposing meaning, organization, and structure upon experience" (Popp & Portnow, 2001, p. 55).

Kegan's (1982, 1994) constructive-developmental theory of self-evolution in adulthood describes these underlying structures as "the organizing principle[s] we bring to our thinking and feeling and our relating to others and our relating to parts of ourselves" (p. 29). Learning and growth are the products of the *transformation* of the underlying meaning-making structure rather than the accumulation of knowledge, skills, and *information.* What distinguishes movement from one structure to the next are relationships between what is "subject" and "object."

Subject refers to "elements of our knowing or organizing that we are identified with, tied to, fused with, or embedded in" (Kegan, 1994, p. 32). Subject is a basic principle that a person could demonstrate, but not tell you about. It is inseparable from the self. Object, on the other hand, is that which gets organized. It "refers to those elements of our knowing or organizing that we can reflect on, handle, look at, be responsible for, relate to each other, take control of, internalize, assimilate, or otherwise operate upon" (p. 32). As individuals gradually shift what they unconsciously held as subject to conscious consideration as object, the underlying structure of their meaning-making becomes more complex. As a person moves through these subject-object transitions, qualitative changes occur in one's reasoning patterns and how one views one's self and one's relationships. For example, persons who use what Kegan calls "socialized," or third-order meaning-making, organize their experiences in a manner that involves co-construction of self with others and ideas. From a socialized perspective, individuals have an abstract sense of self that is accompanied by a sense of loyalty to ideas, people, and groups with which one is identified. The socialized perspective relies on external authority for "standards, values, acceptance, belonging, and a sense of identity" (Popp & Portnow, 2001, p. 60). With the growing capacity to reflect on this co-construction and these external demands, what was subject moves to object and the self-authoring capacity emerges.

The capacity to be aware of one's socialization—to hold it as object—enhances one's ability to negotiate the effects of socialization (Abes, Jones, & McEwen, 2007; Torres & Hernandez, 2007). Baxter Magolda's (2001, 2009) longitudinal participants demonstrate the role of personal and contextual nuances that Kegan notes in the activity of meaning-making. Because individuals *"are* the meaning-making context" (Kegan, 1982, p. 11, italics in original), their personal characteristics play a significant role in how they interpret their experiences. Personal characteristics include personality traits (e.g., extrovert, risk-taker, task-oriented), socialization (e.g., gender, class, race or ethnicity, sexual orientation, faith tradition), and meaning-making structures. Baxter Magolda's participants' personal characteristics mediated how they engaged in the experiences they encountered in their personal, professional, and community lives (for an example, see Cara's story in Chapter 2 of this volume). Their personal characteristics also influenced the type of experiences that they sought out as well as how they interpreted all of their experiences. For example, those who used self-authored meaning-making were more open to considering new perspectives as a result of experience than were those who used externally defined meaning-making. Thus, the activity of meaning-making, and subsequently the journey toward self-authorship, varied widely among participants.

Self-evolution also varies according to people's life and work contexts. Baxter Magolda's participants experienced multiple work, family, and social cultures, or what Kegan refers to as holding environments. The degree to which these cultures offered challenges to participants' meaning-making and sufficient support to address these challenges shaped participants' growth. Participants who encountered more challenge than support struggled, whereas those who experienced minimal challenge stagnated. Conflicting expectations from various holding environments sometimes sparked development if support was available or if the person was at a point of readiness for transformation. Personal and contextual influences intersect such that the developmental journey can vary widely.

The role of personal and contextual influences in meaning-making informs the question of how self-evolution theories might relate to adults in multiple cultural contexts because many theories were generated from interviewing predominantly White American adults. Many constructive-developmental theorists explicitly advise against generalization (e.g., Baxter Magolda, 1992, 2001, 2009; Belenky, Clinchy, Goldberger, & Tarule, 1986; Perry, 1970) beyond their participants. Insight into how cultural influences shape meaning-making have emerged from studies involving adults who immigrated to the United States (Drago-Severson, & Berger, 2001; Helsing, Broderick, & Hammerman, 2001; Portnow, Diamond, & Pakos Rimer, 2001), bicultural individuals (Goldberger, 1996), adults and late adolescents from underprivileged socioeconomic classes (Belenky, 1996; Pizzolato, 2003), Latino/a college students (Torres & Hernandez, 2007), lesbian college students (Abes & Jones, 2004), and college students of color (King & Baxter Magolda, 2007). Although these studies reveal similar core meaning-making structures, patterns of self-evolution vary with personal and contextual influences. Further research, some of which is reported in this volume, is necessary to further explore the nature of self-evolution in general—and self-authorship in particular—in multiple cultural contexts. Studying the nuances of personal and contextual influences in self-authorship requires integrating the epistemological, intrapersonal, and interpersonal dimensions of development into a holistic conceptualization of the complexities of adult development.

Self-Authorship as Integrating Epistemological, Intrapersonal, and Interpersonal Development

This volume focuses on self-authorship as the integration of epistemological, intrapersonal, and interpersonal developmental dimensions. Rich traditions of research exist in each of these developmental arenas that inform theorizing about self-authorship. Although theorists in these traditions focus primarily on one dimension, many note relationships among the three dimensions. In this section, we synthesize these traditions and highlight how the three dimensions of development become integrated in self-authorship.

Personal epistemology considers how individuals come to know, the theories and beliefs they hold about knowledge, and the manner in which their assumptions about knowledge influence thinking and reasoning processes (Hofer, 2004; Hofer & Pintrich, 1997; Pintrich, 2002). Theories of epistemological development include assumptions about knowledge and its acquisition, descriptions about how knowledge is constructed as well as where knowledge resides, and explanations about the certainty, justification, and structure of knowledge (Baxter Magolda, 1992; Duell & Schommer-Aikins, 2001; Hofer, 2002; King & Kitchener, 1994; Perry, 1970). Several authors in this volume discuss epistemology in relation to the broader construct of cognition, in particular, King (Chapter 10) and Pizzolato (Chapter 11).

Most researchers who study epistemology conclude that a developmental progression occurs as individuals mature from adolescence to adulthood, particularly for those who attend college (e.g., Baxter Magolda, 1992; King & Kitchener, 1994, 2002, 2004; Perry, 1970). Across various research methodologies, samples, and study designs, there is agreement that individuals' views about knowledge progress from one in which knowledge is right or wrong to a position of relativism, and then to a position in which individuals consider knowledge grounded in context. At this stage, they actively construct meaning based on evidence and make commitments in a relative world. In most theories, these stages are hierarchical, with the successful attainment of one stage presumed to be a prerequisite for movement to the next stage (Hofer & Pintrich, 1997). Many theories assume this progression is irreversible as it involves structural changes in epistemic assumptions and one cannot return to a previous position because development alters perceptions and the structures for meaning-making (Pascarella & Terenzini, 2005).

Perry (1970), who studied American male college students in the 1950s and 1960s, offered the first theory of epistemological development and found connections among epistemological, intrapersonal, and interpersonal development. Perry described epistemological growth as a new form of responsibility in decision making, which involved accepting the limits, uncertainties, and dissolution of established beliefs. This new responsibility may also include relinquishing "the wish to maintain community in family or hometown values and ways of thinking . . . and most importantly the wish to maintain a self one has felt oneself to be" (p. 52). Even though Perry examined intellectual development, students in his study described different motives for their growth, some that related to their intrapersonal and interpersonal development, such as "a wish for authenticity in personal relationships; a wish to develop and affirm an identity" (p. 51). Furthermore, Perry observed the absence of an integrated description of personal development, and noted "as a strategy of growth it would seem to deserve prominent place, not only in a theory of cognitive development but also in consideration of emotional maturity and the formation of identity" (p. 110).

Likewise Belenky, Clinchy, Goldberger, and Tarule (1986), who expanded on Perry's work to study women's epistemological development, found intersections of epistemology, intrapersonal, and interpersonal development. Their study demonstrated that in each epistemological perspective women experienced a new context in which to consider issues of identity, relationships, and authority. In the earliest positions—silence and received knowing—women's sense of self was embedded in external definitions, and knowers sought gratification in pleasing others and measuring up to external standards because they lacked an authentic and centered self. The quest for self became primary in subjective knowing, but individuals lacked tools for expressing and supporting perspectives. They adopted procedural knowing, either in a separate or connected style, to deliberately analyze knowledge. Women integrated subjective and objective knowledge in constructed knowing—the final position—and considered questions of "how I want to think" and "who I want to be," and achieved the fundamental insights of constructivist thought that "*all knowledge is constructed, and the knower is an intimate part of the known* (Belenky, et al., p. 137, italics in original).

Many intrapersonal development theories also have a common emphasis on developing an internal, structurally mature sense of self as contrasted to an externally established identity that is determined by circumstances or internalized by early identifications with authority (Marcia, 1993). These theories are often associated with Erickson (1968), who outlined developmental stages that mapped internal biological and psychosocial changes and societal expectations. Erickson defined identity formation as a developmental task of adolescence, in which individuals develop a stable, consistent, and reliable sense of self and commitments. Initial studies of identity development based on men revealed a pattern of increasing autonomy and independence from others (Chickering, 1969; Erickson, 1968), whereas investigations of women indicated that the formation of healthy relationships was essential to achieving autonomy and interdependence (Chickering & Reisser, 1993; Josselson, 1987, 1996). Across these theories, individuals who formulated identities through exploration were more likely to develop a sense of self as distinct from others' perceptions, had the capacity to openly engage challenges to their views and beliefs, and experienced greater tolerance for uncertainty and increased capacity for growth and change.

Baxter Magolda's (1998, 2001) longitudinal study also demonstrated links among epistemological, intrapersonal, and interpersonal development. Participants who had expressed complex ways of knowing often struggled to use them until they developed complex ways of seeing themselves and relating with others. Most participants initially adopted externally defined expectations about who they should be without a full exploration and constructed their identities primarily through external forces. Participants needed to ground their internal sense of self by finding, listening to, and constructing an internal self-authored perspective as a source of personal identity and an internal compass to guide decisions about how they came to know. These self-authored voices became a source of knowledge and offered an internal perspective to use when deciding what to believe and how to view themselves. A similar process occurred interpersonally as relationships that had been constructed from an externally defined identity emphasized what others wanted, whereas relationships constructed from an internally defined identity included what the self wanted that was negotiated with others.

Other theories of holistic development also describe the intersection of epistemology, identity, and interpersonal development. One such model illustrates how meaning-making capacity interacts with the perceptions and salience of college students' multiple social identities, such as race, sexual orientation, religion, and social class (Abes, Jones, & McEwen, 2007). Participants who had complex meaning-making capacity were more capable of filtering contextual influences, such as family background, peer culture, social norms, and stereotypes, and determining how these contexts influenced their identity. Integrating these strands of theory, King and Baxter Magolda (2005) proposed that increased complexity in each dimension leads to intercultural maturity.

Kegan (1982, 1994) and Baxter Magolda (2001, 2009) explicitly articulated the intersections of these three dimensions in a holistic portrait of the evolution of self-authorship. To illustrate the foundational assumptions and integration of the three dimensions in the evolution of self-authorship, we use narratives from Baxter Magolda's 22-year longitudinal study (2001, 2009) and Boes's (2006) study with contemporary college students next.

The Evolution of Self-Authorship

The internal authority of self-authorship develops gradually as individuals extract themselves from depending on external authorities for their beliefs, identities, and social relations. Understanding the way in which people depend on external authorities is a necessary starting point for exploring the emergence from this dependence. We turn to Boes's participants to examine the ways of making meaning that precede self-authorship.

Following External Formulas: The Absence of Self-Authorship

The importance of making "right" versus "better" decisions was important to Mike, a college junior who was searching for summer work in either the financial sector or with a political campaign. He explained, "I take myself very seriously, and my future is important to me. I tend to be a perfectionist, and want to make the best decisions, so I get torn a lot. . . . I think it's important to make the right decision" (Boes, 2006, p. 161). In this process, Mike sought the advice of a former supervisor and political expert, saying, "I felt very obligated to leverage my [previous campaign] experience. When you work on a winning campaign you're supposed to leverage that. You're not just supposed to drop it" (Boes, 2006, p. 161).

After this meeting, Mike decided to pursue political work, although he then faced another choice: whether to travel with an "advance" team or to organize voter turnout in the "field." Mike considered what each position offered:

> [Working with the advance team] is a little more flashy and exciting. You're in a new place, you're kind of bossing people around. But . . . I'm interested in politics for politics. And [working in] the field is as grassroots politics as you can get. Working [with the advance team] is like concert promotion and is more fun, and certain people have said it would even be better to do. But everyone says that field work is a better way up the [political] ladder. (Boes, 2006, p. 162)

Although Mike could identify what was most important to him—"politics for politics"—he was significantly influenced by what "everyone says." The opinions and approval of external sources weighed on him because he wanted to make a choice that was perceived as good preparation for his future career. Mike's narrative illustrates the challenge of developing an internal sense of what is best to do in light of others' advice. Those who make meaning through following external formulas rely on those formulas for what to believe, how to construct their identities, and how to guide their social relations. They tend to privilege others' perspectives, to define themselves in ways that others will see as successful, and to act in relationships to gain others' approval. Mike's feeling of being torn between what he is "supposed to" do and his own sense of what is best highlights the limits of his meaning-making system and demonstrates that he has not yet developed self-authorship.

Crossroads: Emerging Self-Authorship

The transitional space between relying on external formulas and achieving self-authorship is the phase of the journey Baxter Magolda identifies as the crossroads (2001). This phase is characterized by meaning-making in the transition between the socialized mind and self-authorship. Jane, a 20-year-old Harvard student, daughter of Taiwanese immigrants and a participant in Boes's (2006) study, offers a window into this perspective:

> Jane: I have a boyfriend that my parents don't know about. So I've been seeing him since July of last year. That is a long time.
>
> Interviewer: Why don't your parents know about him?
>
> Jane: Because he doesn't go [to school] here. When people ask me like, where he goes, it's like, "community college." He grew up in a small town . . . and has four other siblings and his parents didn't finish high school and have [custodial jobs]. . . . He was originally going to go to Boston College or Northeastern or something like that. And then he decided like, no, I need to help my mom out with expenses. So he decided to join the Air Force instead. He tried to go back to school while he was in the Air Force, but then he kept on getting reactivated. Well, anyway, so now he's going to community college, and [working] at the same time. So with this is a person that I'm dating I think that there's a real class issue. I didn't know what it was for a long time. I just knew my parents probably wouldn't be happy that I wasn't dating

someone who was at Harvard or MIT. And then I realized it was a huge class issue. When I go home it's hard enough not putting people in cubbyholes and being like, so this is my Cambridge life, and this is home life. Ideally, I would want to integrate the two. But once again, it's like I'm being such a bad person by not introducing him to my parents. But I saw my brother go through so much when he started going out with his girlfriend that [my parents] didn't approve of, that I just . . . cost benefit analysis . . . .

Interviewer: So are you considering telling them?

Jane: So then I'm like okay, so maybe [I should tell] my parents. . . . I mean, they raised me for 20 years, and they are looking out for the best. And then my best friend's kind of like, "Well, you know, there's a time when you're going to come into disagreement with your parents and you're going to have to decide what you want to do. And this is a case in point, right? Every kid goes through this. You just have to decide." Right?

Jane discusses her dilemma in a way that demonstrates how the epistemological, interpersonal, and intrapersonal dimensions are integrated in the journey toward self-authorship. The conflict she is experiencing is between the values she is developing that are integral to her sense of self and the demands she experiences in the roles and relationships with her parents, friend, and boyfriend. Jane draws on her understanding of social class to conceptually frame and stand apart from these demands. She identifies the change she is trying to make and suggests that the source of the change needs to come from herself—an internal source. While she seeks support from a friend who encourages her to decide for herself, Jane also shares that she wishes to develop a more integrated sense of self that can resolve her external differences in expectations and demands between her college and home lives. Her recognition of one self constructed in her home context and another constructed in a school context, along with her desire to integrate the two, reflects the crossroads she traverses as her internal authority emerges.

Individuals in the crossroads have a tendency to take responsibility for others' expectations and feel guilty when they do not meet them. Recognizing this tendency and seeing an alternative way to frame others' expectations is crucial to movement out of the crossroads into self-authoring. Robert Kegan (personal communication, April 30, 2008) described a conversation with a client that illustrates these two ways of making meaning. The client reported dreading an upcoming conversation with colleagues because he expected to feel guilty about not meeting their expectations. Kegan described their interaction:

> There was a box of Kleenex between us. And so I said, "This is sort of the picture I get. . . ." And I pulled [one] out of the box, and I said, "This is what it is like when people pull their emotions out of the box of their self, and they pass it along in front of you. And you just can't help yourself, you just go (inhaling) . . . and there's another one (inhaling) . . . and you just keep taking them." For months afterward, he kept referring to this metaphor and by our being able to sort of laugh at it and put it out there (visualize it), he could say, "Yes, they put it out there, and it's ME who kind of . . . it is I who (reaches out) and gobbles it up." That raised a whole other possibility that you just let the thing float by. . . . "Yes, this is how you feel . . . yes, this is how you feel. . . ." It created this whole other possibility.

Initially the client was subject to others' feelings. The idea of letting others' emotions and expectations exist without absorbing and taking responsibility for them created the possibility of standing apart from them, or making them object. It created the possibility of self-authorship.

Self-Authorship

When internal authority moves to the foreground to mediate external influence, individuals become self-authoring. Dawn, a participant in Baxter Magolda's longitudinal study (2001, 2008, 2009), articulates finding her internal authority through her work in the theater:

> I have had opportunities to play more than one type of character. The thing that's involved in that is exploring different parts of yourself, learning about how many different types of people you are within yourself and being able to apply that to a script that someone has written. . . . The technique comes in as transferring all that is within you to this character, your abilities to speak the character's truth from, probably, your truth. (Baxter Magolda, 2001, p. 151)

Discovering parts of herself led Dawn to finding her truth, which in turn led her to be comfortable using her internal authority. In her mid-twenties she reported:

The more you discover about yourself, the more you can become secure with it. And that obviously leads to greater self-confidence because you become comfortable with who you really are. My confidence level is so much better than it ever has been. I'm more willing to express my ideas and take chances expressing my ideas . . . when you're confident, you are more willing to say, "This is my opinion; this is why I hold this opinion. You may agree with it or not, but this is what—with my mind I have formulated this opinion and that's how I think and feel." I'm not as afraid to be willing to say that because of what I am this is how I feel. . . . And I think self-awareness too, because you realize that it doesn't really matter if other people agree with you or not. You can think and formulate ideas for yourself and ultimately that's what's important. You have a mind and you can use it. That's the most important thing, regardless of the content of what your thoughts and opinions are. (Baxter Magolda, 2001, pp. 152–153)

Dawn expressed comfort with her identity that enabled her to express her ideas. Cognitively she recognized that she can construct her ideas using her own mind. No longer fearing others' perceptions, she is freer interpersonally to disagree with others. Self-authoring her knowledge, identity, and relationships helped her in coming out as she shared in her late twenties:

One of the biggest things was accepting the fact that my sexual orientation is out of the mainstream. It has taken me probably five years to feel solid. Now, I don't care if you know if I'm gay. It doesn't matter and this is who I am. That has contributed a great deal to how I see things and how I think. Getting to where I am now, the confidence thing; you know you have the inner strength to stand apart from the mainstream. I don't have to be a duck in a row, following what everyone else is doing. Whether it has to do with being gay or not. The best way I can explain it is learning to walk. You get stronger and finally run. It is a release, where you are willing to let go of clutter that people throw at you. (Baxter Magolda, 2001, pp. 182–183)

Dawn is clearly able to stand apart from others' expectations and express her internal authority. Although she uses being gay as an example, she suggests that having the inner strength to stand apart from the mainstream is actually a broader dynamic of letting go of clutter of all kinds to make up her own mind. Interviews with Dawn and her peers through their thirties led Baxter Magolda to identify three elements within self-authorship: trusting the internal voice, building an internal foundation, and securing internal commitments (2008).

Self-Authorship: Trusting the Internal Voice   Baxter Magolda's participants described a point at which they realized that although reality was beyond their control, they could control how they reacted to it. They recognized that they were responsible for interpreting experiences that happened to them by using and coming to trust their internal voices to decide how to feel and react. For Dawn, this took shape when she was diagnosed with multiple sclerosis at age 33. She described her reaction:

> For quite a long time I've been introspective, pursuing that knowledge of self, sense of self, spiritual centeredness—this has evolved over time, but the MS diagnosis accelerated it even more. I think it is fulfilling something that I've always wanted; never thought I'd get it quite this way. You follow the Tao of life, Zen moment, go with the flow, take on whatever comes your way—I always wanted that and I'm finally getting it. There are days when I don't have it, but for the most part I do. I'm trying to make something better out of myself and make the world a better place with me in it. I feel more deeply connected to my spiritual center than I ever have before in my life. . . . Finding the balance between [going with the flow] and me saying I have control over myself, not letting this condition get the best of me. Knowing how to make things happen and let things happen. When you find the balance between those things, life is spectacular. That is kind of a trust thing—trusting that you know yourself enough to dance that line. Know when to make something happen and when to let it happen. Trusting yourself that you know that space. I don't quite know myself enough to trust that yet. I'm working on it. I'm getting close. That deepest self-knowledge to know you can stay there at that middle point and have that balance. That is a constant process for me. To be able to say this is my life and it's on my terms; I love that. (Baxter Magolda, 2004, pp. xx–xxi)

Dawn's sense that she is close but doesn't quite trust herself to know this boundary reflects the fluidity she and her peers experienced in coming to trust their internal voices. Although it was a constant process, they began to build internal foundations when they felt they trusted their voices sufficiently to do so.

Self-Authorship: Building an Internal Foundation   Building internal foundations involved embracing one's personal characteristics and sense of self as a cornerstone for developing a philosophy of life. Dawn took up cooking in her twenties to supplement her meager theater income. In her early thirties, she began to realize her talents in cooking as well as other positive aspects of herself:

> I work magic in the kitchen, and my therapist would be so happy to hear me speaking in such really incredible terms about myself. Now I'm realizing too that what I've held onto all along is that it is very much a creative and artistic outlet for me, which is why I started cooking professionally in the first place because my theater work wasn't making me a lot of money and I had to support myself. I started cooking, and it's just like a huge opening to all of the wonderful things in life that I am. Also, opening to myself, being a wonderful person, and enough of this downplaying it. Life is short. You've got to celebrate every moment that you have. Part of that also has been like this acceptance, even three years into it, of the whole MS thing. I'm sure I denied it a little bit, but just accepting that it is a part of me. It does not have to rule my life in any stretch of my imagination. It will not rule my life. I just feel such a complete sense of settling into myself and everything about me. This is the most peaceful I have felt, I think, in a very, very long time, if ever, you know? But it had to be my willingness to change that, to stop the downplaying, to really just kind of embrace myself for all the amazing things that I can do. Even celebrating the little things that may not be necessarily categorized by some people as amazing but, like the fact that I get up every morning and ride 15 miles on my bike. That's pretty amazing in its own right. So there's been a big shift in that approach to myself and my life. (Baxter Magolda, 2008, pp. 276–277)

Dawn described consciously building a philosophy and an infrastructure for her life that afforded her stability and freedom simultaneously. Embracing her talents and MS, she built a framework from which to organize her career, relationships, and her sense of herself. Trusting her internal voice, she consciously constructed a philosophy through which to view life and interpret her experiences.

Self-Authorship: Securing Internal Commitments   Dawn and her peers articulated another shift: one from holding convictions in their minds to holding them in their hearts. They described this as stemming from living one's convictions so that they became second nature. Dawn framed it like this:

> It's starting to feel—more like wisdom than knowledge. To me knowledge is an awareness of when you know things. You know them as facts; they are there in front of you. When you possess the wisdom, you've lived those facts, that information so fully that it takes on a whole different aspect than just knowing. It is like you absorbed that information into your entire being. Not just that you know things. It is something deeper. Knowledge is brain—wisdom comes from a different place I feel like. Something deeper connecting with your brain so that you have something different to draw from. A point where knowing you are going to do something—the knowledge has a deeper level—internal, intuitive, centered in entire being, the essential part of you that just—makes the basic knowledge pale by comparison. (Baxter Magolda, 2007, p. 71)

Securing internal commitments helped participants cope with whatever challenges came their way. Simultaneously, it made them more open to growth, as Dawn described when discussing the relationship arena:

> I know what I want in a partner and what I need to bring to the table. These are the things that I need to work on. I still am kind of discovering how. Within myself I have been . . . safe. But then, when you have to deal with someone else and knowing that that's something that you want, I definitely would love to be in a long-term relationship, a very caring, open, nurturing, communicative relationship with someone. When you find someone who is that and you're not, it's like, okay, I got some work to do here. I'm pushed up against some big edges and, it's like, okay, you have a choice. You either stay here and be miserable or you can cross over and yes, it's scary, and yes, it's risky, but what's on the other side would be absolutely blissful. And so risk-taking has also been a big, big part of the last couple of months. It's like every big decision that I've made in the past couple of months has all led to other decisions, big decisions to be made and a lot of other things connecting. Once you decide to move the boulder, it's going to start rolling; that's the choice you made. You took the risk; you pushed it. . . . Everything that comes along with it, you just have to be there for. Getting specific about some very big things—my business and this relationship, moving. Making these big decisions has all just kind of created this . . . this chaos but it's a wonderful chaos. There's a connectedness and it's just not so much casting yourself into

the great beyond and whatever happens, happens. Now it's just like, well, let me do this, and then I'm going to watch what happens. It's more engaged and okay, now I'm going to do this, and I'm going to watch what happens. I'm just kind of moving through it seeing how everything's going to kind of settle down into place and it's great. (Baxter Magolda, 2009, pp. 64–65)

Dawn knew her internal commitments well enough to know what she wanted in a relationship. She also knew her areas for growth. She was secure enough to take risks, to move the boulder, and to stay engaged for what happened.

These narratives suggest that self-authorship emerges when external influence moves from subject to object. This transformation enables the internal voice to move to the foreground to mediate external influence on beliefs, identity, and relationships. Self-authorship evolves as one trusts one's internal voice, uses that trust to build an internal foundation of beliefs, identity, and relationships, and deepens those commitments over time with experience.

Expanding and Refining the Concept of Self-Authorship

This book is a product of a working conference, Self-Authorship Theory Development and Assessment Across the Lifespan and Across Cultures, held in Riva San Vitale, Switzerland in May 2008. The purpose of the Riva conference was to bring together scholars interested in further refining the concept of self-authorship across cultures. The constructive-developmental approach to self-evolution we have summarized here offers a foundation from which to do so because it emphasizes the interaction of personal characteristics and contextual influences as persons actively construct their knowledge, identities, and relationships. As we have noted here, the developmental trajectory from external to internal definition, or to self-authorship, routinely appears in both holistic studies of self-evolution and in studies that focus on a particular dimension of self-evolution. The process of making object the parts of one's thinking, feeling, and relating that were previously subject enables increasingly complex ways to know, view oneself, and engage in relationships. These foundational assumptions of constructive-developmental theory address the *structure* with which adults actively construct and reconstruct their interpretations of experience and thus do not specify the content of adults' meaning-making. Once adults come to trust their internal voices, the nature of those particular voices guides building internal foundations and securing internal commitments. Thus the constructive-developmental approach offers multiple possibilities for understanding the evolution of self-authorship in multiple personal and social contexts. Accessing how particular individuals make meaning in their personal and social contexts enables further study of the intersections of epistemological, intrapersonal, and interpersonal dimensions and how they combine to help adults self-author their lives. The remaining chapters offer multiple perspectives on the potential evolution of self-authorship.

References

Abes, E. S., & Jones, S. R. (2004). Meaning-making capacity and the dynamics of lesbian college students' multiple dimensions of identity. *Journal of College Student Development, 45*(6), 612–632.

Abes, E. S., Jones, S. R., & McEwen, M. K. (2007). Reconceptualizing the Model of Multiple Dimensions of Identity: The role of meaning-making capacity in the construction of multiple identities. *Journal of College Student Development, 48*(1), 1–22.

Baxter Magolda, M. B. (1992). *Knowing and reasoning in college: Gender-related patterns in students' intellectual development.* San Francisco: Jossey-Bass.

Baxter Magolda, M. B. (1998). Developing self-authorship in young adult life. *Journal of College Student Development, 39*(2), 143–156.

Baxter Magolda, M. B. (2001). *Making their own way: Narratives for transforming higher education to promote self-development.* Sterling, VA: Stylus.

Baxter Magolda, M. B. (2004). Preface. In M. B. Baxter Magolda & P. M. King (Eds.), *Learning Partnerships: Theory and models of practice to educate for self-authorship* (pp. xvii–xxvi). Sterling, VA: Stylus.

Baxter Magolda, M. B. (2007). Self-Authorship: The foundation for twenty-first century education. In P. S. Meszaros (Ed.), *Self-Authorship: Advancing students' intellectual growth, New Directions for Teaching and Learning* (Vol. 109, pp. 69–83). San Francisco: Jossey-Bass.

Baxter Magolda, M. B. (2008). Three elements of self-authorship. *Journal of College Student Development, 49*(4), 269–284.

Baxter Magolda, M. B. (2009). *Authoring your life: Developing an internal voice to meet life's challenges.* Sterling, VA: Stylus.

Belenky, M. F. (1996). Public homeplaces: Nurturing the development of people, families, and communities. In N. Goldberger, J. Tarule, B. Clinchy, & M. Belenky (Eds.), *Knowledge, difference, and power* (pp. 393–430). New York: Basic Books.

Belenky, M., Clinchy, B. M., Goldberger, N., & Tarule, J. (1986). *Women's ways of knowing: The development of self, voice, and mind.* New York: Basic Books.

Boes, L. M. (2006). Learning from practice: A constructive-developmental study of undergraduate service-learning pedagogy. Unpublished Doctoral Dissertation. Harvard University.

Chickering, A. W. (1969). *Education and identity*. San Francisco: Jossey-Bass.

Chickering, A. W., & Reisser, L. (1993). *Education and identity, second edition*. San Francisco: Jossey-Bass.

Drago-Severson, E., & Berger, J. G. (2001). "Not I alone": The power of adult learning in the Polaroid cohort. In Adult Development Research Group (Ed.), *Toward a new pluralism in ABE/ESOL classrooms: Teaching to multiple "cultures of mind"* (pp. 379–475). Cambridge, MA: National Center for the Study of Adult Learning and Literacy, Harvard Graduate School of Education.

Duell, O. K., & Schommer-Aikins, M. (2001). Measuring of people's beliefs about knowledge and learning. *Educational Psychology Review, 13*(4), 419–449.

Erickson, E. H. (1968). *Identity, youth, and crisis*. New York: Norton.

Goldberger, N. R. (1996). Cultural imperatives and diversity in ways of knowing. In N. R. Goldberger, J. M. Tarule, B. M. Clinchy, & M. F. Belenky (Eds.), *Knowledge, difference, and power: Essays inspired by Women's Ways of Knowing* (pp. 335–371). New York: Basic Books.

Helsing, D., Broderick, M., & Hammerman, J. (2001). A developmental view of ESOL students' identity transitions in an urban community college. In Adult Development Research Group (Ed.), *Toward a new pluralism in ABE/ESOL classrooms: Teaching to multiple "cultures of mind"* (pp. 77–228). Cambridge, MA: National Center for the Study of Adult Learning and Literacy, Harvard Graduate School of Education.

Hofer, B. K. (2002). Personal epistemology as a psychological and educational construct: An introduction. In B. K. Hofer & P. R. Pintrich, (Eds.) *Personal epistemology: The psychology of beliefs about knowledge and knowing* (pp. 3–14). Mahwah, NJ: L. Erlbaum Associates.

Hofer, B. K. (2004). Epistemological understanding as a metacognitive process: Thinking aloud during online searching. *Educational Psychologist, 39*(1), 41–45.

Hofer, B. K., & Pintrich, P. R. (1997). The development of epistemological theories: Beliefs about knowledge and knowing and their relation to learning. *Review of Educational Research, 67*(1), 88–140.

Josselson, R. (1987). *Finding herself: Pathways to identity development in women*. San Francisco: Jossey-Bass.

Josselson, R. (1996). *Revising herself: The story of women's identity from college to midlife*. New York: Oxford University Press.

Kegan, R. (1982). *The evolving self: Problem and process in human development*. Cambridge, MA: Harvard University Press.

Kegan, R. (1994). *In over our heads: The mental demands of modern life.* Cambridge, MA: Harvard University Press.

King, P. M., & Baxter Magolda, M. B. (2005). A developmental model of intercultural maturity. *Journal of College Student Development, 46*(6), 571–592.

King, P. M., & Baxter Magolda, M. B. (2007). *Experiences that Promote Self-Authorship among Students of Color: Understanding and Negotiating Multiple Perspectives.* Paper presented at the Association for the Study of Higher Education.

King, P. M., & Kitchener, K. S. (1994). *Developing reflective judgment: Understanding and promoting intellectual growth and critical thinking in adolescents and adults.* San Francisco: Jossey-Bass.

King, P. M., & Kitchener, K. S. (2002). The Reflective Judgment Model: Twenty years of research on epistemic cognition. In B. K. Hofer & P. R. Pintrich (Eds.), *Personal epistemology: The psychology of beliefs about knowledge and knowing* (pp. 37–61). Mahwah, NJ: Erlbaum.

King, P. M., & Kitchener, K. S. (2004). Reflective judgment: Theory and research on the development of epistemic assumptions through adulthood. *Educational Psychologist, 39*(1), 5–18.

Kohlberg, L. (1969). Stage and sequence: The cognitive-developmental approach to socialization. In R. A. Goslin (Ed.), *Handbook of socialization theory and research* (pp. 347–480). New York: Rand McNally.

Lincoln, Y. S., & Guba, E. G. (2000). Paradigmatic controversies, contradictions, and emerging confluences. In N. K. Denzin & Y. S. Lincoln (Eds.), *Handbook of qualitative research, second edition* (pp. 163–188). Thousand Oaks, CA: Sage.

Marcia, J. E. (1993). The status of the statuses: Research review. In J. E. Marcia, A. S. Waterman, D. R. Matteson, S. L. Archer, & J. L. Orlofsky (Eds.), *Ego development: A handbook for psychosocial research* (pp. 22–41). New York: Springer-Verlag.

Pascarella, E. T., & Terenzini, P. T. (2005). *How college affects students: A third decade of research.* San Francisco: Jossey-Bass.

Perry, W. G. (1970). *Forms of intellectual and ethical development in the college years: A scheme.* Troy, MO: Holt, Rinehart, & Winston.

Piaget, J. (1952). *The origins of intelligence in children.* New York: International Universities Press.

Piaget, J. (1965). *The moral judgment of the child.* New York: Free Press.

Pintrich, P. R. (2002). Future challenges and directions for theory and research on personal epistemology. In B. K. Hofer & P. R. Pintrich, (Eds.). *Personal epistemology: the psychology of beliefs about knowledge and knowing* (pp. 389–414). Mahwah, NJ: L. Erlbaum Associates.

Pizzolato, J. E. (2003). Developing self-authorship: Exploring the experiences of high-risk college students. *Journal of College Student Development, 44*(6), 797–812.

Popp, N., & Portnow, K. (2001). Our developmental perspective on adulthood. In Adult Development Research Group (Ed.), *Toward a new pluralism in ABE/ESOL classrooms: Teaching to multiple "cultures of mind"* (pp. 43–75). Cambridge, MA: National Center for the Study of Adult Learning and Literacy, Harvard Graduate School of Education.

Portnow, K., Diamond, A., & Pakos Rimer, K. (2001). "Becoming what I really am": Stories of self-definition and self-expansion in an Even Start ABE/ESOL family literacy program: A developmental perspective. In Adult Development Research Group (Ed.), *Toward a new pluralism in ABE/ESOL classrooms: Teaching to multiple "cultures of mind"* (pp. 229–377). Cambridge, MA: National Center for the Study of Adult Learning and Literacy, Harvard Graduate School of Education.

Torres, V., & Hernandez, E. (2007). The influence of ethnic identity development on self-authorship: A longitudinal study of Latino/a college students. *Journal of College Student Development, 48*(5), 558–573.

2

THE INTERWEAVING OF EPISTEMOLOGICAL, INTRAPERSONAL, AND INTERPERSONAL DEVELOPMENT IN THE EVOLUTION OF SELF-AUTHORSHIP

Marcia B. Baxter Magolda

Abstract: This chapter uses an in-depth longitudinal narrative to illustrate how the three dimensions of development intertwine in the development of self-authorship. It serves as an in-depth introduction to the nuances of the evolution of self-authorship and how personal and contextual dynamics create divergent pathways toward and through self-authorship.

How do I know? Who am I? What relationships do I want? These were the driving questions for my longitudinal study participants in their twenties (Baxter Magolda, 2001). Their questions reflect the epistemological, intrapersonal, and interpersonal dimensions of development that Robert Kegan integrated in his holistic portrayal of adult development (1994). Consistent with Kegan's theory, my participants initially considered these questions on the basis of what others wanted from them. In their early-to-mid-twenties, they realized the need to answer these questions with their own internal voices. The capacity to internally generate beliefs, identity, and social relations is what Kegan called self-authorship. One participant, Mark, articulated it like this:

> Making yourself into something, not what other people say or not just kind
> of floating along in life, but you're in some sense a piece of clay. You've been
> formed into different things, but that doesn't mean you can't go back on the
> potter's wheel and instead of somebody else's hands building and molding
> you, you use your own, and in a fundamental sense change your values and
> beliefs. (Baxter Magolda, 2001, p. 119)

How do young adults use their own hands to mold themselves? My 22-year
longitudinal study offers one window into how participants work with the
three driving questions to author their own lives.

Longitudinal Study Methodology and Method

The self-authorship theory advanced here emerged from my 22-year longitudinal study of young adults from the age of 18 to 40 (Baxter Magolda, 1992,
2001, 2004, 2008, 2009). I interviewed 101 traditional-age students
(51 women and 50 men) when they began college in 1986 at a Midwestern
public university in the United States (see Baxter Magolda, 1992). Gradual
attrition resulted in 30 participants, all of whom are Caucasian, by year 20.
Of these 30, 2 were single, 1 was in a committed relationship, 26 were married, and 2 were divorced (one of whom remarried). Of these 18 women and
11 men, 22 had children. Seventeen pursued advanced education: 12 had
received master's degrees in such fields as education, psychology, social work,
business administration, and economics. One had completed seminary,
2 received law degrees, 1 completed medical school, and one completed a
doctorate. The most prevalent occupations were business (16) and education
(9). Areas within business included sales in varied industries, financial work,
public services, real estate, and marketing. Educators were primarily secondary school teachers and administrators; one was a college professor. The
remaining participants were in social work, law, homemaking, and Christian
ministry.

The annual interview focused on important experiences that participants
identified; it became increasingly unstructured (Fontana & Frey, 2000) as the
study progressed and addressed what life had been like for participants since
we talked last. These conversations included discussion of the dimensions of
life they felt were most relevant, the demands of adult life they were experiencing, how they made meaning of these dimensions and demands, their

sense of themselves, and how they decided what to believe. Inherent in these dimensions was their sense of themselves in relation to others and their involvement in significant relationships. Interviews were conducted in person during college and by telephone after college; each interview ranged from 60 to 120 minutes.

My constructivist approach to this project and the partnership developed over the course of the study with participants (Baxter Magolda, 2004) both mediate data interpretation. My constructivist approach led to using grounded theory methodology (Charmaz, 2003; 2006) to analyze interview responses (see Baxter Magolda, 2008). Credibility of the themes and patterns is enhanced through prolonged engagement to build trust and understanding and also through member checking to assure accuracy of interpretations. I negotiate interpretations with study participants; because I have shared publications with them for 20 years they are in a position to share their perspectives on my theorizing. Full involvement with participants yields rapport and understanding. Yet Clandinin and Connelly emphasized that researchers "must also step back and see their own stories in the inquiry, the stories of the participants, as well as the larger landscape on which they all live" (2000, p. 81). Thus I bring my perspective to the interpretation yet simultaneously work to be true to participants' narratives, and from the two, construct a theoretical perspective.

Longitudinal Study Overview

Interviews during participants' twenties yielded three phases of the journey toward self-authorship integrating epistemological, intrapersonal, and interpersonal dimension: following external formulas, the crossroads, and self-authorship (Baxter Magolda, 2001). These three phases, each representing a qualitatively different meaning-making structure, portray a gradual shift away from authority dependence toward a capacity to internally generate one's beliefs, identity, and social relations. Most participants followed external formulas when they left college and encountered the crossroads when their internal voices collided with external influence in their mid-twenties. Most spent the majority of their twenties extracting themselves from external influence to move toward self-authorship. Interviews with participants through their thirties yielded a refined portrait of three distinct elements of self-authorship—trusting the internal voice, building an internal foundation, and securing internal commitments (Baxter Magolda, 2008, 2009). Trusting the internal voice to determine one's beliefs, identity, and social relations—the initial element—becomes the basis for using the internal voice to build and solidify an internal belief system, which is the intermediate element. Refining and strengthening this internal system so it becomes the core of one's existence is the focus of the advanced element. Personal characteristics and contextual dynamics mediated developing self-authorship. Participants portrayed this journey as weaving back and forth, rather than taking a straightforward path to securing internal commitments. This chapter explores how the epistemological, intrapersonal, and interpersonal dimensions of development intersect throughout those three elements.

Epistemological, Intrapersonal, and Interpersonal Intersections Within Building a Self-Authored System

The longitudinal narratives reveal that progress toward self-authorship varies by developmental dimension. Often participants achieved growth in one dimension ahead of the corresponding growth in the other two. Participants seemed to "default" to different dimensions depending on their personal and contextual dynamics. Because these nuances are visible through in-depth narratives, one participant, Cara, is featured here to illustrate the interrelationships of the three dimensions within the process of building a self-authored system. The experience of other participants is woven around her story because Cara represents only one of many pathways through self-authorship. I begin Cara's story as she moves toward self-authorship because the intersection of her three developmental dimensions there sets the stage for her process of building a self-authored system.

Emerging Self-Authorship

Cara pursued a master's and doctoral degree during her twenties. Her classes were male-dominated and her male peers did not listen to her. She hesitated to interrupt others in class to participate and was careful not to do anything that would interfere with her educational progress. She encountered a major dilemma, however, when one of her professors expressed a romantic interest in her. She did not want to ruin her chances of working in his area, but she did not want to get involved either. Cara processed this experience via her epistemological dimension, analyzing past relationships and making a conscious choice to stop allowing others' interests to interfere with her own. She found it difficult to implement, however, because of her interpersonal desire for others' approval. She knew on an epistemological level that she should listen to herself, saying, "If I went on my own intuition, I'd be okay" (Baxter Magolda, 2001, p. 117). She elaborated:

> I have had a good intuitive sense but have ignored it; like in bad relationships; my stomach would clench. Then I'll have a logical or rational voice saying you are overreacting. In the last 6 months I've tried to listen more; spend 20 minutes a day and do breathing exercises. I'm used to reading to help myself; read what someone else is saying rather than listening to myself. The more I'm listening to myself, I'm allaying fears. I'm paying more attention to me than to other people; I made some bad decisions as a result of listening to others. I changed my major to psychology to stay at home with a boyfriend. I'm sick of listening to others! Then I think, "I'm not honest with my parents." When am I going to stand up for myself and be who I am instead of trying to make people happy? Or share my reaction when people aggravate me? Expression of my opinion is seen as creating a scene. If a man said it, they'd say "good point." I am at the start of this—not there—an invisible force, I'm pushing against it, what is it? I don't know, but it is there though. (Baxter Magolda, 2001, p. 118)

Cara consciously worked on her intrapersonal dimension by trying to listen to and cultivate her own voice. The invisible force was external influence, which was made important by her interpersonal construction of wanting validation from others. If expressing her opinion meant risking others' disapproval, she hesitated to do it. She found support to transition into trusting her own voice from her boyfriend, whom she did marry. She also found a female mentor—a first in her educational journey—who encouraged her to listen to herself. Commenting on a quote on this woman's desk, Cara reported:

> Patricia has a quote on her desk—"care too much about others' opinions and you'll be their prisoner." I obsess about what others think. I think about that, and say to myself, "don't go there." My husband said the same thing to me, but I discounted it. Of course he is going to say that, he's married to me. It had more validity to me coming from her. (Baxter Magolda, 2001, p. 118)

Cara again turned to her epistemological dimension to analyze her intrapersonal and interpersonal assumptions. She recognized herself in the quote and kept reminding herself not to "go there." At the threshold of self-authorship, Cara continued to push against the invisible force. This conversation within her would continue across her thirties as she tried to get her intrapersonal, interpersonal, and epistemological development in sync with one another.

Trusting the Internal Voice

In her late twenties Cara completed her doctorate, married her boyfriend, and started kickboxing. Each of these contexts helped her come to trust her internal voice. Talking about finishing her dissertation, she offered:

> I feel like a somewhat different person than I did in my twenties. In high school, I was somewhat confident; in my twenties this took a downward swing, and now I'm back to how I used to be. [There were] different pieces up in air—they've come together now. Finishing my dissertation was great—some say it was a let down; it was huge to me. Part of it was getting rid of the negative, getting it off my back; and feeling like, "I did this." It was not the dissertation itself, but just to finish it. I was visualizing myself as—not fragmented as in schizophrenia—just not grounded. I felt like every external event, I was swaying with it. I don't feel that way anymore. I'm not impervious to external events, but I don't feel that way. (Baxter Magolda, 2001, p. 163)

Cara recognized she had been swaying with reality instead of managing her reactions to it. The dissertation process had been complicated by external realities: the death of one of her committee members and departmental changes. Finishing her dissertation felt like a major accomplishment that strengthened her perception of her professional competence. Acquiring a faculty position upon graduation also affirmed her competence, although she shared that gender issues continued to haunt her. Reflecting on her struggle to value her own voice, she said:

> I was thinking about how important the gender stuff really was for me, just how my perception of being female and what that means played into my insecurities. Part of my reactions related to how I saw being female, and I think I saw that as in some ways weak or less strong or impressive. It is funny all the comments I've had on my size, yet I am not a willowy crea-

ture in any way. For example, on my interviews people commented on my size! In one place I met a man who said, "Wow, you are a lot smaller than I thought you would be from your vita!" Someone else in the middle of my job talk said that I could stand to gain some weight. No one asked my husband about his marriage status and most places asked me and wanted to know what my spouse did. It's like being female is often emphasized and not in ways that are necessarily empowering.

Cara knew these questions and comments were inappropriate, yet they still complicated her work to empower her own voice. Cara took up kickboxing in part to resolve some of her sense of not being strong enough:

> I started kickboxing—martial arts. I have always run and jogged—but this made me feel like a stronger person. . . . It has given me better self-confidence and presence—all my life people have commented on my height. This related to the whole "I'm weak, not professional enough" aura. That has helped me feel more confident. I carried a 150-pound woman around the gym; I weigh 110. . . . I'm not as weak as people make me out to be. Apparently I had a ton of aggression I didn't realize. (Baxter Magolda, 2001, pp. 164–165)

Cara's physical strength helped her build her sense of professionalism and overcome the perception of weakness that was constantly reinforced by (primarily) men in her work contexts. She used her keen epistemological sense to analyze the effects gender bias had on her internal voice, which allowed her to reconstruct her intrapersonal sense of herself.

Cara's marriage was another major factor in her trusting her own voice. Her husband's perception of her was crucial:

> One thing is like when you marry someone—he is so grounded and stable—when someone loves you despite your flaws—it is an amazing thing. That is how he is. [Our relationship] isn't without problems, but when someone loves you unconditionally, it is healing. It changed my perception of myself. How I see that he sees me, has changed how I see me. Isn't there a theory of social reflection? See yourself mirrored in other people. (Baxter Magolda, 2001, pp. 163–164)

As was typical, Cara used her epistemological bent in framing her relationship in the theory of social reflection. Her husband's unconditional love helped Cara alter her intrapersonal sense of herself—something she had been working at with minimal support for a decade. She reported that the dilemmas associated with marriage (e.g., religious differences, expectations of in-laws) also strengthened her internal voice. Faced with making important decisions in this context, Cara was able to bring her values and convictions to the forefront to react to reality. Her internal voice was strong enough to express these convictions even if it meant she and her husband had to work through them. She had finally pushed past the invisible force when she was able to express what she viewed as the truth and no longer sway to external events. This strengthening of her intrapersonal dimension translated to more open relationships in which she was willing to disagree and work out conflicts. Doing so helped her see more clearly who she was. Thus her intrapersonal and interpersonal dimensions mutually reinforced each other.

Cara's professional success, strong relationship with her husband, and personal work (both mental and physical) she had engaged in during her twenties helped her trust her internal voice. Her epistemological shift to realizing she could control her reactions to external realities led to her intrapersonal work on listening to her own voice, which in turn strengthened her interpersonal dimension. As was the case with many participants, Cara struggled more in the interpersonal dimension and in personal contexts to hear and trust her internal voice. Cara's strength in analyzing her situation was a positive factor in trusting her voice enough to begin building an internal foundation.

Building an Internal Foundation

Cara's faculty position offered a context for continued professional success and for synthesizing dimensions of her development into an internal foundation in her thirties. Despite the typical hesitations about teaching effectively and publishing enough to achieve tenure, Cara excelled at academic life. She stuck to what she thought was right in the face of disagreement. Colleagues coached her to cut her hair and dress like a man to garner more respect in the classroom. She refused, saying,

> I'm not a man. I don't want to look like a man to have students respect me and I don't want to act like a drill sergeant to have some kind of control over the classroom. So that's been kind of annoying.

An even bigger issue was her university's attitude about changing student grades to avoid student complaints. As a new faculty member she was advised to raise her grades, and she reported that in general she gave grades that were higher than what she thought appropriate, in order to be consistent with the university grading culture. She reported one situation in which she felt doing so was wrong. A student harassed her and two of her students who worked with him on a project. She reported:

> He told me he had a really bad temper and if I didn't change a grade he didn't know what he'd do about it. In the college people said, "Well, next time you'll know just to raise his grade when they complain," and so I'm sure he's done this before and gotten away with it. I dug my heels in.

From an epistemological standpoint Cara thought his behavior was wrong. Her intrapersonal determination not to be pushed around strengthened her motivation to act on her internal foundation even when that did not yield others' approval. These professional dilemmas helped Cara clarify and solidify her internal foundation and demonstrated that her interpersonal development was more closely aligned to the other dimensions.

Cara's personal life also contributed to building her internal foundation. Her professional goals and personal life intersected as she worked to clarify her internal feelings about having children. At 33, Cara struggled both mentally and physically with having children. On the one hand, Cara wanted children, in part because she felt time was getting away from her. On the other hand, she was not sure she was ready. Cara relied on her epistemological bent to explore her internal feelings about whether she wanted children:

> I don't want to wake up when I'm forty-five and think, "I wish we would have had kids." It really worries me that that will happen. Or we could adopt—that sounds like a really good idea to me—yet when I talk to other people who really want kids, if they couldn't have kids they would need therapy. I'll think why am I not like that? Why don't I have that urge? I don't feel like I have it like they do and I'm not sure why that is. There are other women close to my age that I've met now in the academic community, so we're all kind of the same like that, and I wonder why. Is it like the job that's made us like this? I just got a Ph.D. I worked all this time and maybe it's a selfish thing, but the idea of giving up some of that freedom sounds awful to me . . . .like, do I have

like any female hormones in me? That's been something I've been thinking about a lot. (Baxter Magolda, 2009, p. 235)

Here Cara used her epistemological framework to analyze her intrapersonal sense of herself as an academic and possibly a mother. She also analyzed how her feelings played out in interpersonal settings:

> My parents really want a baby, and I'm the only child, so I'm the only one they're going to get. When I talk about adoption, they just look crushed. I talked to them the other night and said: "Look, to have a baby we might have to go all the way to in vitro, which I just don't know if I'm willing to do. I'm not that desperate for a baby." And they look at me like, "Well, it can work. We know lots of success stories," not really hearing what I'm saying. (Baxter Magolda, 2009, p. 236)

> Also the reaction of some of my female friends, who could not wait to quit their jobs to have babies and they were excited that was kind of a bonus of having a baby, whereas I'm thinking, "Ooh, how does that impact my career?" I live in this academic world here, and then I'll go back home and see my friends there and it's completely different. The men and women separate and go off in different groups, and the women talk about babies, and the men talk about things that I really want to be talking about. It's kind of like switching who I am . . . not who I am, but just being a different side of me maybe.

Cara was struggling internally to reconcile who she was (her intrapersonal dimension) with what others wanted from her (her interpersonal dimension). I asked Cara how her internal struggle related to our earlier conversations about extracting herself from external expectations. Her immediate reaction was:

> Oh no! I'm back, aren't I?! It's really true. Professionally, I feel really competent or at least confident in what I'm doing. But I don't know why I don't have that same confidence about this. . . . I do think part of it's a need or a desire to really connect with other people. I do feel uneasy when I don't have that kind of connection, and this is one way [to connect]. . . . I have two grandmothers that are alive still and . . . my grandfather died last October, and one of the oddest reactions I had was I felt so sad that we hadn't had a baby by then for him to meet. And I got in this panic where I was like, "OK, we have to have a baby so [the grandmothers] can meet him or her." Well, when I thought this out, having a child for your grandparents? Because this would make them so happy? I get the

sense from my parents that they're hoping that that happens, too, which is really nutty. I realize it's nutty, but yet at the same time, I can still feel that kind of pressure to make them happy. (Baxter Magolda, 2009, pp. 236–237)

Cara's immediate reaction conveys her epistemological capacity to reflect on her own development and recognize the gap between her professional and personal confidence. She takes responsibility for her need for connection, a reflection of both her intrapersonal and interpersonal dimensions. She acknowledges that emotionally she would like to please her grandparents, yet epistemologically she recognizes this as "nutty" decision making. Cara's thought process suggests that she is cycling back to trusting her internal voice in the personal arena, particularly as it relates to having children. At the same time, she still has her internal foundation from which to reflect on this process.

Cara's internal foundation was both crucial and continually challenged a year later when she had surgery for endometriosis, a condition she figured out through Internet research and then confirmed with her doctor. This prompted her to assume she could not become pregnant, but then she became pregnant unexpectedly and had a miscarriage. She reported feeling depressed despite continued professional success. When I asked why, she offered:

> I don't even know. I just feel like I don't know what I want to do. I don't know if I want to have children or not. I feel like I have to now make that decision because of my age, and now that it's an option. Before I didn't even think it was really an option so it really wasn't that much of a struggle. It's interesting, too, about the kid. We did three ultrasounds before the miscarriage. If you see it, you really connect with this thing. I still am really pro-choice. It's not a small issue for me; it's pretty big. You see the ultrasound and you're like, "Oh." It's really weird because I'm connecting, yet I would still argue this now, but especially in the past, but it's not a baby. But then you're grieving for something, but really at the stage that I had the miscarriage, it was still really small, I mean an inch. Really it's a huge sense of loss. You almost feel kind of hypocritical, for in the past, people would say, "It's a baby," you know, "How can you get rid of a baby?" I'm like, "It's not a baby." And then now that was me. But it's also different; I wasn't making a choice. (Baxter Magolda, 2009, p. 238)

Cara had to reevaluate her feelings about pregnancy now that it was an option. She also had to reevaluate her pro-choice beliefs. She remained committed to that belief although she recognized through her own intraper-sonal feelings the grief associated with a miscarriage. The epistemological and intrapersonal dimensions of her internal foundation sustained her through this traumatic experience. As she noted, the interpersonal dimension was always the hardest to manage:

> We did tell some people. And everyone was so happy, this huge deal in our families, huge celebration, and then all my girlfriends that have children that I told . . . just really happy and wanted to talk to me all the time. And I realized . . . this goes back to the connection thing . . . .how much more in common I suddenly had with them. It was just like this big celebrating time, and then how crushed my family was when I had the miscarriage. So, it's getting in the way of my knowing what I want because I feel so much pressure that part of me wants to react to that and say, "I'm not having chil-dren," almost in a reaction—you can't push me into doing this. So it's childish. It's a huge issue. What kind of decision making is that? But there's always so much noise around me that I'm having a hard . . . which is some-thing I think I've always struggled with . . . like pushing that out to see what I really want. So, I mean it's the same struggle I've had, but now it's in this situation. And then I'm mad that it's even an issue, you know? It irri-tates me that this is taking up so much of my time and my worry. (Baxter Magolda, 2009, p. 238)

The interpersonal noise was still a challenge for Cara. The other parts of her internal foundation were clouded by it, but they were strong enough for her to be aware that she had to push the noise out to hear herself. She was irri-tated with herself that she reacted the way she did to external pressures.

Another miscarriage further complicated the choice of biological child-birth or adoption. Cara described the effects that led her and her husband to choose adoption:

> The first one didn't hit us the same way, but that second one just really hit us hard and we talked about just wanting to be parents, just wanting a child, not needing a genetic connection and that we were just tired of risk. It's just that we wanted the baby.

Their analysis of the risks of pregnancy and their lack of need for a genetic connection led Cara and Jack to pursue adoption. She described the effect of this process on her relationship with her parents and her sense of herself:

> It was a very huge growing up process for us even though we were thirty-six. It was kind of a separation from them that was probably needed, like we are doing this. You are either on board or you're not, which we've really never done before firmly. (Baxter Magolda, 2009, pp. 238–239)

Cara's internal foundation had been in her head for a long time; she could construct it epistemologically prior to being able to act on it intrapersonally. She worked to refine her internal voice to determine her beliefs, identity, and relationships. She altered her thinking about how to respond to external pressures and realigned her life choices with her internal voice, even as she struggled to know it clearly in the case of having children. Her struggle illustrates that building an internal foundation often requires revisiting trusting one's internal voice. Synthesizing her epistemological, intrapersonal, and interpersonal development into one internal foundation formed a cohesive system through which she could coordinate parts of her self into an integrated, consistent whole. This enabled her to act on her internal foundation from her heart and to move toward securing her internal commitments.

Securing Internal Commitments

Cara was securing her internal commitments at the age of 36 when she and Jack brought their new 11-month-old daughter home from China. Cara was surprised that Melissa initially gravitated toward Jack and had to force herself to stop researching attachment disorder. Although the baby's hesitancy to connect with her bothered Cara, she was secure enough to be patient and allow Melissa to adjust. Despite these challenges, Cara found the adoption and the baby to be an amazing experience that altered her perspective:

> [Before] anything at work could just send me flying over the edge, every success, every negative, politics, meetings, just tunnel vision. Having Melissa, just, [I'm] completely much more mellow about those things. I'm still very achievement driven, but when you go to China, you see this is how people are living. This is what's going to happen to other babies. And then you see this child. She says and does the funniest things, and she's loving, and then it's like this whole other part of your brain is firing, like okay, Cara,

open your mind. There is joy; there is fun . . . you can be playful. You don't have to be so serious. I'd say more balanced, which I had wanted, and just like a kinder, more patient than I was. I care more about my own behavior. I can't come home on some rampage from work because that affects her, so I have reined in a lot of those negative traits . . . worked on disciplining my mind more than I have before. I focus more on positives because I would like her to have a more optimistic view. I think about the way I was raised, what I would like from that and what I don't want, and that's kind of pushed me to behave differently. (Baxter Magolda, 2009, p. 239)

Visiting China and experiencing Melissa gave Cara perspective in the epistemological, intrapersonal, and interpersonal arenas. She recognized that her daily problems were not worth getting worked up about relative to bigger issues. The joy she felt with Melissa allowed her to be less serious. Her desire to do what was right for Melissa also caused her to evaluate and monitor her own behavior. Her change of perspective permeated how Cara saw herself and her interactions with others. This led her to "speak what I think is true, regardless of [others'] reactions." Given her longstanding struggle with this issue, I asked to what extent she could do so. She replied:

Ooh, that's more, definitely, than I used to be able to, and actually to a point where I feel good about it, not that there's not room for growth. Before when I said things, part of what I was doing was wanting something back, wanting to be validated, wanting to be heard and then I would think there would be no point in saying anything unless people changed based on what I said. I don't need that as much anymore, or I can catch myself sometimes getting into that cycle. Say what you think, where you are, regardless of whether they agree or not because I would rather others do that for me too. I would rather know them even if they don't agree. I can't imagine running around thinking the only way I would speak would be to change somebody. Part of it too . . . sometimes I don't need to speak. Before, I think, I needed to engage more than I do now. I needed to battle it out. [Now] I'm more able to hear other people. I can just listen. I don't need to say anything, or I don't need to say as much as I used to. So, that's kind of paradoxical. Like on one hand, I feel more free to speak, but then on the other hand, I don't feel like I have to speak or I don't regret as much not saying things sometimes because I think there's a time not to say anything. So, that has been big, and it feels a lot better to not care as much or to not obsess and ruminate, not that I don't do those things, but not like I used to. (Baxter Magolda, 2009, pp 239–240)

Cara was able to reflect on her earlier intrapersonal need for validation. Securing her internal commitments led to speaking to let others know her rather than to change their thinking. This epistemological shift reduced her need to battle it out and heightened her ability to listen. Changes in her intrapersonal and epistemological dimensions led to a greater sense of mutuality in her interpersonal relations.

Cara had found her way through the external noise in her life. I asked how she came to this point:

> There was something about the process of Melissa. I'm not exactly sure what it was except that at some point I just realized . . . it kind of just hit me on the head. Part of it was simply you are 36 years old, and now you have your own child, and this isn't just going to happen naturally unless you start making this kind of emancipation happen. You just have to do it. It is something that I really worked on, that I thought like I'm going to go one of two ways. I'm either going to be driving myself crazy and worrying and anxious all the time, or I'm going to try to get a grip on this, and so part of it was deliberate and doing some work on that. (Baxter Magolda, 2009, p. 240)

Cara seemed to default to her epistemological dimension when it was time for a change. She recognized that she needed to do something to control her anxiety and she took action to work on it. She anticipated my next question about what this work involved:

> I was doing a paper on moral disengagement and ethics. Why do we do bad things and the processes that we go through to disengage ourselves. That's what got me on this track. I started reading these books, seven perfections according to Buddhism. That's where I learned the calm my body, calm my mind thing. One thing that I've really picked up from this book that I just love was this notion of how do you stay engaged with people or the world without being smothered by it, but then also not fully disengaging? That really fascinated me because that really spoke to me about how I saw myself as somebody that would get so engaged, be crushed under the weight of whatever it was and then the only way I knew how to get out of that was to disengage completely. And so this perspective that you could actually have some equanimity, like you could sit and be engaged with somebody or something and let it go up and down, but you didn't have to come with it, and that was just huge, like the biggest, wow, that's obvious, but it wasn't.

You don't need to be so extreme. You can stay engaged and still be separate. (Baxter Magolda, 2009, pp. 240–241)

Previously Cara lost herself when she was highly engaged in something and then felt the need to disconnect to keep from drowning. Now that she had a strong internal foundation and was securing her internal commitments, she was ready to consider the possibility that she could separate herself from that intense level of engagement. She began to listen to a series of tapes in the car called *Your Buddha Nature.* Tensions with her family enabled her to hear the messages in the tapes:

> Things were really intense emotionally with our families. I felt like I was drowning in my family and I felt panicked. At that point, it was very intense, and that kind of worked its way in and I really heard it, and I'm not sure I would have heard it before. I started doing yoga. . . . It's about balance and breathing. So there's something that goes on with yoga. I don't know what it is, but for me, at least, there is something about working through that same set of postures over and over, progressing through them and then doing really difficult postures. You do the same postures on each side, which is very balancing, and then some days you can do one thing, but then the next time you can't do it. It's maddening at first, like I could just do this, but it's like life. Go back and forth. You make progress; you come back. You make progress; you come back. (Baxter Magolda, 2009, p. 241)

Cara deliberately worked on calming her mind and her body in order to manage the intensity of all her emotions. She used insights from Buddhism and yoga to keep herself grounded in her internal foundation. She made conscious decisions from her epistemological foundation to create the intrapersonal self she desired and the relationships she wanted. She used this approach in parenting, teaching, and interacting with her colleagues. She also used it to stay grounded through the trauma stemming from a violent murder of a member of her extended family. Throughout this tragedy, Cara reported, "when I would feel myself getting sucked that way or angry at what they were doing, I was able to get re-centered" (Baxter Magolda, 2009, p. 241). Living her internal commitments even in the most challenging circumstances was possible because they had become the core of her being. Like many participants, Cara had blurred the boundaries of the epistemological, intrapersonal, and interpersonal dimensions such that her internal commitments seemed second nature. Yet Cara's analogy of making progress and going back captured the cyclical nature of participants' journeys. Returning to build trust in the internal voice was common while participants built their internal foundations, and returning to reconstruct some aspect of the internal foundation was typical while they secured internal commitments. As they secured internal commitments, they became increasingly open to listening to others because of their own personal security. Thus rethinking one's beliefs, self, and relationships became an ongoing quest.

Relationships Among Dimensions

Typically participants had a default, or a "home," dimension that was in the foreground of how they constructed their lives. Some, like Cara, used the epistemological dimension as their initial means of analyzing their circumstances. Others who were highly self-reflective used their intrapersonal dimension, and those who were highly relational used their interpersonal dimension. Those who relied heavily on the epistemological dimension privileged the "How do I know?" question. Cara's conscious decision in graduate school to stop allowing external realities to control her, her long quest to look inside to determine whether she wanted children, and her use of thinking to calm her mind and body are examples of defaulting to the epistemological dimension even when the issues are entangled in the intrapersonal and interpersonal dimensions.

In contrast, Dawn's intrapersonal default led her to privilege the "who am I?" question. As a theatre professional she was always looking for her internal voice to bring to her characters. As she came to trust her internal voice in the intrapersonal realm, it helped her build her belief system in the epistemological realm. Like Cara and many others, Dawn struggled with the interpersonal dimension as it lagged behind the others for her. When interpersonal crises arose, she turned to her intrapersonal analysis and epistemological beliefs to work through them.

Some participants' interpersonal dimension was in the foreground of their development and often overwhelmed movement on the other dimensions. For example, Kurt focused heavily on relationships because he relied on others' perceptions for his self worth. He was aware of the dilemmas this created, yet it took him the decade of his twenties to strengthen his internal voice sufficiently to put others' perceptions in the background. He used his epistemological and intrapersonal dimensions to work through this to resolve the significant problems it created in his work as a supervisor.

Regardless of which dimension was in the foreground, participants typically constructed their beliefs epistemologically before being able to integrate those into their identity intrapersonally; in other words, convictions were in their heads before they could live them in their hearts. Even when crises emerged from the intrapersonal or interpersonal arenas, participants often initially dealt with them epistemologically. Making decisions about what to change was usually a precursor to doing the intrapersonal and interpersonal work to implement the change. This implies that the epistemological dimension is necessary to process beliefs about self and relationships. Achieving self-authorship in the interpersonal dimension seemed to be the most challenging for participants.

Securing internal commitments required integration of all three dimensions. Most participants experienced progress in one dimension that then created tension in another, prompting them to actively work on the dimensions that were lagging behind. For example, Cara's frustration with her professor led to her awareness of her obsession with what others thought about her (an interpersonal issue). Her conscious decision to stop allowing others to control her thinking (an epistemological construction) led her to work on listening to herself (the intrapersonal dimension). She routinely used her epistemological dimension to sustain her intrapersonal dimension as she struggled with the interpersonal dimension. Many participants, including Cara, found that using their internal voices was often easier in work than it was in personal life. It was not until all three dimensions became integrated that participants were able to act on their internal foundations consistently across contexts.

Collectively the longitudinal narratives reveal multiple possibilities for how the epistemological, intrapersonal, and interpersonal dimensions of development intersect as participants moved through trusting their internal voices, building internal foundations, and securing their internal commitments. Gaining access to multiple pathways through the three elements based on participants' default dimension and how they move among the dimensions to respond to the questions of their lives offers a rich perspective of how self-authorship may evolve.

References

Baxter Magolda, M. B. (1992). *Knowing and reasoning in college: Gender-related patterns in students' intellectual development.* San Francisco: Jossey-Bass.

Baxter Magolda, M. B. (2001). *Making their own way: Narratives for transforming higher education to promote self-development.* Sterling, VA: Stylus.

Baxter Magolda, M. B. (2004). Evolution of a constructivist conceptualization of epistemological reflection. *Educational Psychologist, 39*(1), 31–42.

Baxter Magolda, M. B. (2008). Three elements of self-authorship. *Journal of College Student Development, 49*(4), 269–284.

Baxter Magolda, M. B. (2009). *Authoring your life: Developing an internal voice to meet life's challenges.* Sterling, VA: Stylus.

Charmaz, K. (2003). Qualitative interviewing and grounded theory analysis. In J. A. Holstein & J. F. Gubrium (Eds.), *Inside interviewing: New lenses, new concerns* (pp. 311–330). Thousand Oaks, CA: Sage.

Charmaz, K. C. (2006). *Constructing grounded theory: A practical guide through qualitative analysis.* Thousand Oaks, CA: Sage.

Clandinin, D. J., & Connelly, F. M. (2000). *Narrative inquiry: Experience and story in qualitative research.* San Francisco: Jossey-Bass.

Fontana, A., & Frey, J. H. (2000). The interview: From structured questions to negotiated text. In N. K. Denzin & Y. S. Lincoln (Eds.), *Handbook of qualitative research, second edition* (pp. 645–672). Thousand Oaks, CA: Sage.

Kegan, R. (1994). *In over our heads: The mental demands of modern life.* Cambridge, MA: Harvard University Press.

3

LINKING LEARNING CONCEPTIONS TO SELF-AUTHORSHIP AND BEYOND

Rebecca Hamer and Erik Jan van Rossum

Abstract: We link our six-stage model of students' views on learning and good teaching to epistemological models. We place self-authorship with our fourth learning-teaching conception. Each way of knowing forms an epistemological ecology in a temporary but fairly robust balance of many closely interrelated beliefs, learning approaches and outcomes.

Some 25 years ago we first published a five-stage developmental model of learning conceptions, linking the qualitatively different ways that students perceive the meaning of learning (learning conceptions) to study strategies and the quality of learning outcomes (van Rossum & Schenk, 1984). By the end of the 1980s, our studies on students' views on good teaching led to expansion into a six-stage developmental model of linked conceptions of learning and good teaching (van Rossum, Deijkers, and Hamer, 1984; van Rossum, Deijkers, and Hamer, 1985; van Rossum and Taylor, 1987) and over the decades we refined it further. The six-stage learning-teaching conception model presented in this chapter (van Rossum & Hamer, 2004; in press) is based on the views on learning and teaching of over 600 students in Dutch universities and higher professional education, collected over almost three decades. We link this six-stage model to major developmental epistemological models that each draw heavily on Perry's seminal publication (Perry, 1970), primarily the "ways of knowing" described by Baxter Magolda (1992, 2001) and Belenky, Clinchy, Goldberger, and Tarule (1997), and the broader approach taken in Kegan's (1994) model of orders of consciousness.

We propose that learning and teaching conceptions describe an essentially identical development as the previously mentioned epistemological models, relating a similar progress along at least three dimensions: epistemology, interpersonal relationships, and the sense of self (intrapersonal). This chapter not only links our model to self-authorship, but it also offers an alternative perception of self-authorship as a stage within epistemological development. We further propose that this development is more complex than the three-pronged advancement along the dimensions defined previously, introducing the concept of an epistemological ecology; a dynamic system of closely interrelated beliefs, approaches, and outcomes in a precarious, but often self-correcting balance. Finally, we close with the proposition that it is possible to link the models discussed here to adult intellectual development.

Epistemological Ecologies: Perspectives in Precarious Balance

In research, quite often assumptions are made regarding what drives intellectual development. For instance, the literature on self-authorship focuses on the three dimensions mentioned earlier. Elsewhere, distinction is made between peripheral and core beliefs, with the latter more fundamental to development (Hofer & Pintrich, 1997). Finally, some epistemological research implies probable causal directionality based on little else than apparent logic. For example, when Hofer (2001) suggested that beliefs regarding knowledge underlie the preference for a particular learning environment, directionality is assumed from epistemology to learning and teaching. However, in other research (e.g., van Rossum & Hamer, in press; Hofer, 2004) students indicate that a more constructivist learning environment "forces" them to change their views on (good) teaching and learning, making them realize that knowledge may be something else than they thought before, implying just the opposite causal direction.

We propose that personal epistemology, learning and teaching conceptions, learning approaches and outcomes, motivation, assessment conceptions, self-confidence, and conceptions of self are closely intertwined. This system of closely interrelated beliefs, approaches, and outcomes moves as one dynamic whole and each temporary balance influences the way people see the world at a particular moment in time. In a sense this complex system seems to behave like an ecology. This notion of an epistemological ecology implies that to perturb a way of knowing sufficiently to cause a considerable change of structure—a new balance, a higher order of consciousness, in short an expanded awareness—it is necessary to put substantial pressure on as many aspects of the current ecology for as long as possible, while providing a supportive environment conducive of change in the desired direction.

A Developmental Model of Students' Learning and Teaching Conceptions

Learning conceptions play an important role in students' study behavior because "we view the world through the lenses of our conceptions, interpreting and acting in accordance with our understanding of the world" (Pratt, 1992, p. 204). In 1979, Roger Säljö used the phenomenographic method devised by Ference Marton, and found that five categories were sufficient to describe the views on learning prevalent within a heterogeneous group of respondents. The six stages of our model—the first five of which were initially based on Säljö's five learning conceptions (Säljö, 1979)—are listed in Table 3.1 (van Rossum & Hamer, 2004; in press).

The six stages of this model consist of two groups of three. The first three are basically reproductive and quantitative in nature: learning lacks real personal involvement; knowledge remains unchanged by the learner, and vice versa. The next three stages are characterized by more constructivist views on learning and teaching; knowledge is constructed by the learner and the learner's self becomes increasingly involved with what is learned. The basic

TABLE 3.1
Van Rossum and Hamer's Six-Stage Model of Learning Conceptions

Learning Conceptions	Säljö's Original Labels
1. Increasing knowledge	Learning as the increase of knowledge
2. Memorizing	Learning as memorizing
3. Reproductive understanding/ application or Application foreseen	Learning as the acquisition of facts, procedures et cetera, which can be retained and/or utilized in practice
4. Understanding the subject matter	Learning as the abstraction of meaning
5. Widening horizons	Learning as an interpretative process aimed at the understanding of reality
6. Growing self-awareness	

nature of these stages has been confirmed by our own work (e.g., van Rossum, Deijkers, & Hamer, 1985; van Rossum & Taylor, 1987; van Rossum and Hamer, 2004) and that of others (e.g., Marton et al., 1993) and these stages can be found for university as well as higher professional education.

In our model, we discuss the commonalities with other epistemological models by stage. Within the literature on self-authorship, (e.g., Baxter Magolda, 2001) development is described as proceeding along three dominant dimensions, or storylines: epistemological, interpersonal (relationships), and intrapersonal (sense of self). The epistemological storyline is captured in our learning conceptions. The interpersonal storyline underlies the development in teaching conceptions, namely in the description of the relationship with authority. Aspects of the intrapersonal storyline can be found in both types of conceptions, with the learning conception focusing on increasing awareness of the self in learning, and the teaching conception focusing on the development of a student-teacher relationship characterized by equality and mutuality.

Learning-Teaching Conception 1: Increasing Knowledge—Imparting Clear/Well Structured Information

For Ones[1], learning is not reflected upon: it is simply something "everybody does," like breathing. Ones seem not to understand the meaning of the question, and responses often take the form of a list of activities or synonyms.

> It's to increase your knowledge . . . you kind of start with a small bag and there is not much in it, but then the longer you live, the more you fill it up. (Säljö, 1979, p. 13)

Although the complementary view on teaching is not found very often in higher education, students with this learning conception view teaching as the transfer of knowledge. The role of the student is minimal and the teaching-learning process is defined entirely by the teacher. As Femke says:

> Good teaching to me is presenting the subject matter to be learnt in such a way that it is not too dry (presented with humour if possible). The subject

---

[1]For convenience, we refer to the students at a particular level of epistemological development by a capitalized numerical. This means that Ones refers to students who view the world from the perspective of the first learning–teaching conception, etc.

matter needs to be explained well and presented in a well-organised way. Resulting in a situation where further learning by oneself does not lead to problems due to sometimes disorganised and unintelligible teaching. (van Rossum and Hamer, in press)

This epistemological position is characterized by a lack of reflection and a lack of awareness of self, neither learning nor the learner are considered something to think about, they just are. We feel that silence, as found by Belenky and colleagues (1997), comes closest to this learning conception; in particular we recognize the lack of words "that suggested an awareness of mental acts, consciousness or reflection" (Belenky et al., 1997, p. 25) leading to responses that seem to ignore the question. In addition, the relationship (or interpersonal) aspect of silence—(total) obedience to authority—seems an extreme expression of the first teaching conception. The lack of storyline-awareness Kegan (1994) finds characteristic of the first order of consciousness can be recognized in these students' atomistic and relatively arbitrary listing of aspects related to learning. From an epistemological ecology perspective, the characteristic nonreflective and atomistic view of Ones is also found in their motivation to learn, their perception of knowledge, understanding, and application, influencing their study behavior, which in turn is reflected in the quality of learning outcomes. Ones often mention wanting "to know a lot"; collecting knowledge as if it were merely an accumulation of fixed and external items. Understanding is seen as understanding each word and each sentence, application is seen as matching fixed knowledge to reality. We have linked this way of knowing to Biggs' unistructural level of learning outcomes (Biggs, 1979; van Rossum & Schenk, 1984).

Learning-Teaching Conception 2: Memorizing—Transmitting Structured Knowledge, Acknowledging Receiver

To Twos, learning is equal to memorizing and the ability to reproduce what is memorized, usually in a school test setting. Like Ones, Twos see learning in quantitative terms: learning more is being able to reproduce more.

Well, it's to learn what's in the books. In principle it means to learn in order to be able to answer the questions which the teacher gives you. (Säljö, 1979, p. 14)

However, Twos also show a budding awareness of not having to learn every-thing, being able to make a selection of the facts to be memorized: the first signs of reflection, if not on the quality of what you learn, then at least on the quantity. For Twos, teaching must be clear, orderly, efficient, entertain-ing, and must include opportunities to ask questions, implying a limited type of student-teacher interaction in a still very teacher-dominated environment. Anne elaborates:

> I detest it when a teacher shows contempt because you just happen to be not that good in this particular subject. A little bit more attention is more useful than remarks such as "you won't ever learn."

> I really dislike lectures when there is no opportunity at all for students to say something. I don't always need to say something, but the idea that it is possible is agreeable.

> Having a chat or a bit fun occasionally, and for the rest a decent lecture, consequently not too much disruptions.

> (van Rossum & Hamer, in press)

Although the teacher in this conception is still dominant, students want to be recognized as the recipients of the message, and—for example, through posing questions—become a little more involved. Baxter Magolda's absolute knowing also "translates into learning methods that focus on acquiring and remembering information" (1992, p. 37). This fits seamlessly with the main focus of Twos, who are extremely dependent on the teacher to provide the correct clues, correct explanations, and the correct environment to learn. In a sense, although Twos begin to see themselves as learners, listening to the voices of others (the teacher) is dominant. Belenky and colleagues (1997) related this way of knowing—received knowledge—to Perry's dualism (Perry, 1970) in which things are either right or wrong, and teachers, as sources of truth, know the (only) right answer to each question.

For Kegan (1994), the increased complexity of thinking at this second order of consciousness is expressed in that independent elements now become part of a set of related elements—a durable category. In the complex-ity of the second order, understanding takes on the character of a linear nar-rative, a recounting of a string of events (what happened) at a concrete level; application is seen as reproducing what is learned. In van Rossum and

Schenk (1984), learning outcomes related to this level of thinking were found to be multistructural (Biggs, 1979). Such outcomes often take on the form of a recounting of a text as completely as possible; a catalogue (or string) of conclusions "it shows . . . it also . . . it also. . . ."

Learning-Teaching Conception 3: Reproductive Understanding/ Application or Application Foreseen—Interacting and Shaping

For Threes, the process of learning is selecting and memorizing those facts, procedures, ideas, and so on that *may* prove useful later in life. Learning and understanding both are interpreted as being able to apply what is learned in the future. Respondents value this process over the—in their eyes—inferior process of memorizing only for (school) tests. Both aspects are present in the following quote.

> Well I think of learning plain facts which you select from your head more or less that is, as regards studies . . . , but then it is . . . I mean you have to be able to use it if, let's say if you find yourself in a similar situation to the one you were in earlier or if it reminds you of it, then you should be able to pick out the correct facts so to say or the correct way to proceed. (Säljö, 1979, p. 15)

The major focus of learning is still quantitative and reproductive, and neither the learner nor what is learned is changed in any way.

Teaching for Threes is characterized by teacher-dominated discussion, up-to-date examples, cases from practice, and an enthusiastic teacher who shapes and motivates the students using positive and negative feedback. As Jeroen says:

> [In good teaching] lectures need to be short and to the point, be more like a discussion group. Furthermore topics need to be current and connected to practice. I found the Promotion Management lectures were best, because there cases from practice were discussed in relationship to the literature. Following this, a short case—related to the topic addressed in the lecture— was given as an assignment to be made in small groups.

> [An ideal teacher is] a teacher who uses a lot of examples from practice and connects these to the literature, and he/she should invite discussions during the lecture so that sufficient interaction takes place. In addition, I feel it is important that a teacher motivates students for his subject using his

enthusiasm: I feel humour is very important in lectures. Furthermore, it is important that a teacher gives feedback to his students in a positive way. This means not only emphasising the negative, but also evoking the best in his students. (van Rossum and Hamer, in press)

This view on teaching is characterized by a wide range of elements displaying a Three's growing need for involvement in the teaching-learning process and an emergent independence within the student-teacher relationship. Threes attach a lot of importance to being heard, giving them the opportunity to express their opinions. They feel any opinion is as good as any other, linking this learning-teaching conception firmly to Perry's position 4a, multiplicity (Perry, 1970) and to Baxter Magolda's notion of "the emerging voice" that may be used to express a personal opinion characteristic of transitional knowing (Baxter Magolda, 1992). In her 1992 model, understanding is strongly related to the (reproductive) application of knowledge, as it is for Threes. Transitional knowers and Threes feel the need for increased interaction in the classroom, such as working in groups (peer-peer interaction) or group discussions (teacher-student interaction). However, this increased involvement is confined within the teacher's ultimate responsibility for the learning process. In Belenky and colleagues' (1997) subjective knowledge we see the same parallel existence of listening to the voices of others and listening to one's inner voice. When describing subjectivists' views on learning and teaching, they emphasized their preference for learning from direct experience, and for personal involvement with the subject matter, which is very similar to Threes' preference for experiential learning, simple application, and sharing personal opinions.

The shaping aspect of Threes' preferred teaching is consistent with the focus on socialization as one of the main themes of Kegan's third order of consciousness. Kegan illustrates the difference between third and fourth order education as a difference between socialization and command of a discipline (or ideology), warning that socialization may lead to "education for inauthenticity, since one learns the right moves and the right words but accomplishes no 'inside out' [fourth order] mastery of the locality's discipline" (Kegan, 1994, p. 289). Threes' preference for interaction and group discussion, as well as for formulating a personal opinion fits nicely within the third order of consciousness. When asked to "think for yourself," Threes feel they only need to express their opinion. Such opinions need not be grounded in inquiry and evidence. Threes also have difficulty differentiating opinions from the holder of the opinions: at this level one is (embedded in) one's opinion and to deny an opinion's validity is to deny the person.

Learning-Teaching Conception 4: Understanding the Subject Matter— Challenging to Think for Yourself/Developing a Way of Thinking

In our perception, the move to Four represents a major shift in perspective on knowledge and learning. Kuhn (1991) found that probably about half of the adult population with higher education would have experienced this shift at some point in their life. Of all the students from whom we have collected learning and teaching conceptions over almost three decades, less than a quarter could be categorized as Fours at any time. This shift is a *watershed*: the focus shifts from taking in ready-made things (facts, procedures) existing "out there" to constructing meaning. Säljö (1979) described this shift as follows: "Learning is no longer conceived of as an activity of reproducing, but instead as a process of abstracting meaning from what you read or hear" (p. 16). Whereas the process for this learning conception is reaching understanding, through relating ideas within the subject, collecting various viewpoints on the studied material, and so on, the product of this conception is the internalization of a "way of thinking." We feel that this is one of the espoused goals of higher education with its emphasis on the intellectual ability to think coherently, logically, and analytically: an approach to thinking (as a skill) aimed at arriving at an "informed view" (Beaty et al., 1997, p. 156) based on real understanding of the subject matter. See the response below:

> [To] have a process of thought that sort of "sets in motion" when you look at something . . . looking at something new in a far more logical way, and seeing the steps and the moves towards arriving at some sort of conclusion . . . learning is thinking clearer. . . . Perhaps it is just the skill you have learned of thinking more coherently. (Beaty et al., 1997, p. 159)

That this way of thinking goes beyond reproduction is clear from Sara's view on applying your knowledge to solve problems:

> I also saw that what you had learned could not always be applied in a standard way. But the idea behind it could. That made me look at things differently. . . . You come to the conclusion that there are no standard solutions to problems . . . [and] there are no standard problems with matching solutions. (van Rossum & Hamer, in press)

Fours prefer teachers who: (1) challenge students to (start to) think for themselves, (2) encourage students to realize that multiple informed approaches and solutions to problems are possible, (3) encourage and coach students to develop "a way of (disciplinary) thinking" through (4) a less formal—confidence building—interpersonal relationship (Morgan & Beaty, 1997). In Hester's words:

> [Good] teaching invites students to think for themselves about the theory the teacher provided. . . . [The ideal teacher] is a coach/counsellor while the students do assignments/discuss a particular subject. He/she is open to new/other views/explanations of theory and stimulates students to think about the theory and to do something with it. (van Rossum and Hamer, in press)

Fours have become active participants in the teaching-learning process. Student and teacher both focus on understanding and finding solutions within a particular discipline (building expertise). Many aspects of Baxter Magolda's (1992) independent knowing can be identified here; students begin "to think for themselves" and discover the validity of their own distinctive voice. They realize that most knowledge is uncertain, and consequently authorities lose the exclusive ownership of it. Everybody may develop a point of view based on a set of arguments using the rules of the discipline. The matching way of knowing of Belenky et al. (1997) is procedural knowledge.

Kegan (1994) linked his fourth order of consciousness to taking charge of an intellectual discipline and to constructing systems (e.g., a discipline, ideology) containing rules and methods for generating, judging, and relating its parts. Here disciplines "are public procedures for relating to third order constructions" (Kegan, 1994, p. 286). This interpretation displays considerable overlap with Labouvie-Vief's intrasystemic level of thinking where the individual is able to "coordinate the elements that comprise a single abstract system" (Labouvie-Vief, 1990, p. 69). Furthermore, this level is very similar to Perry's position 4b or our learning-teaching conception 4, in the sense that the core lies in learning to think for oneself and developing a systemic way of thinking. Kegan links the concept of personal authority or self-authorship to this capacity to think for oneself.

Self-authorship is a key term in Kegan's 1994 model of orders of consciousness. In 2002 in an interview with Debold, Kegan described that self-authorship involved becoming "the writer of a reality that we then are faithful to" (Debold, 2002, quoting Kegan, p. 150). However, Kegan put self-authorship in perspective when he stated that "the capacity of mind that permits a measure of personal authority in one's learning is the same capacity that would permit a learner the cognitive sophistication to master the knowledge-generating and knowledge-validating processes of an intellectual field or discipline" (Kegan, 1994, p. 285). Kegan stated that self-authored learners see a discipline or ideology as "a method, procedure or system of interpretation for reflecting on hypotheses, evaluating values and validating knowledge" (1994, p. 286). The disciplinary boundary Kegan put on self-authorship and on the fourth order of consciousness is further elaborated where Kegan observed that some constructivist teachers may end up over-asking and confusing their students when they deliver "a message about the limitations of ideology and systemic procedure," thereby "transcending the fourth order" (1994, p. 292). And again (1994, Table 8.1, p. 291) Kegan limited self-authorship to a "discipline's system or systems for creating [disciplinary] knowledge, generating, regarding, evaluating, and relating [third order] inferences" (p. 291). This led us to link self-authorship to one, and only one, level of thinking or way of knowing: learning-teaching conception 4. This is also why we argue that here we go beyond self-authorship, as we proceed to describe the remaining two constructive learning-teaching conceptions.

Learning-Teaching Conception 5: Widening Horizons—Dialogue Teaching

At this level another boundary is crossed, and only a very small proportion of our students experienced this change. Taking all our studies together, about 6% of our students were categorized as Fives at any time. Säljö observed that for Fives learning acquired a more personal meaning as opposed to the relatively technical view of learning in the previous stage.

> What's most important really, that's the connection between what I read and what I do and see otherwise during the days. I guess I have discovered this in some way, I guess it's the strategy. I've worked a little bit with problems like these in companies. . . . I mean with problems of learning and teaching new things and then I have tried to . . . well if you don't see connections between what you read and your own situation, not very much will happen really. In some way I think I've found out that you learn things twice somehow. The first time could have been at school really, the second time is the connection, I mean it becomes conscious in some way. (Säljö, 1979, p. 18)

Marton and colleagues (1993) and Beaty and colleagues (1997) expanded on Säljö's original interpretation of the fifth learning conception, referring to notions such as broadening one's outlook on things, opening one's mind, widening horizons, or looking "at the world with those eyes" (Beaty et al., 1997, p. 156). In our opinion, this conception of learning, with its truly rela-tivist flavor, matches Perry's fifth position (Perry, 1970) and Baxter Magolda's contextual knowing (1992). Gwen included the personal aspect, the ongoing process of widening horizons and a discipline-relativist way of knowing in her response:

> As you hear more people's opinions, you piece together what you really think. Who has the valid point? Whose point is not valid in your opinion? And come to some other new understanding from a more dimensional per-spective. . . .
>
> I realized that it is ongoing learning and that every time you think you are comfortable and think you understand—for me, those are always the times when I try to shake things up again so I'm forced to push a little further. (Baxter Magolda, 1992, p. 59 and 61)

Fives appreciate a teaching environment based on dialogue, where teach-ers and students become equal partners in the mutual construction of knowledge. This emphasis on dialogue is central in the quotes below from Diana:

> Good teaching is—in my opinion—teaching that involves the students as much as possible in the subject. Consequently not that a teacher reels off his lectures while the students listen quietly—at least that's what you hope. So, I think that dialogue teaching is best, for me too. Then you stay involved in the subject. There's less chance that your thoughts wander. Furthermore I think that a teacher should be open to criticism, especially when it comes from the students: that he remains the teacher without putting himself on a pedestal. (van Rossum & Hamer, in press)

The juxtaposition of dialogue and a personal perspective seen here is compa-rable to the blending of communion and agency that Baxter Magolda sees as the essence of contextual knowing and internal foundation (see Baxter

Magolda, 2004). For example, contextual knowers, while engaging in relationships with teachers or peers, stress interdependency, characterized by equality and ongoing dialogue. We expect that contextual knowers will prefer dialogue teaching (teaching conception 5) or learning partnerships (Baxter Magolda, 2004).

In Belenky and colleagues' constructed knowledge, women "must 'jump outside' the frames and systems authorities provide and create their own frame" (1997, p. 134). In an epistemological sense, these women often ask themselves in what way *they* are going to approach the world as a learner, and they have to decide how *they* want to think. In constructed knowledge, a woman's own voice—"her own way of expressing what she knew and cared about" (p. 133)—is the integration of the voices of others, intuition, and reason: here women integrate received, subjective and procedural knowledge. The emphasis Belenky et al. placed in this way of knowing on "relativism," "moving beyond systems," and "personal frames of reference," is clearly similar to the central themes in our learning-teaching conception 5 and Perry's position 5 (Perry, 1970).

If self-authorship is sufficient to meet the demands of modern life, Kegan felt that it is insufficient to meet the demands of postmodern life, which is defined to include a rejection of absolutes and the celebration of difference (or relativism) (Kegan, 1994, p. 325). In order to cope with the postmodern world, the cognitive sophistication of taking charge of a discipline (fourth order) must now be subordinated to the realization of the relative nature of intellectual disciplines (fifth order). One must now stand aside and reflect upon one's discipline from a perspective "outside ideology": at the fifth order of consciousness people realize "that each way of knowing is a way of not knowing, that each discipline is itself an ideology offering the power of explanation but at the price of inevitably advantaging someone or something and disadvantaging someone or something else" (Kegan, 1994, p. 290). Kegan linked the capacity to reflect critically on "the discipline itself, subjecting its prevailing theories to analysis not just from the perspective of another contending theory but from a perspective 'outside ideology'" to the "5th order of consciousness (trans-system structures)" (1994, p. 291). This emphasis on relativism is consistent with Perry's fifth position and our own fifth learning-teaching conception. In describing the move into the fifth order of consciousness as one where—after realizing that one's self-authored system is not definitive or objective—one builds a system that is much more "able to hold on to multiple systems of thinking" (Debold, 2002, p. 151, quoting Kegan), Kegan again places postmodernism (fifth order) firmly beyond the fourth learning-teaching conception and beyond self-authorship, identifying it as a separate way of knowing as we have here. Labouvie-Vief's intersystemic level (1990) would seem to describe this way of knowing as well.

Kegan described the shift from the fourth order of consciousness to the fifth, as the move "from the self-authoring self to . . . the self-transforming self" (Debold, 2002, p. 151, quoting Kegan). To return to the metaphor of "writing a reality" used for the fourth order, it seems that in the fifth order one realizes the self can "write" (or author) different realities using different systems. In a sense the self is then transforming the perception of reality depending on the system used to "author" this perception: "you start to build a way of constructing the world that is much more friendly to contradiction, to oppositeness" (Debold, 2002, p. 151, quoting Kegan). In Kegan's interpretation, this fifth order of consciousness holds in itself two structures: a negative form of relativism he called deconstructive postmodernism, and a more positive brand of postmodernism, reconstructive postmodernism. Reconstructive postmodernism, which Kegan sees as the end point of the shift from four to five, is characterized by a "capacity for reconnecting to these ideologies [of four] and recognizing that each of them is partial. You're building relationships among them rather than holding on to one and projecting the other" (Debold, 2002, p. 152, quoting Kegan). We feel (see below) that reconstructive postmodernism in fact describes another, sixth order of consciousness, and not the end point of the fifth order of consciousness.

Learning-Teaching Conception 6: Growing Self-awareness—Mutual Trust and Authentic Relationships: Caring

This most sophisticated learning conception that we have found in our student data is characterized by an existential dimension, the self of the learner seems to have become the focus of learning.[2] This position is extremely rare; only slightly more than 1% of all our students studied over about three decades was identified as making meaning in this way. The process aspect of

---

[2] We feel that the transformation here is sufficiently large to consider a change of context, from learning-teaching conceptions to conceptions of being, with this position forming the first conception of being.

this conception is growing self-awareness, looking for answers to the question "Who am I?" The self has become the ultimate object of reflection. The product is self-realization: becoming the person you feel you are (van Rossum, Deijkers, and Hamer, 1984; van Rossum & Taylor, 1987; van Rossum and Hamer, 2004). Responses are often remarkable with regard to the language used: combining organic metaphors with the feeling of agency and "being in charge." Both aspects can be seen in the quote below:

> [Learning is] something personal and it's also something that's continuous, once it starts it carries on and it might lead to other things. It might be like a root that has other branches coming off it . . . it is for the person before and for the person afterwards sort of thing. . . . Learning is self-realisation. . . . When I've been made aware of something . . . the effect of learning how I feel . . . I've got more positive views and more positive ideas and I know which side of the fence I am on. (Beaty et al., 1997, p. 158)

The feeling of "being in charge" of one's own life (or destiny) is very similar to trusting the internal voice, a concept used by Baxter Magolda (2008) to describe what she sees as the first element of self-authorship. Marton et al. (1993, p. 293) described exactly this as the most radical form of the sixth learning conception: the realization of the "fundamental change from seeing oneself as an object of what is happening . . . to seeing oneself as an agent of what is happening." In Baxter Magolda's interpretation of self-authorship, trusting the internal voice, internal foundation, and securing internal commitments reflect full self-authorship and the endpoint of the developed fourth order of consciousness (personal communication).

Good teaching to Sixes seems to be defined almost exclusively in language referring to emotion, autonomy, and reciprocal relationships and it boils down to mutual trust and caring while showing an almost dismissive approach to teaching techniques and methods. Cora's comment is a good example:

> I don't really have an idea of what good teaching is. I do know, that (this refers more to learning from people than to teaching) as soon as someone tells me 'you have to do it this way or that way' I start to bristle. I feel: Just

show me what, who, how and why you are, do, feel et cetera. . . . Live as
you think is right and if I can learn from that (what is almost sure to happen) then I can pick that up myself.

I can only become wiser when I want to, you can't make me. I do feel the
latter is valid within teaching. Good teaching is presenting the subject matter in such a way that [for] those already interested it stays that way or
becomes more so. (van Rossum & Hamer, in press)

Sixes experience for the first time that influence they give to external
authorities on decision making is within their complete control. Some of
Baxter Magolda's participants (2001) described a feeling of "coming
home." On the interpersonal aspect, internal foundation shows clear similarity with the sixth teaching conception: we recognize "a sense of communion (. . .) evident in the ability to connect meaningfully and mutually
with others while maintaining an authentic self" (Baxter Magolda, 2001,
p. 184) as an expression of the need for authentic relationships often mentioned by Sixes.

Both Belenky et al. and Kegan described this level of thinking without
identifying it as a separate category of description. In van Rossum and
Hamer (in press) we dubbed this sixth way of knowing as "constructing a
meaningful life" (Belenky et al., 1997, pp. 150–151) and "reconstructive postmodernism," respectively (Kegan, 1994). In personally rejecting deconstructive postmodernism, Kegan (1994) introduced reconstructive
postmodernism, but immediately acknowledged that the move from deconstructive to reconstructive postmodernism could not be made without "dis-
turbing the self" (Kegan, 1994, p. 332). The latter in our opinion indicates
that this move is in fact a step to a higher order of consciousness. In reconstructive postmodernism the need to make choices, to seek an internal foundation, is recognized and so it is very similar to our sixth learning-teaching
conception. And finally Perry (1970) also acknowledged that the transition
from relativism to a level of thinking where one starts to define oneself in
choices made, or, in Perry's terminology, commitments, is driven by the
need to find a way to stop drifting and make "my own decisions in an uncertain world with no one to tell me I'm Right" (Perry, 1981, p. 79). Perhaps it
is bold to suggest that following self-authoring (fourth order) and self-transforming (fifth order), this stage could be called self-self-defining (sixth
order).

In Table 3.2 we have summarized our learning-teaching conception model, and offered our interpretations of its links to epistemological models of interest to our current readers. We define key concepts for the three developmental dimensions: epistemology, relationships (interpersonal), and sense of self (intrapersonal).

We believe it is possible to link this six-stage developmental model to models of adult intellectual development. Elsewhere we postulated (Hamer & van Rossum, 2008; van Rossum & Hamer, in press) a further four stages of development using the concept of subject-object perspective shift introduced by Kegan. This ten-stage model then consists of two distinct developmental paths: the first five stages covering the epistemological development; the remaining stages describing an existential development. We have used biographical, gerontological, and philosophical literature, as well as insights from research into elder tales (Chinen, 1997) to flesh out this existential development. In his interview with Debold, Kegan theorized about developments far beyond the fourth order (and self-authorship), culminating in a "complete emptying of the subject into the object, so that there is, in a sense, no subject at all" (2002, p. 147). In our provisional life-span developmental model the eyes turn inward first, with the epistemological development focusing on increasing "tolerance of uncertainty of knowledge" and "significance of an autonomous self," the latter reaching its pinnacle in Sixes. Then the eyes turn outward again, first toward other humans, then to living organisms, and culminating in a relatively insignificant, but intact self in relationship with the universe. Tornstam (2005) observed a similar pattern noting a U-shaped correlation between self-centeredness and age.

TABLE 3.2

Relating Students' Learning-Teaching Conceptions to Ways of Knowing and Orders of Consciousness

Hamer and van Rossum (2008)							
Learning Conception	Teaching Conception	Epistemology (Knowing)	Relationships (Interpersonal)	Sense of self (Intrapersonal)	Baxter Magolda	Belenky, et al.	Kegan
1. Increasing knowledge	Imparting clear/ well structured knowledge	—	Obedience	—	—	Silence	First order
2. Memorizing	Transmitting structured knowledge (acknowledging receiver)	(selecting for) Memorization	Asking questions, subservient	Seen through the eyes of others	Absolute knowing	Received knowledge	Second order
3. Reproductive understanding/ application or Application foreseen	Interacting and Shaping	(reproductive) Applying	Interacting and discussing	Having a personal opinion	Transitional knowing	Subjective knowledge	Third order Traditionalism

4. Understanding subject matter	Challenging to think for yourself/ developing a way of thinking	The way of thinking within a discipline	Actively participating	Thinking for yourself, personal authority	Independent knowing	Procedural knowledge	Fourth order Modernism (self-authoring self)
5. Widening horizons	Dialogue teaching	Relativism or Realization of multiple perspectives	Engaging in true dialogue	Constructing a personal perspective	Contextual	Constructed knowing	Fifth order knowledge Postmodernism (self-transforming self)
6. Growing self-awareness	Mutual trust and authentic relationships: Caring	Paradoxical thinking and emergence of wisdom	Compassion and caring	Coming home (to yourself)	Internal foundation	Constructed meaningful life	Reconstructive Postmodernism

References

Baxter Magolda, M. B. (1992). *Knowing and reasoning in college: Gender-related patterns in students' intellectual development.* San Francisco: Jossey-Bass.

Baxter Magolda, M. B. (2001). *Making their own way: Narratives for transforming higher education to promote self-development.* Sterling, VA: Stylus.

Baxter Magolda, M. B. (2004). Learning Partnerships Model: A framework for promoting self-authorship. In M. B. Baxter Magolda & P. M. King (Eds.), *Learning partnerships: Theory and models of practice to educate for self-authorship* (pp. 37–62). Sterling, VA: Stylus.

Baxter Magolda, M. B. (2008). Three elements of self-authorship. *Journal of College Student Development, 49*(4), 269–284.

Beaty, E., Dall'Alba, G., & Marton, F. (1997). The personal experience of learning in higher education: Changing views and enduring perspectives. In P. Sutherland (Ed.), *Adult Learning: A Reader* (pp. 150–165). London: Kogan Page.

Belenky, M. F., Clinchy, B. M., Goldberger, N. R., & Tarule, J. M. (1997). *Women's ways of knowing: The development of self, voice and mind.* 10th anniversary edition. New York: Basic Books.

Biggs, J. B. (1979). Individual differences in study processes and the quality of learning outcomes. *Higher Education, 8,* 381–394.

Chinen, A. B. (1997). *In the ever after.* Wilmette, IL: Chiron Publications.

Debold, E. (2002). Epistemology, fourth order consciousness, and the subject-object relationship. *What is Enlightenment?* Fall-Winter 2002, 143–154.

Hamer, R., & Van Rossum, E. J. (2008). *Learning to be: Conceptions of being. Beyond relativism and postmodernism.* Paper presented at the Self-authorship, Theory Development and Assessment Across the Lifespan International Conference. Riva San Vitale, Switzerland. May 18–21, 2008.

Hofer, B. K. (2001). Personal epistemology research: Implications for learning and teaching. *Journal of Educational Psychology Review, 13*(4), 353–383.

Hofer, B. K. (2004). Exploring the dimensions of personal epistemology in differing classroom contexts: Student interpretations during the first year of college. *Contemporary Educational Psychology, 29,* 129–163.

Hofer, B. K., & Pintrich, P. R. (1997). The development of epistemological theories: Beliefs about knowledge and knowing and their relation to learning. *Review of Educational Research, 67*(1), 88–140.

Kegan, R. (1994). *In over our heads: The mental demands of modern life.* Cambridge, MA: Harvard University Press.

Kuhn, D. (1991). *The skills of argument.* Cambridge, UK: Cambridge University Press.

Labouvie-Vief, G. (1990). Wisdom as integrated thought: Historical and developmental perspectives. In R. J. Sternberg (Ed.), *Wisdom, its nature, origins and developments* (pp. 52–83). Cambridge (UK): Cambridge University Press.

Marton, F., Dall'Alba, G., & Beaty, E. (1993). Conceptions of learning. *International Journal of Educational Research, 19*(3), 277–300.

Morgan, A., & Beatty, L. (1997). The world of the learner. In Marton, F., Hounsell, D., & Entwistle, N (Eds.). *The experience of learning* (pp. 217–237). Edinburgh: Scottish Academic Press.

Perry, W. G. (1970). *Forms of intellectual and ethical development in the college years: A scheme.* New York: Holt, Rinehart & Winston.

Perry, W. G. (1981). Cognitive and ethical growth: The making of meaning. In A. W. Chickering and Associates (Eds.) *The Modern American College* (pp. 76–116). San Francisco: Jossey-Bass.

Pratt, D. D. (1992). Conceptions of teaching. *Adult Education Quarterly, 42*(4), 203–220.

Säljö, R. (1979). Learning in the learner's perspective. I: Some common sense conceptions. Reports from the Institute of Education, University of Göteborg, Mölndal, No. 76.

Tornstam, L. (2005). *Gerotranscendence.* New York: Springer Publishing Company.

Van Rossum, E. J., & Hamer, R. (2004). Learning and teaching: A model of linked continua of conceptions. In Rust, C. (Ed.) *Improving Student Learning— Theory, Research and Scholarship* (pp. 121–133). Proceedings of the 2003 11th International Symposium Improving Student Learning.

Van Rossum E. J., & Hamer, R. (in press). *The meaning of learning and knowing.* Doctoral Thesis in preparation (Utrecht University).

Van Rossum, E. J., & Schenk, S. M. (1984). The relationship between learning conception, study strategy and learning outcome. *British Journal of Educational Psychology, 54*, 73–83.

Van Rossum, E. J., & Taylor I. P. (1987). *The relationship between conceptions of learning and good teaching: A scheme of cognitive development.* Paper presented at the Annual Meeting of the American Educational Research Association, April 1987, Washington D.C., U.S.A.

Van Rossum, E. J., Deijkers, R., & Hamer, R. (1984). Aanpassen of Stimuleren— over Kunst en Kunde. [Adaptation or Stimulation—about Art and Ability]. *Onderzoek van Onderwijs, 13*(4), 41–44.

Van Rossum, E. J., Deijkers, R., & Hamer, R. (1985). Students' learning conceptions and their interpretation of significant educational concepts. *Higher Education, 14*, 617–641.

PART TWO

MULTICULTURAL PERSPECTIVES ON SELF-AUTHORSHIP

Peggy S. Meszaros

The five chapters in this section challenge our thinking about the developmental trajectory of self-authorship across cultures of age, gender, and geography. Two studies begin to situate self-authorship in adolescence and the possible connection between dissonance and development in different parts of the world. Weinstock's study of male and female Bedouin and Jewish adolescents raises issues of collectivist versus individualist culture differences in defining authorship of one's self. Meszaros and Lane propose a model of risk and resilience and the role of support to foster self-authorship in African American male and female adolescents in economically depressed areas of the United States who experience dissonance in academic achievement. Dissonance is further explored in a third study as Torres describes her longitudinal study of Latino/a college students and the role of ethnic identity and dissonance as a propellant to self-authorship. Finally, gender and geography come together in two studies. Brownlee, Berthelsen, and Boulton-Lewis foreground development of epistemological beliefs using scenarios with Australian college females preparing to be childcare workers. Hofer's comparative study of Japanese and U.S. college students' epistemic beliefs examines the marked contrasts between the U.S. idea of self as autonomous, Asian conceptions of self as relational and connected and the "fit" with concepts of self-authorship.

This section raises important questions about the need for more cross-cultural collaboration to understand self-authorship development in different cultures and the need to address better measurement and interpretation of results in multiple cultures.

4

INVESTIGATING LATINO ETHNIC IDENTITY WITHIN THE SELF-AUTHORSHIP FRAMEWORK

Vasti Torres

Abstract: This chapter presents a longitudinal study of Latino/a college students and explains the additional developmental tasks Latinos/as experience within the self-authorship framework. These additional tasks are explained within each of the statuses of self-authorship.

Although much attention is given to the demographic information regarding the increase of Latino/a college students, limited research exists on how they develop during the college years. Knowledge from other developmental theories indicates that some different developmental tasks occur for students of color (Cross, 1995; Helms, 1995; Phinney, 1993), yet there is little clarity about what is similar or different for Latino/a college students. The desire to investigate these similarities and differences became the focus of my research.

When I began a longitudinal study of Latino/a college students my intent was to consider the influence of ethnic identity development on the college experience. As I collected years of data and began analysis across the years it became increasingly difficult to separate ethnic identity (or identity in general) from other developmental issues; it was particularly difficult to separate the identity development processes from cognitive development. Around the same time I began to code the data across years using a process called coding for process that allows the researcher to focus on "looking at action/interaction and tracing it over time to note how and if it changes or what enables it to remain the same with changes in structural conditions" (Strauss & Corbin,

1998, p. 163). During this time I was also reading Baxter Magolda's (2001) analysis of her participants past the college years. Though I had previously read Kegan (1982; 1994), it was Baxter Magolda's work that brought the concept and journey toward self-authorship to life in a manner that related to the college experience and to me as a researcher and faculty member in higher education. At this point, I was unsure that considering the self-authorship framework with Latino/a students was appropriate because the sample used by Baxter Magolda was predominantly White. This hesitation regarding a theory based on a majority population required significant reflection and risk. As a result, I considered aspects of development and applied the framework to partial processes, such as the phenomenon of changing negative images to positive images among some of the participants. This first attempt to consider the link between the processes in self-authorship and ethnic minorities was a result of an emerging finding early in the data analysis—the need for some students to reconstruct negative messages about being Latino into positive interpretations. This led to the consideration of the self-authorship framework as a plausible tool to use in interpreting what had occurred with these students. The consideration of multiple dimensions and the interactions among the dimensions allowed a more complete picture to emerge. This initial use of the self-authorship framework resulted in a journal article that related the cognitive processes to the identity processes involved in ethnic identity development (Torres & Baxter Magolda, 2004). Testing the applicability of the framework on aspects of development among Latino college students allowed me to feel more comfortable applying the framework to the entire sample of Latino/a college students.

Subsequently, more examples emerged during data analysis where the self-authorship framework would help in the interpretation of data by allowing consideration of all three dimensions of development. This chapter highlights the research that evolved considering the role of ethnic identity within the self-authorship framework. It is important to note that the framework was never imposed on the data as a priori theory; rather it emerged as a tool to analyze and interpret the data about these Latino/a students' development.

In order to provide the information necessary to understand these developmental processes, I begin with an overview of the research study and methodology. I then report the findings that add to the literature and understanding of the journey toward self-authorship. The focus is on what is different from the populations previously considered by Baxter Magolda (2001).

Longitudinal Study of Latino/a College Students

The longitudinal study used interviews to gather data over a span of three to five years. For the first-year interview I gathered data from 83 students and by the end of the study 29 students (35%) continued to participate for at least three years. This chapter focuses on the 29 self-identified Latino/a college students with multiple-year interviews, which allows for across-year analysis. The majority of the students included in this analysis were from four urban universities and three of the students began their higher education at community colleges, eventually transferring to urban universities. Because the majority of the participants were from the urban universities, the description of the context focuses on these universities. Two of the universities were predominantly White institutions (PWI) with Latinos/as making up approximately 4% of the student population. One of the universities is considered diverse with approximately 25% Latino/a students and is classified as a Hispanic Serving Institution (HSI). The fourth institution was a monocultural university with Latinos/as making up approximately 95% of the student population; this institution is also a HSI. The students who self-identified as Latino/Hispanic first-time-in-college freshmen on their institutional information were mailed a request to participate. I interviewed the participants each spring for the three to five years the participant stayed in the study. Some students (9) began their participation in the study in 2000, some (13) in 2002, and the remaining (7) began in 2003. The majority of the participants were women (19) and most were born in the United States (23). Four of the students transferred at some point during the study period and six stopped out for at least one semester during the three to four years that they participated in the study.

Method

Methodology   I see myself as a constructivist researcher who uses grounded theory as a methodology (Charmaz, 2000; Strauss & Corbin, 1998). By using a constructivist epistemology I acknowledge the meaning-making of the individual student and the understanding that this process is socially constructed (Crotty,1998). Using grounded theory allowed me to acknowledge a personal relationship with the individual participants as well as assume that theoretical understanding would emerge from the data (Charmaz). The theoretical influence of the self-authorship framework could be seen as a form of what Strauss and Corbin call a theoretical comparison. "It is not that we use experiences or literature as data rather that we use the properties and dimensions derived from the comparative incidents to examine the data in front of us" (Strauss & Corbin, p. 80).

Data Analysis   Data were analyzed using open coding followed by coding for process across the years (Strauss & Corbin, 1998). The open coding process allows for a large number of initial codes to emerge. Coding for process organizes the initial codes into patterns over time and is thus a more appropriate technique in longitudinal research. During the coding for process the research team began using the framework of self-authorship to assist in coding individual students' development. The process entailed reading all years of data for each student at one time and identifying processes that were cognitive, identity, or interpersonally oriented. The research team discussed these processes across the years, thus allowing us to test whether there was a commitment to more internally defined developmental thinking or if there was wavering among the developmental statuses or dimensions. Once the coding was completed, each student's development was depicted on an individual sheet of paper (summary sheets) with the three dimensions and the four statuses used by Baxter Magolda (2001). For each student the research team identified behaviors that illustrated each dimension and which status the behavior illustrated each year. Therefore a summary sheet would illustrate that while student A began as externally defined in year one (with transcript location of data that exemplifies this level of development) he or she illustrated examples of crossroads thinking in the third or fourth year (again, with transcript location of data exemplifying the development). The summary sheets could be physically sorted by dimensions to see if the framework was useful in explaining the development of Latino/a students and to examine if new patterns emerged. The summary sheets were also color coded by institutional type to investigate whether any potential pattern existed within institutional environments (none were found). Prior to the sorting by dimensions and statuses, the research team agreed that if patterns did not emerge within the self-authorship framework, the analysis would begin again, thus not forcing the students' stories to fit the framework.

Once the summary sheets were sorted by status at the end of the study for each dimension, the research team discussed the patterns and whether the patterns indicated similar or different processes than the predominantly White sample used by Baxter Magolda. At this time the research team was able to discuss specific students' developmental issues and what they each had in common with the others. Part of the discussion also focused on whether sufficient evidence emerged to see a pattern of development. These discussions ultimately resulted in understanding movement points as well as additional tasks these Latino/a students experienced during their college years.

Trustworthiness and Positionality of the Researcher   My positionality as a researcher provides insight into the lens used to consider the trustworthiness of this qualitative study (Jones, Torres, & Arminio, 2006). Although I am an immigrant Latina, I acknowledge that I have lived the majority of my life in the United States. Although I am bilingual and continue to be a strong member of the Latino community around me, my level of education and economic status identify me as an outsider for the participants who are first generation in college or low income. The annual interview allowed me to develop a relationship with the participants and allowed me to follow up on personal matters as these types of issues emerged in the interview and in the meaning-making process they were related to the study's goal of understanding the student's college experiences. A summary of the findings was provided to the students each year as a way to engage them in a member-checking activity. This provided me with some feedback about my analysis and allowed me to check my understanding. Once the participant read and responded to the summary, the interview would resume and provide additional data.

Findings

The results from data analyses of longitudinal interviews revealed several tasks beyond identity formation within the developmental process. The processes that occur within these tasks illustrate the interwoven nature of development within the cognitive, interpersonal, and intrapersonal dimensions. Common patterns of development were evident between phases and in all dimensions among the students in this study and those in Baxter Magolda's study. The students who transitioned from external formulas to crossroads during the research study timeline recognized that the plans formulated by authorities were not working and that they needed to adapt their plans (Torres & Hernandez, 2007). The distinction for these students is the realization that occurred as a result of being introduced to new worldviews and definitions of *Latino*. For the purposes of illustrating how the self-authorship framework was useful in the interpretation of data, the distinctions are highlighted in Table 4.1.

TABLE 4.1
Matrix of Holistic Development Including Latino/a Cultural Choices
(reprinted with permission from the *Journal of College of Student Development*)

		External Formulas	Crossroads	Becoming Author of One's Life	Internal Foundation
How do I know	Cognitive	• Family and known peers are the authority	• Expands own views to recognize multiple perspectives • Recognizes racism	• Recognizes their own cultural reality and internalizes choices between cultures to create their own principles	• Knowledge and decisions are contextually interpreted and inclusive of cultural choices
Who am I	Intrapersonal (Ethnic Identity)	• Geographic definition of identity • Identity is determined by family • May believe negative stereotypes of Latinos	• Recognition of stereotypes and deliberate about how they influence self • Understanding of positive and negative cultural choices	• Integration of cultural choices into daily life—an informed Latino/a identity • Advocate for Latinos	• Comfortable illustrating culture in behavior and choices • No longer intimidated by differences
What relationships do I want with others	Interpersonal (Cultural Orientation)	• Avoid anything outside of comfort zone • Dichotomous view of culture (either Latino or Anglo) • Negative support to try new experiences	• Change in environment (place or friends) brings about new diversity that is incorporated into social circle • Manages family influence • Ease with individuals from multiple perspectives	• Renegotiate relationships that are more consistent with an informed Latino perspective	• Living an interdependence that maintains own cultural values within the context of a diverse environment

External Definitions   These Latino/a college students' view of authority included some faculty and administrators in power positions, but they showed a preference for family members and trusted authorities. Jebus illustrated his externally defined cognitive ways of thinking about his educational process by not considering the consequences of his behaviors or actions in selecting a major, seeing an advisor about course selection, and focusing on what he needed to get done. He stated: "It's not really scary at all. I'll be in school longer, but I'm not really worried about it. Advisors and everyone else told me that I'll end up changing my major around 6 or 7 times possibly" (Torres & Hernandez, 2007, p. 562). Jebus did not change his external definitions or investigate alternative paths until his third year of college when his friends were getting close to graduating with bachelor's degrees, and he realized he had been attending college full time for three years and was still at least two years away from graduating with his associate's degree. It was not until this comparison came alive for Jebus that he began to see his advisor regularly and make more intentional decisions about his course selection and trajectory.

Within the intrapersonal dimension the externally defined students described their ethnicity as geographically related or by whatever terms their parents used to describe their background. When asked what meaning they attached to the term, they offered an explanation of who or what gave them this language. For example, Martin defined being Mexican American as "a Mexican born in the United States" (Torres & Hernandez, p. 564). When asked if he felt that the label had any additional meaning, he responded with "no, not really" (p. 564). These students were not able to attach personal meaning to ethnic labels and had not yet come to recognize how society may view these labels. Other students articulated externally defined views of ethnicity by linking the term to food, language, or music.

Another aspect of an externally defined intrapersonal dimension was the potential to believe the negative stereotypes associated with being Latino. Sagi illustrated this internalized negative belief about having a Spanish accent when she spoke English:

> I feel ashamed . . . because I have an accent, I am confused, people judge me more, because you have accent. But if you are an American and you say something and it doesn't come out right then they say, well, can you explain that a little more and they can explain it. They have more words to explain

it. And when you are a second language learner, you don't. Besides when [the professor] gives you this look, then she makes you feel embarrassed, it makes it hard to come up with a word. (Torres & Baxter Magolda, 2004, p. 338)

Sagi felt that she would not be able to complete college because she was not as intelligent as her English-speaking peers. She had internalized the belief that having an accent meant that you were not as smart.

The students in the externally defined interpersonal dimension avoided anything outside of their comfort zone. For many of these students, this included avoiding interactions and, in some cases, contact with the majority White Anglo culture. Alejandra was born in the United States, yet she had a slight accent when she spoke English. For this reason she felt self-conscious around Anglos and described her preference for spending time with other Latinos/as. She explained that when she met someone new she would think "there might be a chance that they know Spanish, so I can talk to them at least to get some connection" (Torres & Hernandez, p. 567). For others their lack of contact with differences allowed them to accept images of others in the manner that they are portrayed in the media. Without contact or the ability to interact with those who are different, the externally defined students stayed with others like themselves and seldom ventured beyond their families and peer groups.

Crossroads   The students who entered into the crossroads were often propelled there as a result of changing their environments. For Nora her transition came when she transferred from her monocultural institution to a predominantly White institution (PWI). She described how she began to explore multiple perspectives.

Actually I just think that since I've met these people and you get to see their points of view and the way they're going through life and you actually start making sense to who you are. I get to see what they feel like and what they're going through and I get to see it from another point of view, from other people, from other countries. Sometimes I feel like "Wow, I'm not that bad," or "I'm not suffering as much as they are." And you get to see the good side of your nationality and it's definitely good because all of them want to speak Spanish. I'm like "Yeah, sure," they'll try to say something right and it's off and I get to make fun of them, it's kind of cool. (Torres & Hernandez, p. 562)

Her change in environment required that she consider diverse worldviews because she was confronted with peers who were not like her at the PWI. When she realized that some of her credits would not transfer, Nora exhibited crossroads cognitive behaviors when she switched her major to align more closely with her desire to graduate earlier while also doing something in her academic area of interest. She was able to seek out information and evaluate the options in order to decide for herself what would best serve her needs.

Within the intrapersonal dimension the Latino/a students in this study had to make meaning of negative stereotypes associated with being Latino/a in the context of the majority Anglo society. As a part of this recognition process, they also needed to make deliberate choices about how these stereotypes would be interpreted. This was a more complex way of seeing identity because it required students to make meaning of the idea that both positive and negative choices are available to them in defining their ethnic identity. While the positive choices focused on family, cultural expressions, and other ethnic icons, such as food and music, the negatives included leaving the family and their comfort zone in order to get an education.

Mauricio's fair skin gave him an outward appearance that is not typical for a Latino. He was not always perceived as Latino when he interacted with the majority Anglo world. During his college years, family circumstances required Mauricio to become head of household for his younger siblings. The added family responsibilities seemed to provide the dissonance necessary to propel Mauricio into developmental tasks and to consider how negative comments about Latinos applied to him:

> Sometimes, people look at me like . . . [why] are you standing up for them? But the people don't know . . . what I am. They don't know that I'm Latino. They don't know where I come from. So they think, "Oh yeah we can just make fun of them." I stand for them . . . because first of all they are my friends. And second, we are all Latinos. (Torres & Hernandez, p. 565)

It should be noted that this level of understanding within the intrapersonal dimension did not occur for Mauricio until his fourth year of college. He was attending college in his hometown and living at home during his college years. It was not until his fourth year that he experienced enough dissonance to make him begin to question his previous understanding of the world around him. This level of dissonance did not occur for Nora until she transferred to a PWI where she was for the first time a minority:

> The fact that I am a minority . . . and people have told me, friends of mine, that there are still people that don't like Mexicans or any other culture. I guess they think Mexicans are all the same, they always describe them as short, lazy, you know? Like I said, there are still people that don't like the way we are. (Torres & Hernandez, p. 565)

The recognition of negative images and the desire to make meaning of this propelled Nora to become more aware of her ethnicity. She became prouder of her identity and began to recognize racist comments, helping her to avoid internalizing the negative stereotypes that others might hold.

In the interpersonal dimension students entered the crossroads when they were able to incorporate multiple perspectives and not be completely driven by family expectations. These students did not desire to ignore their family expectations; rather they had to develop techniques to manage the familial influence. For many Latino/a students, their parents can seem very strict when compared with the Anglo countertypes. Rosalie came to a point where she was able to discuss her choices with her mother instead of feeling like she had to be told what to do. She described how she managed her relationship with her mother by stating: "And with my mom, I just tell her, you know I know her obsessions, but 'this is what's happening, this is what's going on, this is how it's going to be,' we just work things out like that" (Torres & Hernandez, p. 568).

The crossroads was often prompted by change in environment or life circumstances. Many of these students attended college in their own communities and lived at home. This allowed them to have little dissonance and therefore they could maintain previous ways of knowing for longer periods of time.

Becoming Authored   The students who were able to transition from crossroads to becoming authored showed evidence of a stronger method of decision making that considered their values and needs as a result of responding to crisis. Within the cognitive dimension, Antonio illustrated his ability to construct his own plan of action while also considering the realities of his situation as an undocumented college student. Because of his legal status in the United States, Antonio understood that his options could be limited, and therefore he chose a major that would allow him to have a profession regardless of his legal status.

Because that way I might be able to find some more help to pay for my school. A lot of the medical schools, when one graduates from a four-year university, a lot of medical schools require that the student have a social security number or something like that. And besides, medical school is very, very expensive, so if I was to have papers, the government might be able to help me, and I might be able to apply for scholarships which require me to have a social security number. So more doors will be open for me to study medicine. (Torres & Hernandez, p. 563)

Antonio recognized that his dream of being a doctor may not be realistic given his legal status. As a result he created an alternative plan and changed his major so that his legal status would not necessarily hinder his professional path. Although this could be seen as not being true to his interest, his decisions were based on sound and realistic thinking. He balanced his options with the realism of his residency status and made a decision that would benefit him in the long term as well as provide direction in the short term. The realism illustrated his understanding of the world around him and the decisions he did have control over.

Students who entered this phase of development were also more willing to advocate for other Latinos/as, and many felt a need to give back to their communities. Antonio gave speeches to civic groups that could influence the passing of the DREAM Act, a legislative initiative to allow temporary residency to academically promising undocumented college students.

In the intrapersonal dimension, the few students who entered this phase were able to integrate their cultural choices into their daily living experiences. For example, Susie cut previous attachments to her former gang friends and realized that it was not bad to be seen as a "nerd"—she explained by saying, "It's not so bad, because nerds actually get somewhere" (Torres & Hernandez, p. 565). This integration also extended to the interpersonal dimension where students began to associate with others who also had an understanding of their culture and were comfortable having discussions about culture. Maria, who transferred from a community college to an urban university, described her relationships by saying:

I definitely feel really comfortable with Dominicans who don't feel like they're American at all, and then I definitely feel less comfortable with Americans who have no connection with their ethnic background or anything like that. But I definitely understand that I'm definitely American, like I know that. (Torres & Hernandez, p. 568)

In this case, Maria understood her blended cultural identity while also acknowledging that she was more comfortable with people who understood their cultural backgrounds. She was less comfortable with Anglos who did not understand the influence of their cultural background because she valued this journey to know who you are and where you come from. Again, it is important to note that this level of understanding did not occur for Maria until her fourth year of college and after she left home.

Internal Foundations   Only a few students from this study entered the Internal Foundations phase by the end of the study, or their fourth-year interview. These students were able to reflect on how their choices considered context, values, culture, and personal desires. Within the cognitive dimension, Jackie illustrated this intersection by explaining how she goes about making decisions about potential job offers:

> I think about where it would be best. I mean if different options come up, I consider them and I say okay, if I do take this path, you know, what is it going to offer me? And how am I going to better my career and myself as a person? (Torres & Hernandez, p. 563)

For the few who were internally defined, their intrapersonal dimension embedded culture within their daily choices and behaviors. Vanessa, a nontraditional student with children, achieved such a level of comfort with her ethnic identity that she began having conversations with her children about being Latino and the fact that they chose not to learn Spanish. She told the story of her children trying to blame her for not speaking Spanish. Her response was:

> Now that we go to family get-togethers . . . they ask him [son], "Why don't you speak Spanish?" and he's like "I don't know." So later on when we're alone he's like, "Ma, it's your fault." He blames me for not teaching him. I'm like, "How is it my fault? I spoke to you [in Spanish]; your grandfather and grandmother spoke to you. Why didn't you pick it up?" and he is like "I don't know." So then don't blame me. (Torres & Hernandez, p. 566)

This statement illustrates Vanessa's ability to differentiate her responsibility as a parent and her son's responsibility as a learner. She was not willing to accept the blame, but instead helped her son understand how his choices influenced the fact that he did not speak Spanish. This more in-depth understanding of herself and the choices that occur within a Latino/a person's life span was consistent with an internally defined identity.

In the interpersonal dimension, only two students reached an internally defined understanding of their relationships with others. In the case of Jackie, she was intentional about having a diverse group of friends, and her interest in doing community service increased as she became more internally defined. When describing her peer-group, she stated that: "We do a lot of community services which I have always been interested in" (Torres & Hernandez, p. 568). She surrounded herself with peers who shared her values, but was also able to work with peers in her academic program who did not share her values. She could differentiate between friends and coworkers in an internally defined manner.

The few students who were able to develop an internal foundation were no longer afraid of being different or being around difference; rather they found that diverse communities and intellectual environments were desirable and added to their sense of self.

New Patterns in Development

Although some commonalities in developmental tasks existed among the Latino/a students and samples used in previous studies, it is important to note that new patterns emerged within this study. The primary differences in the patterns focus on two issues: (1) student development was not always linear, but fluctuated between growth, regression, and stagnation as a result of environmental or societal pressures, and (2) development never progressed within one dimension more than one phase ahead of the other dimensions.

This first pattern is illustrated by students who coped with crisis by avoidance, or who lacked the support to deal with it, and therefore tended to stagnate in their development. Other students who were unable to make meaning of racist incidents could regress to an externally defined level of defining oneself as a way to avoid the dissonance caused by racism. This fluctuation in growth was always a result of a student's inability to make meaning of a negative situation. Within these fluctuations insufficient support, and in some cases, devastating negative messages could present a circumstance too difficult for students to work through on their own. When students received negative support for attempting new things, they were more likely to stagnate. For example, Jebus thought about leaving home for college, but his family members provided negative support for this behavior and made him feel like that would be a bad idea. Within this sample of students the negative support for new experiences occurred most often for students who lived at home and needed to balance their parents' expectations with their own goals about educational attainment. Support was provided for education, but not for changing the dynamics within the family.

Although students regressed in this study as a result of avoiding racist situations, it should be noted that the regression of development only occurred between external definitions and crossroads. The research team believed that once the students' cognitive abilities were sufficiently developed to work through these types of crisis they were better able to cope with the issues that arose and therefore progress in their development (Torres & Hernandez).

The second pattern focuses on students' progression at different rates among the dimensions. None of the students in this study progressed more than one phase in one dimension without positive development in the other dimensions. For example, the few students who were able to create Internally Founded definitions in the intrapersonal dimension were at least at Becoming an Author in the other dimensions. This provides some evidence of a synergistic relationship among the dimensions that must be considered as part of the developmental journey (Torres & Hernandez).

Synthesis and Implications for Research

The findings in this longitudinal study of Latino/a college students reveal some additional developmental tasks that should be considered within the development of Latino/a college students' sense of self-authorship. Although in this study the Latino/a students faced racism as a developmental task, all adults need to consider how social status influences them and others (King & Baxter Magolda, 2005). Previous research has not fully explored the influence racism or the understanding of privilege (for majority students) can have on the development of the cognitive, intrapersonal, and interpersonal dimensions. This study indicates that an influence does exist, and the meaning-making process for an individual can either advance development or regress it.

The final implication to consider is the role environmental dissonance provided for these students. The students who experienced major environmental changes were propelled into the meaning-making process and therefore were better able to create more internally defined aspects of themselves. Those who had little dissonance in their environment seemed to take longer, waiting until an incident prompted them to question their previous assumptions about knowledge, themselves, and others, thus promoting development toward more complex ways of thinking. Unfortunately for some of these students with little environmental dissonance, the incident that did create dissonance came about as a result of not making sufficient academic progress or other negative consequences that can occur within the college career.

Although the meaning-making process of being a minority within the U.S. culture did propel development for some of the students in this study, it also prompted others to regress or stagnate. For this reason, new issues arise regarding the role of minority status, and this phenomenon deserves greater attention in the research literature surrounding self-authorship. It is difficult to make comparisons, but it is also difficult to say that Latino/a students in this study developed more or faster than other groups. What can be learned from this study is that minority status provided additional developmental tasks that can propel students, but this is dependent on the student's willingness and ability to tackle these difficult developmental situations.

As researchers gain greater understanding of the holistic view of development, it is imperative that different social identities be considered within this developmental process. This study adds to the literature by considering Latino/a college students, yet other social identities should also be considered.

References

Baxter Magolda, M. B. (2001). *Making their own way: Narratives for transforming higher education to promote self-development.* Sterling, VA.: Stylus.

Baxter Magolda, M. B. (2004). Evolution of a constructivist conceptualization of epistemological reflection. *Educational Psychologist, 39*(1), 31–42.

Charmaz, K. (2000). Grounded theory objectivist and constructivist methods. In N. K. Denzin & Y. S. Lincoln (Eds.), *Handbook of qualitative research* (2nd ed., pp. 509–536). Thousand Oaks, CA: Sage.

Cross, W. E. (1995). In search of Blackness and Afrocentricity: The psychology of Black identity change. In H. W. Harris, H. C. Blue, & E. E. H. Griffith (Eds.),

Racial and ethnic identity: Psychological development and creative expression (pp. 53–72). New York: Routledge.

Crotty, M. (1998). *The foundations of social research: Meaning and perspective in the research process.* Thousand Oaks, CA: Sage.

Helms, J.E. (1995). An update on Helms's White and People of Color racial identity models. In J. G. Ponterotto, J. M. Casas, L. A. Suzuki, & C. M. Alexander (Eds.), *Handbook of multicultural counseling* (pp. 181–197). Thousand Oaks, CA: Sage.

Jones, S. R., Torres, V. & Arminio, J. L. (2006). *Negotiating the complexities of qualitative research in higher education: Fundamental elements and issues.* New York: Brunner-Routledge Publishing.

Kegan, R. (1982). *The evolving self: Problem and process in human development.* Cambridge, MA: Harvard University Press.

Kegan, R. (1994). *In over our heads: The mental demands of modern life.* Cambridge, MA: Harvard University Press.

King, P. M., & Baxter Magolda, M. B. (2005). A developmental model of intercultural maturity. *Journal of College Student Development, 46*(6), 571–592.

Phinney, J. S. (1993). A three-stage model of ethnic identity development in adolescence. In M. E. Bernal & G. P. Knight (Eds.), *Ethnic identity formation and transmission among Hispanics and other minorities* (pp. 61–79). Albany: State University of New York Press.

Strauss, A., & Corbin, J. (1998). *Basics of qualitative research techniques and procedures for developing grounded theory* (2nd ed.) Thousand Oaks, CA: Sage.

Torres, V., & Baxter Magolda, M. B. (2004). Reconstructing Latino identity: The influence of cognitive development on the ethnic identity process of Latino students. *Journal of College Student Development, 45*(3), 333–347.

Torres, V. & Hernandez, E. (2007). The influence of ethnic identity on self-authorship: A longitudinal study of Latino/a college students. *Journal of College Student Development, 48*(5), 558–573.

5

AN EXPLORATORY STUDY OF THE RELATIONSHIP BETWEEN ADOLESCENT RISK AND RESILIENCE AND THE EARLY DEVELOPMENT OF SELF-AUTHORSHIP

Peggy S. Meszaros and Crystal Duncan Lane

Abstract: Risk and challenge, resilience and support, and the early development of self-authorship in a group of 115 academically at-risk adolescents enrolled in a summer training academy are explored in this study. Both the quantitative and qualitative responses point to self-authorship development within some of the adolescent participants.

I would listen to both sides and when I hear both sides I will figure out what advice fits me best.

When two people who both know me give two different suggestions on what to do with my life I would sit down and think about what has been told to me and compare and contrast the options. Then I will decide which option best suits me.

These quotes come from two adolescents who, along with their 113 classmates, were rising high school freshmen and sophomores from urban and rural high school districts in economically depressed areas of southwest Virginia. They, like adolescents in general, were trying to make sense of their lives and who they were becoming. All were participating in a three-year youth development program called the Virginia Tech Summer Training Academy for Rising Students (VT STARS), which ran from 2005–2007.

The purpose was to prepare academically at-risk high school students from economically depressed regions to pursue advanced education related to science, technology, engineering, or math (STEM). This residential experience was followed in the subsequent year with supportive academic mentors at their high schools and parents or guardians in their homes. The purpose of this chapter is to explore the relationship between the risks and challenges in their lives and their development of resilience, their support, and signs of development of self-authorship.

In recent years researchers are increasingly interested in the tremendous risks and opportunities inherent in early adolescence, which is defined in Merriam-Webster's Dictionary (2008) as the period of life from puberty to maturity terminating legally at the age of majority. It is a period during which many young people face risky behaviors and challenges as they mature intellectually, make decisions, and set priorities that can shape their life course. This developmental period presents an opportune time to explore the possible existence and role of self-authorship in adolescence.

Achieving intellectual maturity is an educational learning outcome goal that typically includes effective citizenship, critical thinking, complex problem solving, interdependent relations with diverse others, and mature decision making (Baxter Magolda & King, 2007). Achieving this maturity begins in earnest in adolescence as young people begin to make meaning of their lives. Research into the development of self-authorship has almost exclusively involved college students, with Baxter Magolda's twenty-two—year longitudinal study of young adult development and learning being a prime example. Although researchers have studied adolescents' epistemological and identity development, searching the literature resulted in only one study of self-authorship within adolescence (Pizzolato, 2006). In this study, Pizzolato followed four eighth-grade girls through a short story unit designed to help develop metacognitive awareness. Results were promising as the girls experienced seeking ways to meet others' expectations while still honoring and including their own ideas, thus opening the door for further investigation of emerging self-authorship in early adolescence. Pizzolato's early work also offers the greatest insights into understanding high risk college students (Pizzolato, 2003), and her investigation of the provocative moment (Pizzolato, 2005), provides context for the current study. Students in Pizzolato's studies experienced varying levels of support as they journeyed toward self-authorship. The eighth-grade girls were supported by their teacher, college students experiencing a provocative moment were supported by family or college advisors, whereas the high-risk college students with low privilege often lacked parental support.

This connection between challenge and support is central to Baxter Magolda's (2004) Learning Partnerships Model (LPM), which illustrates the process of self-authorship development. Specifically, through a learning partnership between the student and a supportive other, the student is able to develop "an internal belief system, internal identity," and "share authority and expertise in a mutual relationship," with the supportive other who "validates the learners' capacity to know, situates learning in the learners' experience," and "defines learning as mutually constructing meaning," (p. 41). The learning partnership between the student and the supportive other is crucial to allowing the student to face the challenge, disequilibrium, or even *risks* at hand and build *resilience* through the support offered as a protective factor. It is this hypothesized connection between challenge/support, risk/resilience, and the self-authorship development process that is at the heart of our study.

Rationale and Need

As our model shows (see Figure 5.1), we believe there is a relationship between adolescent risk/challenge, resilience/protective factors as encompassed by support, and emerging self-authorship. Although the relationship between the development of self-authorship and support exemplified in the LPM is documented in college students, it is not known if this relationship exists for adolescents. The purpose of this study is to examine the relationship between risk/challenge and resilience as mediated by support in a group of previously mentioned adolescents who were academically at risk. It is our

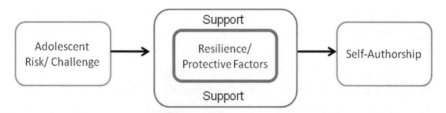

Figure 5.1. Process Model of LPM and Risk/Resilience in Adolescents

hope that finding a relationship between risk/resilience and challenge/support as defined by Baxter Magolda (2004) will situate self-authorship within adolescence, thus expanding the breadth of practice for the LPM and demonstrating an approach for emerging self-authorship in adolescents.

Defining the Model

The following constructs are present in our model: adolescent risk/challenge, resilience/protective factors, support, and self-authorship.

Risk/Challenge

According to Rolf and Johnson (1990), risk factors are defined as those variables that "have proven or presumed effects that can directly increase the likelihood of maladaptive outcome" (p. 387). This definition may be applied at any systemic level. Walsh (2003) identifies risks as "multiple, recursive influences involving individuals, families, and larger social systems," (p. 402). More specifically, risks may take the form of a physical illness, sociocultural variables such as poverty, or having some form of minority status. They may be the result of vulnerabilities associated with normative life-cycle events such as puberty, navigating parental control, transitioning between schools, and factors associated with school success.

For the purposes of this study, risks are defined as being an adolescent, being academically at risk, in poverty, and risks associated with race and class. With regard to being academically at risk, maternal education, income, and occupational status are shown to have significant effects on outcomes such as achievement test scores, course failures, and completed years of schooling (McLoyd, 1990, 1998); thus our use of these variables here.

We define the constructs of risk and challenge in our model as closely related. Risk and challenge may also be akin to Pizzolato's (2005) provocative moment, disequilibrium, or dissonance, which forces the adolescent to develop internal formulas for dealing with the problems they are facing when no external solutions/formulas are readily available. Although the concept of adolescent risk is usually couched in terms of the outcome of resilience and the mediating variable of support, so too does Baxter Magolda (2001) couch challenge and the relationship between challenge and support with the outcome of self-authorship.

Resilience

Walsh (2003) defines resilience as the "ability to withstand and rebound from disruptive life challenges" (p. 399). Garmezy (1993) views resilience as a protective factor for individuals and families identifying three recurrent factors: temperament factors; families marked by warmth, cohesion, and a caring adult who may take the place of absent parents; and a well-defined social support network of external support that may be a teacher, neighbor, parents, peers, or an institutional structure such as a caring agency or church. Along with these authors we posit that resilience and protective factors, enmeshed within a strong support network; are keys to buffering the risk/challenge within an adolescent's life; thus building the resilience needed to advance along the journey of self-authorship.

Applying the Model to Adolescents Who Are At Risk

Alhough literature linking self-authorship to adolescence is minimal (Pizzolato, 2006), studies connecting support with risk and resilience in adolescents who are at risk are numerous. The examination of this relationship is a trend in social sciences literature (Gutman, Sameroff, & Eccles, 2002; MacTavish & Salamon, 2006; Walsh, 2002; Woolley & Bowen, 2007).

Woolley and Bowen (2007) use Coleman's (1988) definition of social capital to conceptualize the impact of supportive adults on the school engagement of middle school students from families of lower socioeconomic status (SES) who are racially diverse. The authors conceptualized teachers, adults in the students' neighborhood who were perceived as caring, and involved parents as the social capital of these students, and found that this social capital was integral for dealing with risk in these students' lives. This social capital appears to be similar to Baxter Magolda's (2004) definition of support.

Gutman et al. (2002) found similar performances in those youth 10–14 years of age with regard to self esteem, grade point average, test scores, and class attendance of African American (AA) and Caucasian American (CA) adolescents *until* the middle school transition. At this point the authors found a decrease in performance in those AA adolescents who lacked consistent discipline from parents, and support from sources outside the family.

Walsh (2002) discussed resilience findings in those adolescents who were at risk and noted the "crucial influence" (p. 130) of skilled others such as coaches and teachers who believed in their potential and encouraged them toward success. This support was vital for those adolescents who were at risk and whose families were not able to meet most of their physical, emotional, and cognitive needs.

MacTavish and Salamon (2006) found results regarding the importance of supportive others in the lives of adolescents who were at risk. Their study however was unique in that it focused on adolescents living in a rural trailer park. The authors found a strong link between support of adults in the neighborhood and school environments and discuss the impact of this support in terms of whether the participant was *flourishing* (earning high grades, socially successful, and not associated with the trailer park), *floundering* (associated with the trailer park and failed academically), or *static* (demonstrating qualities of flourishing and floundering youth and having the potential for success).

This study is of particular interest as our participants come from a rural, economically depressed area of the southeastern United States, and demonstrate the qualities of *static youth*. They were judged by their school counselors and principals as academically at risk and were neither *A* students nor *F* students. We believe that static youth such as those in our study can develop the qualities of flourishing youth, capable of making informed decisions if the support in their lives increases and deepens in quality.

Method

Sample   Participants were 115 students enrolled in three cohorts (2005–2007) of the VT STARS residential youth development program. Participants consisted of 54 (49%) males and 56 (51%) females, with five missing responses, who were enrolled in 11 urban and rural high schools in economically depressed areas of southwest Virginia. Their average age was 15 years old. A majority of the sample was AA, with 70 (60.9%) students claiming this racial identity, and 33 (28.7%) were CA. The sample included one report each of Hispanic and Asian American race, two "other" responses, and eight missing responses. All students were identified as academically at risk and recommended for VT STARS by an advisory team in each school district made up of school principals, counselors, and teachers. All selected students had parental permission to participate and an agreement from parents to attend special sessions to develop parental support strategies and the final presentations at the end of the summer program. Criteria for student selection included specific measures to identify and attract females, persons with disabilities, and members of any minority population within the participating school district. Students selected for the program were categorized as *students in the middle,* neither achieving nor failing but in danger of dropping out of school. Their high school experiences thus far were disappointing given their potential as judged by school personnel. The mission of the VT STARS program was to strengthen the academic, interpersonal, and technical skills of participants and to improve their motivation and ability to attain a college degree and entry-level qualifications for the knowledge economy. All selected students received a copy of the mission statement, a schedule of planned events for the on-campus summer program, and subsequent expectations for participation throughout the following academic year with after-school enrichment activities, civic projects, and teacher involvement. Students and their parents signed commitment contracts for full participation in all phases of the program.

Participant Families   Family variables included marital status, highest level of education of mother and father, and number of sisters/stepsisters and brothers/stepbrothers. Specifically, most students lived with their married parents (38.3%), with the second and third largest groups of students living with parents who were divorced/separated (31%) or who had never married (29%) parents. These numbers do not reflect single-parent families, as stepparents and live-in partners are not accounted for in this analysis. A majority of mothers (40%) held high school or equivalent degrees, associate's degrees (25.2%), and bachelor's degrees (18.3%), as did fathers, with percentages of 53.9%, 17.4%, and 6.1%, respectively.

Measurement   All data used in this study are a subset of data from the *Career Decision-Making Survey* developed in the initial stages of a five-year study funded by the National Science Foundation to explore the relationship between self-authorship and students' career decision making (Creamer, Burger, & Meszaros, 2004). The VT STARS program translated the original survey into an online format. Only two of eleven subsets of this original 2005–2007 survey were analyzed in the current study and both subsets were from the decision orientation section. The *Setting Priorities* subset is a 12-item Likert type scale measuring priority-setting when making decisions through agreement/disagreement to statements such as "I am confident about my ability to set my own priorities about schoolwork." The *Decision Making* subset is a 6-item multiple choice section assessing the influence of diverse viewpoints when making decisions such as "What do you see as your primary role in making an educational decision, like the choice of a major or career?" Answer choices to this question include, "To seek direction from informed experts, To acquire as much information as possible, To rely primarily on personal judgment, and To make a decision considering all the available information and my own views." A narrative question, "Sometimes people receive conflicting advice about career options that fit their skills, interests, needs, and values. In a couple of sentences, would you tell us what you think it means when two people, who both know you and both care about you, give you entirely different advice?" was added to the online survey to assess how participants made meaning of conflicting opinions and advice.

Data Collection Procedure   This study received IRB approval in 2005. Students completed the online *Career Decision-Making Survey* as a preassessment prior to the start of the summer experience. Surveys were completed individually in two-hour sessions at on-campus computers. Data analyzed for this study are only from this preassessment.

Quantitative Analysis   Statistical procedures including descriptive and inferential analyses were used in this study, with a critical value of 0.05%. All analyses were conducted using the Statistical Package for the Social Sciences (SPSS) version 13.0.

The coefficient alpha is used to assess the reliability of the two subsets of questions used in this study. The alphas for the Decision Making and Setting Priorities sections were 0.54 and 0.21, respectively. This is admittedly a low level of consistency, which may be one reason why we found few significant results in our quantitative analyses.

Qualitative Analysis   Our definitions and examples of coding for pre–self-authorship, emerging self-authorship, and self-authorship are informed by Baxter Magolda's explanation of self-authorship (2008). We analyzed responses independently using open coding (Strauss & Corbin, 1998) to uncover key themes in individual responses, and we cross-coded all responses to maximize the consistency and accuracy. We initially reached agreement on 75% of the coding categories, discussed rationale for differences, and finally reached consensus on all responses.

Findings

Quantitative Results   The only quantitative analysis with significant results was the chi square analysis of the *Setting Priorities* questions with significant differences between responses to these questions according to ethnicity. Although no other inferential analyses had significant results, a descriptive review of the two sub-parts of the survey suggests the *potential* for self-authored decisions in this population.

The majority of responses in the *Setting Priorities* subsection point to self-authored responses, and this becomes clearer when "Slightly Agree" and "Agree" are combined into one total score, and "Slightly Disagree" and "Disagree" are likewise combined. At least 60% of participants chose a self-authored response for every question with the combined total range of responses to the most self-authored question being 60–97%. Similarly, a majority of participants chose the most self-authored response in five out of the six decision-making subsection questions. Response rates differed, however, by ethnicity, and we believe further in-depth analyses with a larger population are required before positing a reason for this occurrence. Along with this, a discrepancy is evident between the frequency of responses to the self-authored statements in the survey, versus what are judged to be self-authored statements given in response to the narrative question. This may be explained in two ways. Students may be answering survey questions from a social desirability perspective with answers they perceive are "right" and what the researchers are looking to see. Or it may be that students can recognize statements that reflect a higher level of development than they can actually produce. They may simply be recognizing questionnaire items that "sound right" even though their narrative responses when recounting how they resolved a complex issue do not produce the same level of self-authorship. This is likely a measurement issue and will involve the design of better survey instruments.

Qualitative Results   Ninety participants responded to the narrative question. Open coding of the responses resulted in a judgment of 64 instances of pre–self-authorship, 14 judgments of emerging self-authorship, and 12 students judged to exhibit self-authorship. Clear contrasts were evident between responses judged to be in each category. For instance, an example of pre–self-authorship was:

> I would know that those persons are wrong because if they are my friends or whatever they should stick by me and my choices no matter what goes down. If not, I don't think we should be friends.

This statement is judged as pre–self-authorship because it demonstrates the use of external formulas. The multiplicity of choices is not considered, nor is the ability of the student to be right *or* wrong, and the student does not demonstrate a willingness to consider suggestions or alternatives to their reality from others. The student also does not claim responsibility for making the choice.

An example of an emerging self-authorship response was:

> I think you should consider both of the persons' advice. That does not necessarily mean that you have to take both of their advice.

Unlike the student judged to be in pre–self-authorship, this student is willing to consider the suggestions of others, and is thus willing to accept the possibility of multiple realities. However, the student does not claim the choice as his or her own, and therefore, this statement is judged to be in emerging self-authorship.

Selected examples from the 12 responses judged to be in the self-authored range are:

> I would listen to both sides. When I hear both sides I will then figure out what advice fits me best.

> I would take them both under consideration. Also, I would make a pros and cons list of what would be best for me.

> When two people who both know me give two different suggestions on what to do with my life I would sit down and think about what has been told to me and compare and contrast the options. Then I will decide which option best suits me.

These three statements all suggest existing self-authorship within these students. Not only are the students willing to consider suggestions from others (and thus various forms of reality), they also claim the responsibility of the choice as their own.

Although it was not possible to fully interview these students, and our analysis relied upon one narrative question, we can begin to see some possible development of self-authorship among a small percentage of these at-risk high school students.

Discussion

Although generalizability is limited for the quantitative results and discrepancy exists between those results and the qualitative results, it does appear that emerging self-authorship is evident in the adolescent participants. Further, qualitative responses to the narrative question appear to mirror levels of self-authorship as demonstrated by responses to the quantitative questions. Like Pizzolato's (2006) study of adolescent girls engaged in a short story unit where a clear shift in meaning-making occurred, this study also demonstrates potential evidence for a similar shift among our participants.

This population of adolescents faced the challenge of being academically at risk, and had supportive others in their lives in the form of parents who supported their participation in VT STARS and principals, school counselors, and teachers who referred them. Though we cannot know if the youth truly experienced dissonance or a provocative moment when they realized they were academically at risk, they clearly knew they were being invited to have an experience to improve their academic standing, and this may have created some disequilibrium. They also knew they were singled out for a program to strengthen their academic, interpersonal, and technical skills and prepare them to attain a college degree. The provocative moment for them may have been this direct knowledge that they were not measuring up to standards and needed to improve to be successful. It seems possible that their choice of the self-authored responses in the quantitative survey, along with the reflection of this in a small percentage of their narrative responses may be a result of the combination of the challenge of being academically at risk or "static youth," (MacTavish and Salamon, 2006) and the support or "social capital" (Coleman, 1988) in their lives.

These two factors along with a very possible provocative moment may contribute to the emerging and self-authored responses in the results. Though generalizability is again limited, these data reflect prior studies regarding the relationship of support to the navigation of risk and outcome of resilience (Gutman et al., 2002; MacTavish & Salamon, 2006; Walsh, 2002; Woolley & Bowen, 2007) in disadvantaged youth. Further, they reflect prior findings regarding emerging and actual self-authorship in those who face a provocative moment (Baxter Magolda, 2004; Pizzolato, 2003, 2005, 2006). Unlike Pizzolato's study of upper-class, mostly white youth, however, this study appears to be unique in that it focuses on a population that is mostly minority youth from an economically depressed region. This not only has implications for understanding the way risk is successfully navigated by disadvantaged resilient youth, but is possibly a new area for intervention in the lives of youth with the *potential* for resilience as well, and is further evidence of self-authorship emerging in adolescence.

Limitations   This exploratory study has some limitations to note. First, it was a cross-sectional design, with a small convenience sample limited to one economically depressed region of one state and one type of risk: academic risk. Future studies with larger samples and larger numbers of diverse at-risk adolescent populations as well as different risk categories would improve the design and ability of researchers to draw generalizations.

A major limitation was that the survey was in an early stage of development when administered. Another potential limitation was the online format for the survey, as Dillman (2000) notes some concerns about using online surveys. However, all participants in each of the summer cohorts of the VT STARS program were seated together in a computer lab at the time of administration and directions were given to the entire group with sufficient time to complete the survey. All students were high school students and knowledgeable about computers, thus minimizing the potential impact of this limitation.

Finally, this exploratory study is a first attempt by the authors to examine the relationship of risk and challenge and resilience and support to the early development of self-authorship.

Areas for Future Research   Along with further exploration of the relationship between risk, resilience, and self-authorship in the lives of youth with risk factors in their lives, two areas for future exploration seem possible: Mezirow's Transformative Learning Theory (2000) as a strategy for strengthening family functioning to support development of self-authorship, and the more central inclusion of parental support in developing self-authorship in adolescents. We ponder whether there is a role for this theory as a method for developing the support piece in the LPM. Briefly, Mezirow's theory describes how expectations, cultural assumptions, and experiences, and the presence of a disorienting dilemma "directly influence the meaning we derive from our experiences," (Taylor, 1998, p. 6). A disorienting dilemma is much like Pizzolato's provocative moment in that it is a situation whereby usual expectations, assumptions, and coping mechanisms do not provide an adequate solution to a problem (Mezirow, 2000) and new solutions or formulas must be formed. Mezirow (2000), states that transformative learning is a process whereby we transform our "frames of reference," and make them more "inclusive, discriminating, open, emotionally capable of change, and reflective" (pp. 7–8). The purpose of the LPM is to do this very thing: respect different frames of reference, and develop a healthy, supportive partnership. This theory also emphasizes the importance of what Goleman (1998) terms *emotional intelligence* as a precursor to participating in reflective discourse, or mutual meaning-making. Emotional intelligence encompasses "knowing and managing one's emotions, motivating oneself, recognizing emotions in others and handling relationships, as well as clear thinking," (Mezirow, 2000, p. 11). Although this is a leap for adolescents to achieve, we believe the support inherent within the LPM may make this emotional intelligence possible, emphasizing again the potential of transformative learning as the method of the supportive other.

Whereas most of the literature regarding support in the lives of youth with risk factors focuses on external sources that are outside the family, we believe a family focus may also be an area of future research. Although many authors (Gutman et al., 2002; MacTavish & Salamon, 2006; Walsh, 2002; Woolley & Bowen, 2007) posit that social support *outside of the family* is the answer to supporting adolescents as they face the risks in their lives, this well-intentioned assertion potentially communicates a bias against the families of these adolescents because it does not involve them in the intervention. It is our belief that parents/guardians/families of these adolescents can learn to support their youth toward emergent and self-authored meaning-making. For those parents/guardians/families who appear to struggle with providing for the needs of their adolescents in particular, we believe interventions may be put in place to guide these families to more process-oriented support of their adolescents. Beyond shifting the meaning-making of the adolescents, this intervention may also *strengthen the families.*

References

Baxter Magolda, M. (2001). *Making their own way: Narratives for transforming higher education to promote self-development.* Sterling, VA: Stylus Publishing, LLC.

Baxter Magolda, M. (2004). Learning partnerships model. In M. Baxter Magolda and P. M. King (Eds.) *Learning partnerships: Theory and models of practice to educate for self-authorship* (pp. 37–62). Sterling, VA: Stylus Publishing, LLC.

Baxter Magolda, M. B. (2008). Three elements of self-authorship. *Journal of College Student Development, 49,* 269–284.

Baxter Magolda, M. B., & King, P. M. (2007). Interview strategies for assessing self-authorship: Constructing conversations to assess meaning making. *Journal of College Student Development, 48*(5), 491–508.

Coleman, J. S. (1988). Social capital in the creation of human capital. *The American Journal of Sociology, 94,* Supplement: Organizations and Institutions: Sociological and Economic Approaches to the Analysis of Social Structure, S95–S120.

Creamer, E. G., Burger, C. J., & Meszaros, P. S. (2004). Characteristics of high school and college women interested in technology. *Journal of Women and Minorities in Science and Engineering, 10*(1), 67–78.

Dillman, D. A. (2000). *Mail and Internet surveys—The tailored design method.* New York: John Wiley & Sons, Inc.

Garmezy, N. (1993). Children in poverty: Resiliency despite risk. *Psychiatry 56*: 127–136.

Goleman, D. (1998). *Working with emotional intelligence.* New York: Bantam Books.

Gutman, L. M., Sameroff, A. J., & Eccles, J. S. (2002). The academic achievement of African American students during early adolescence: An examination of multiple risk, promotive, and protective factors. *American Journal of Community Psychology, 30,* 367–399.

MacTavish, K. A., & Salamon, S. (2006). Pathways of youth development in a rural trailer park. *Family Relations, 55,* 163–174.

McLoyd, V. C. (1990). The impact of economic hardship on black families and children: Psychological distress, parenting, and socioeconomic development. *Child Development, 61,* 311–346.

McLoyd, V. C. (1998). Socioeconomic disadvantage and child development. *American Psychologist, 53,* 185–204.

Merriam-Webster Dictionary Online. (2008). *Definition of adolescence.* Retrieved May 4, 2008 from: www.merriam-webster.com/dictionary/adolescence.

Mezirow, J. (2000). Learning to think like an adult: Core concepts of transformation theory. In J. Mezirow (Ed.), *Learning as transformation: Critical Perspectives on a theory in progress* (pp. 1–33). San Francisco: Jossey-Bass.

Pizzolato, J. E. (2003). Developing self-authorship: Exploring the experiences of high risk college students. *Journal of College Student Development, 44*(6), 797–812.

Pizzolato, J. E. (2005). Creating crossroads for self-authorship: Investigating the provocative moment. *Journal of College Student Development, 46*(6), 624–641.

Pizzolato, J. E. (2006). Crafting stories, constructing selves: Supporting girls' development through structured short story writing. *Identity: An International Journal of Theory and Research, 6,* 187–206.

Rolf, J. & Johnson, J. (1990). Protected or vulnerable: The challenges of AIDS to developmental psychopathology. In J. Rolf, A. S. Mastern, D. Cicchetti, K. H. Nuechterlein, & S. Weintraub (Eds.). *Risk and protective factors in the development of psychopathology* (pp. 384–404). Cambridge, UK: Cambridge University Press.

Strauss, A., & Corbin, J. (1998). *Basics of qualitative research: Techniques and procedures for developing grounded theory* (2nd ed.). Thousand Oaks, CA: Sage.

Taylor, E. W. (1998). *The theory and practice of transformative leaning: A critical review. Information series no. 374* (Report No. IN 374). Columbus, OH: Center on Education and Training for Employment. (ERIC Document Reproduction Service No. ED423422).

Walsh, F. (2002). A family resilience framework: Innovative practice applications. *Family Relations, 51,* 130–137.

Walsh, F. (2003). Family resilience: Strengths forged through adversity. In F. Walsh (Ed.) *Normal family processes: Growing diversity and complexity* (3rd ed., pp. 399–459). New York: The Guilford Press.

Woolley, M. E. & Bowen, G. L. (2007). In the context of risk: Supportive adults and the school engagement of middle school students. *Family Relations, 56,* 92–104.

6

TOWARD SELF-AUTHORSHIP IN CHILD CARE STUDENTS
Implications for Working With Children and Their Families

Joanne Brownlee, Donna Berthelsen,
and Gillian Boulton-Lewis

Abstract: Using self-authorship as a theoretical framework, this chapter examines the relationship between personal epistemology and beliefs about children's learning for students studying to be child care workers in Australia. Scenario-based interviews were used to investigate how students' views of knowledge, identity, and relationships with others were related to beliefs about how children learn. Implications for vocational education are discussed.

A large body of research now demonstrates that the formal pre-service education of early childhood teachers is one significant way in which quality child care and outcomes for children can be improved. In particular, the beliefs that early childhood teachers hold about relationships with children seem to be related to beliefs about children's learning and personal epistemology (Brownlee & Berthelsen, 2004). This chapter examines the relationship between personal epistemology and beliefs about children's learning for students studying to be child care workers in Australia. We focus on self-authorship theory to understand students' sense of ownership of knowledge, identity, and relationships with others, in the development of their epistemological beliefs (Pizzolato & Ozaki, 2007). In this chapter we emphasize the nature and development of students' epistemological beliefs. We take the view that a mature personal epistemology is a prerequisite to being an effective child care practitioner.

Background

Over the last 30 years, a strong research literature has developed in the area of personal epistemology. Personal epistemological beliefs are those beliefs that individuals hold about the nature of knowing and knowledge (Hofer & Pintrich, 1997). From a developmental tradition, many researchers such as Perry (1970); Belenky, Clinchy, Goldberger, and Tarule, (1986); Baxter Magolda (1994); and Kuhn and Weinstock (2002) have demonstrated that individuals change their beliefs over time in a similar way, often as a result of educational experiences.

According to Kuhn and Weinstock (2002), at first individuals hold absolutist epistemological beliefs about knowing. This means that knowledge is viewed as "right or wrong," and does not need to be examined because the source of knowledge simply transmits the "right" information to the individual. Next, individuals with multiplist epistemological beliefs consider knowledge to be founded upon personal opinions. From this perspective, knowledge remains personal, intuitive, and unexamined. Finally, individuals with evaluativistic beliefs about knowledge, like individuals who hold multiplist beliefs, acknowledge that knowledge is personally constructed. However, an evaluativist weighs the evidence to construct this understanding. Knowledge is considered to be evolving, tentative, and evidence-based.

Personal Epistemology and Beliefs About Learning

The personal epistemology research literature has demonstrated that core beliefs about knowing and knowledge influence learning. Brownlee (2001) found, for example, that student teachers with evaluativistic beliefs were more likely to use deep approaches to learning that were focused on making meaning. Other research has also demonstrated links between epistemological beliefs and learning (e.g., Hammer, 2003). Links also exist between epistemological beliefs and teachers' beliefs about children's learning (Doverborg & Pramling, 1996).

Brownlee and Berthelsen (2004) showed that child care workers' epistemological beliefs were related to beliefs about children's learning. Child care workers with evaluativistic beliefs believed that children learn through a process of actively constructing knowledge. Child care workers with subjectivist epistemological beliefs were more likely to think that children learn by modeling behaviors of others and being active (e.g., through play). However, we know that children in constructivist child-centered environments are more likely to have increased motivation and increased problem solving skills compared with children in teacher-centered teaching environments in which teachers take a transmissive stance (Daniels & Shumow, 2003).

Self-Authorship: Beyond Personal Epistemological Beliefs

Although it is important to consider epistemological beliefs and their connections with learning, our global communities require us to interact in ways that go beyond epistemology to encompass respectful and supportive interactions with others. This is considered within self-authorship theory. Self-authorship is central to adult thinking and involves the ability to gather and critique information in the context of one's own personal beliefs (Creamer & Laughlin, 2005). From this perspective, the self is central to development and learning in higher education (Baxter Magolda, 2003). Self-authorship involves a holistic view of the learner (Meszaros, 2007) with a process of meaning-making that includes epistemological, interpersonal (social relationships), and intrapersonal (personal values and identity) dimensions (Kegan, 1994). This means that in order to think in complex ways one must be able to evaluate multiple perspectives (epistemological dimension) in the context of understanding one's personal beliefs and values (intrapersonal dimension), and building healthy social relationships (interpersonal dimension). The construction of knowledge must involve weighing both formal and personal knowledge in social contexts. According to Meszaros (2007), such an approach to learning may provide a platform on which to build a culture change in higher and further education.

This study aimed to investigate self-authorship in child care students in the context of their professional training courses to work in child care settings. It also explored how the development of self-authorship was related to their beliefs about children's learning.

Method

In 2007, all students completing a Diploma of Children's Services at four vocational education institutes, located in a large metropolitan area in Australia, were invited to participate in a federally funded research project[1]. A total of 47 students from the two-year Diploma course agreed to participate, which involved a semi-structured interview that included reflection about a typical behavior management scenario that might occur in a child care setting. The Diploma of Children's Services enables students to work as group leaders in child care centers in Australia. A group leader is expected to take responsibility for the overall management of a group of children in a child care program. All of the modules in the diploma course have a practical focus, although students are also required to show an understanding of how theories of children's learning and teaching in early childhood programs is enacted in teaching practice.

Participants

Of the 47 students who participated in the research, 43 were female. Thirty-eight of the students were under 25 years of age. Most students (n = 32) had completed high school. Twelve students held post-secondary qualifications, such as certificates and diplomas, from disciplines such as business and hospitality. Most students (n = 32) had no previous work experience in child care settings.

Interviews

A common way of investigating epistemological beliefs is through the use of semi-structured interviews (e.g., Belenky et al., 1986). However, Brownlee, Boulton-Lewis, and Berthelsen (2008) reported that many students had difficulties with some interview questions that explore personal epistemology. In an effort to make more concrete and less abstract the ideas about knowledge and learning, we embedded in the semi-structured interview questions a common practice scenario that students might encounter in their field experiences in child care settings. The use of scenarios to explore learners' perspectives has an extensive history in educational psychology, providing opportunity for learners to deal with big ideas that are significant to practice (Sudzina, 1997). Learners consider the situation and the range of perspectives from which it can be understood, as well as the different ways to respond (Dockett & Tegel, 1995, 1996). This approach was based on the work of Stacey, Brownlee, and Thorpe (2005) and Nist and Holschuch (2005), who noted that participants are able to discuss their views more cogently when a familiar scenario is presented. The audio-taped interviews lasted 30 to 60 minutes, and were transcribed verbatim.

The students in the current study were interviewed using the scenario on page 105 (drawn from Stacey et al., 2005).

---

[1] This research was funded by the Australian Research Council 2006–2008.

Daniel Kennedy is 4 years old and he has just arrived with his Mum at his child care center. He is generally very sociable and plays immediately with the other children when dropped off. Today, however, he holds onto Mum's leg, cries loudly, and will not let her go. Mum is becoming upset by this and some other children begin to cry. Mrs. Bennett, the center director, takes hold of Daniel and says, "Just go quickly." His mother does so and Daniel became more upset and hits Mrs. Bennett.

> Do you think that this was the right action by the center director in this sit-
> uation? What would you do? Sometimes people talk about there being "right
> answers" or "truth" in child care practice. What are your views? Do you agree
> with the idea that there are no right answers in child care practice? Do think
> that anybody's opinion is as good as another?

Daniel's behavior did not improve throughout the morning. It escalated when he bit another child. The group leader began talking to Daniel about this incident. However, Mrs. Bennett, who happened to be in the room, thought that this was insufficient. She took Daniel by the arm and took him to the naughty mat and told him to stay there. The group leader was worried about Daniel and tried to speak to Mrs. Bennett.

Mrs. Bennett said, "Experts say that you must be firm with children every time and use time out. It will make him behave better." The group leader was too nervous to raise her objections with Mrs. Bennett. She was unsure about the right way to manage a child in this situation but she remembered reading things like what Mrs. Bennett was saying in textbooks. She thought to herself, "Experts must be right, mustn't they? It doesn't feel right though."

> What do you think is going on in the group leader's mind? Could the text-
> books and Mrs. Bennett be wrong? Do you trust the opinions of experts?
>
> How do you learn? How do you go about learning something that you think
> is important to know that would help you to be a good group leader? How
> do you know when you have learnt something? So can you tell me what you
> think learning is? What are the most important ways in which your current
> course is helping you to learn about child care practice?
>
> How do you think children learn? Can you think of an experience you have
> had with a child where you really noticed that he or she had learnt some-
> thing? How do you know when a child has learnt something?

Analyzing Interviews

We used a deductive (theory-driven) approach to analyze the interviews and to categorize responses that described students' personal epistemology, whereas an inductive (data-driven) analytic approach was used to analyze students' beliefs about children's learning and the intrapersonal and interpersonal dimensions of self-authorship theory.

The deductive approach was used to analyze personal epistemologies because this field has a strong research tradition, and categories to describe beliefs have emerged consistently in the literature over the last 30 years. The categories used for the classification of epistemological beliefs in this analysis were complex evaluativistic thinking, practical evaluativistic thinking, subjectivist thinking, and objectivist thinking.

In contrast, individuals' beliefs about children's learning were not coded deductively because of a paucity of research into beliefs about children's learning. Instead, inductive analysis was used to identify categories in the data. Beliefs about children's learning were classified according to the level of understanding demonstrated that children's learning is a process of making meaning, and that children are competent and active processors of information. Similarly, inductive analysis was also used to identify categories about the intrapersonal and interpersonal dimensions of self-authorship theory that reflected, for the intrapersonal dimension, a sense of a professional identity in being a teacher of young children and, for the interpersonal dimension, the level of evidence reflecting respect for diversity and others' values, including those of family and children, as well as for colleagues in their professional practice.

We used dialogic reliability checking to ensure credible findings (Åkerlind, 2005). A second researcher, who was skilled in epistemological beliefs interview analysis, was asked to analyze a sample of responses using the established categories. Agreement was reached on 94% of the beliefs about children's learning categories and 88% of the categories on the intrapersonal and interpersonal dimensions. When disagreement occurred, differences were resolved through discussion.

Discussion of Findings

The interviews revealed four main profiles of self-authorship beliefs. The findings are presented through these group profiles that represent belief frameworks. These profiles are labeled according to the level of epistemological beliefs held (complex evaluativism, practical evaluativism, subjectivist thinking, and objectivist thinking). Each of these profiles will be discussed in turn, and related to the interpersonal and intrapersonal dimensions of self-authorship, as well as to beliefs about children's learning.

Complex Evaluativistic Thinking Profile

Fifteen students described knowledge as tentative, evolving, and needing to be backed up with theoretical evidence. These beliefs are referred to as *complex evaluativism*. One student who held this profile said:

> Everybody is going to have a different opinion. You can talk to that person and work out why your opinions are different in something. It may change your own opinion by listening to other people if you agree with what they were saying and the way they supported it. You can trust experts if there's evidence to support it and if there's a few different studies or experts who have the same opinion.

It is of interest that although evidence, in particular theoretical evidence, is important in justifying an opinion, this student clearly indicated that informed opinions still had to resonate with her own beliefs.

The students who held this profile believed that there were no "right answers" in child care. They indicated that children, parents, staff, and centers varied enormously and this diversity must be taken into account in relation to teaching practices with children.

> If it's like about how to bring up a child or how to teach a child, there are no right or wrong answers because people have different ways of teaching their children.

Such responses indicated that students were aware of multiple perspectives and the need to work with diversity in child care settings. A sense of professional identity was evident, as well as recognition of the importance of respecting different family and professional values.

Students with a complex evaluativistic profile also described children's learning as a process of making meaning. For example:

> They learn through their own experiences; they learn through experimentation; exploring different items and they figure it out in their own way. No matter what they've got in front of them they're going to figure out something they can do with that item and you may not have even thought of it. I don't know . . . they *figure it out in their own way* and usually it is so amazing what they can do with these things.

Such a view of children's learning indicates that children are competent and active processors of information. It is also evident that linking knowledge to one's personal beliefs is an important component of learning even for children.

The students were considered to hold a complex evaluativistic profile if they analyzed information to arrive at their own opinions using research and theory.

Practical Evaluativistic Thinking Profile

Sixteen students had profiles described as *practical evaluativism*. Their epistemological beliefs focused on analyzing practices rather than being informed by theoretical ideas. For example, the following quote shows how the student would use others' opinions to construct knowledge:

> Probably through discussions and just letting them explain their own beliefs and how to deal with it; then incorporating how you would like to (do it), your own beliefs, and then coming up with something that incorporates both your and their ideas.

These beliefs do not reflect complex evaluativistic beliefs, in which theory and practice are critically analyzed to develop evidence-based knowledge. Students in this group talked about how they would critically analyze the practices of others, although not from the perspective of research and theory. In terms of the intrapersonal dimension of self-authorship, these students reflect what Pizzolato and Ozaki (2007) describe as being in transition, or at the crossroads, between following formulas and self-authorship. They talked about relying on their personal beliefs in the assessment of "experts' practice." In terms of the interpersonal dimension of self-authorship, students with practical evaluativistic profiles emphasized respect for others in their professional practice. They indicated that differences between children, parents, staff, and child care centers meant that they could not rely on having right answers and that varied perspectives needed to be valued and respected. For example:

> I suppose you could say there are no right answers . . . it depends, really, on the question. Right answers, if it's coming down to regulations or rules or something like that, then yes, there's always a definite right answer. If it comes down to how you deal with a child who's showing separation anxiety, there is not a right answer. It depends completely on the child. It depends on the parent. It also depends on the carer and the center in which you are working.

The focus on skills and strategies rather than theory has important implications for the way in which students construct child care practice, how they evaluate the practices of experts in their field, their beliefs about how children learn, and how they interact with children in their child care programs. Rather than examining theory and research, these students evaluated strategies they observed in their professional practice.

These students' views of children's learning present an interesting variation on what was found in the previous profile of complex evaluativism. They talked about children's learning typically as active and based on observing others around them. However, there was no clear indication that they believe children are competent processors of meaning, as was the case for those who espoused complex evaluativistic beliefs. For example:

> The other day I planned this activity for this particular child, just like giving them more experiences. They seemed to become engrossed in what they were doing and learned a lot more because they had so many more things available. I was supportive as well as allowing them to do their own thing and build their skills.

This quote exemplifies the typical view that children learn by being active, but shows no evidence of a belief that children construct their own knowledge.

Subjectivist Thinking Profile

Fourteen students held *subjectivist* epistemological beliefs, in which knowledge is based on one's personal opinions. From this perspective, knowledge is predominantly intuitive, based on feelings, and does not need to be supported with evidence—neither practical nor theoretical. For example:

> Look at other people's opinions; use it to see where other people are coming from. Have a more open view on what people's opinions are. You don't necessarily have to take on their opinion, but you have to show that you have respect for how they feel about situations and, if you're taking care of their child, then to take their opinion into consideration.

These students did not talk about constructing their own beliefs, so it is not clear how their professional identity was developing for teaching in child care contexts. They were not analyzing information or other opinions and so they did not talk about how other perspectives fitted with their own views.

Eleven of these students believed that, on some issues, absolute knowledge exists as to what is right in child care practice, whereas on other issues, personal judgments must be made (no right answers). These students held what appeared to be contradictory beliefs. The beliefs considered to be absolute reflected the importance of adhering to the regulations and licensing requirements set by regulatory authorities. Developmentally, this is a transitional phase for these students as they seek to find a balance about how their personal knowledge about good practice sits with their recognition of their responsibilities to meet regulations. The other three students who held a subjectivist thinking profile took an absolutist position that experts provide right answers that inform child care practice, and did not acknowledge the importance of a personal construction of meaning.

As was evident for the previous two thinking profiles, most of these students believed that it was impossible to rely on absolute knowledge in child care because children, parents, staff, and centers varied extensively and these perspectives must be respected. This suggests that they valued relationships with others in the child care context.

These students typically described children's learning as based on observation and being active:

> Children learn from experiences by actually doing things, you know by hands on, getting in there and trying things.

These views of children's learning do not give any clear indication of a belief that children are competent constructors of meaning. The focus is on repeating what has been observed or simply being active in some way (e.g., investigating, experimenting, and playing).

Objectivist Thinking Profile

Two students held beliefs about knowing and knowledge that were *objectivist* in nature. They believed that child care practice was based only on "black and white" knowledge. This is an absolute position, that experts can supply the "right answers" about good practice in child care. Personal construction of meaning about what is good practice, based on evaluating theoretical and research evidence and reflecting on personal experience, was not expressed in these students' beliefs.

> I mean there are specific right and wrongs. There might be some that are wrong but I think there are more that have got a yes or a no answer than ones that are a maybe.

Their views demonstrated a clear lack of focus on active construction of meaning. This view was also reflected in their descriptions of children's learning as observing and modeling others around them. For example:

> They'll imitate mum and dad, what they do through play or what they've seen their teacher do . . . whatever they have come into contact with they'll use that.

These students did not say that children must be competent processors of information in constructing their own knowledge. They also did not discuss their personal beliefs (intrapersonal dimension). Similar to subjectivist thinking, these students did not talk about their own beliefs, possibly because they were not focused on analysis of other perspectives and how these might fit with their own views. They also did not talk about the interpersonal dimension of self-authorship.

Implications

Students who held evaluativist profiles (practical, $n = 16$, and complex, $n = 15$) described knowing as a process of analyzing other perspectives. Although these students often agreed that all opinions must be respected, there was a clear sense that knowledge must be justified by analyzing opinions in relation to other perspectives, including their own. Even though students with practical evaluativist thinking frameworks may have been more concerned with practice than theory, they clearly indicated that practical knowledge must be evaluated rather than simply accepted, as was the case for students with subjectivist profiles (n = 14) or objectivist profiles (n = 2). Individuals with both subjectivist and objectivist frameworks did not focus on actively evaluating information to develop their knowledge base for practice.

What is also clear is that students who evaluate information in the light of their own beliefs hold more sophisticated views about children's learning. Complex evaluativistic thinkers, in particular, are more likely to describe children as competent constructors rather than receivers of knowledge. A teacher with evaluativist beliefs is more likely to view the meaning of teaching and the roles that teachers have in relation to the construction of meaning. On the other hand, teachers with objectivist beliefs may see their role as transmitting knowledge to children (Chan & Elliott, 2004). We still need to investigate how such beliefs are enacted in child care practice. However, these preliminary findings suggest that complex epistemologies are related to constructivist views about children's learning, which are considered to underpin the provision of quality learning experiences in child care settings. Effective teachers in child care model appropriate language and behavior, and also provide children with experiences that will enable them to derive meaning from these experiences (Siraj-Blatchford & Sylva, 2004).

An interesting finding in this study was the important role played by personal beliefs in the process of learning and knowing. Students with evaluativistic thinking frameworks (both complex and practical) described how they analyzed others' perspectives in the light of their own beliefs. They clearly understood that they could not simply accept someone else's opinions or practices, but that they had to analyze information and connect with what they personally believed. This demonstrated that students are finding and using their own professional voice and values related to child care practice (intrapersonal dimension of self-authorship). However, this was not the case for those students with subjectivist and objectivist thinking profiles. These students did not discuss the need to link knowledge to personal beliefs in their responses, possibly because they were not focused on analyses of others' perspectives and how these might fit with their own views. These students could be described as displaying pre–self-authorship beliefs.

Self-authorship is dependent on healthy social relationships (interpersonal dimension). All but six students in the study indicated the importance of respect for diversity in children, parents, other staff, and centers. This was reflected in the responses to the question, "Are there right answers in child care?" in which they recognized that no right answers in child care practice are possible because of diverse perspectives. However, although awareness is evident, our data does not provide any evidence of the enactment of these beliefs in practice. This is an area of research that must be investigated further. Students who articulated evaluativistic thinking (practical and complex) held sophisticated epistemological beliefs (epistemological dimension) and recognized the role of personal beliefs and values in knowing (intrapersonal dimension). It seems that all students, excluding those with objectivist beliefs, were able to acknowledge the need to accommodate diverse perspectives (interpersonal dimension).

To promote self-authorship we must focus on complex thinking that involves the three dimensions of self-authorship: evaluativistic thinking (epistemological dimension of self-authorship) in the context of maintaining personal beliefs and values (intrapersonal) and healthy social relationships (interpersonal). Self-authorship requires critical personal reflection. This theory may provide a way to promote a culture change in education (Meszaros, 2007). The notion of reflection, particularly how new knowledge is constructed in relation to existing personal beliefs, is important for teachers in the child care context. Learning in practice ideally involves an action-reflection-action cycle to promote effective practice (Boshuizen, 2004). Child care professionals must engage in reflection that goes beyond analyzing a range of different practices to also incorporate theoretical and research perspectives.

One way to promote such reflection is to ensure that assessment in professional preparation programs goes beyond the measurement of skills and competencies. Competency-based assessment that is mandated for vocational education programs in Australia does not require students to engage in extensive reflection. Assessment must challenge students, including how to evaluate competing claims about knowledge and how different claims connect with the development of their own knowledge and how to apply it. As Boshuizen (2004) suggests, we must engage in further research about the nature of complex learning in practical contexts. We argue that this may be accomplished through a focus on self-authorship. Further research using self-authorship theory to understand the development of the professional identity of teachers of young children in child care settings can provide the platform for understanding and promoting more critical reflection and the deep learning required to work effectively in child care contexts.

References

Åkerlind, G. (2005). Variation and commonality in phenomenographic research methods. *Higher Education Research and Development, 24*(4), 321–334.

Baxter Magolda, M. B. (1994). Post-college experiences and epistemology. *Review of Higher Education, 18*(1), 25–44.

Baxter Magolda, M. (2003). Identity and learning: Student affair's role in transforming education. *Journal of College Student Development, 44*(2), 231–247.

Belenky, M. F., Clinchy, B. M., Goldberger, N. R., & Tarule, J. M. (1986). *Women's ways of knowing: The development of self, voice and mind.* New York: Basic Books.

Boshuizen, H. P. A. (2004). Does practice make perfect? A slow and discontinuous process. In H. P. Boshuizen, R. Bromme, & H. Gruber (Eds.), *Professional learning: Gaps and transitions on the way from novice to expert.* Dordrecht, The Netherlands: Kluwer.

Brownlee, J. (2001). Knowing and learning in teacher education: A theoretical framework of core and peripheral epistemological beliefs. *Asia Pacific Journal of Teacher Education & Development, 4*(1), 167–190.

Brownlee, J., & Berthelsen, D. (2004). Working with toddlers in child care: Personal epistemologies and practice. *European Early Childhood Education Research Journal, 12*(1), 55–70.

Brownlee, J., Boulton-Lewis, G., & Berthelsen, D. (2008). Epistemological beliefs in child care: Implications for vocational education and course design. *British Journal of Educational Psychology, 78,* 457–471.

Chan, K., & Elliott, R. (2004). Relational analysis of personal epistemology and conceptions about teaching and learning. *Teaching and Teacher Education, 20*(8), 817–831.

Creamer, E., & Laughlin, A. (2005). Self-authorship and women's career decision making. *Journal of College Student Development, 46*(1), 13–27.

Daniels, D., & Shumow, L. (2003). Child development and classroom teaching: A review of the literature and implications for educating teachers. *Applied Developmental Psychology, 23,* 495–526.

Dockett, S., & Tegel, K. (1995). Situation based learning in early childhood teacher training. *Teaching Review, 3*(1), 40–44.

Dockett, S., & Tegel, K. (1996). Identifying dilemmas for early childhood educators. *Journal of Australian Research in Early Childhood Education, 3,* 20–28.

Doverborg, E., & Pramling, I. (1996). *Learning and development in early childhood education.* Stockholm: Liber.

Hammer, D. (2003). Tapping epistemological resources for learning physics. *Journal of Learning Sciences, 12*(1), 53–91.

Hofer, B., & Pintrich, P. R. (1997). The development of epistemological theories: Beliefs about knowledge and knowing and their relation to learning. *Review of Educational Research, 67*(1), 88–144.

Kegan, R. (1994). *In over our heads: The mental demands of modern life.* Cambridge, MA: Harvard University Press.

Kuhn, D., & Weinstock, M. (2002). What is epistemological thinking and why does it matter? In B. Hofer & P. Pintrich (Eds.) *Personal epistemology: The psychological beliefs about knowledge and knowing.* Mahwah, NJ: Lawrence Erlbaum.

Meszaros, P. (2007). The journey of self-authorship: Why is it necessary? In P. S. Meszaros (Ed.), *Self-authorship: Advancing student's intellectual growth: New Directions for Teaching and Learning,* (Number 109, pp. 5–14). San Francisco, CA: Jossey-Bass.

Nist, S., & Holschuch, J. (2005). Practical applications of the research on epistemological beliefs. *Journal of College Reading and Learning, 35*(2), 84–92.

Perry, W. G. (1970). *Forms of intellectual and ethical development in the college years.* New York: Holt, Rinehart and Winston.

Pizzolato, J., & Ozaki, C. (2007). Moving toward self-authorship: Investigating outcomes of learning partnerships. *Journal of College Student Development, 48*(2), 196–214.

Siraj-Blatchford, I., & Sylva, K. (2004). Researching pedagogy in English preschools. *British Educational Research Journal, 30*(5), 713–730.

Stacey, P. S., Brownlee, J., Thorpe, K., & Class EAB016 (2005). Measuring and manipulating epistemological beliefs in early childhood pre-service teachers. *International Journal of Pedagogies and Learning, 1,* 6–17.

Sudzina, M. R. (1997). Case study as a constructivist pedagogy for teaching educational psychology. *Educational Psychology Review, 9*(2), 199–208.

7

EPISTEMOLOGICAL DEVELOPMENT OF BEDOUINS AND JEWS IN ISRAEL
Implications for Self-Authorship

Michael Weinstock

Abstract: The development of self-authorship entails attainment of a contextual epistemology. Cultural values and practices concerning knowing might influence epistemological development and beliefs. Bedouin-Israeli adolescents, from an authority-oriented culture, displayed different response patterns to an epistemological assessment than did autonomy-oriented Jewish-Israeli adolescents. Such findings prompt consideration of the culture-specificity of self-authorship.

The development of a sophisticated epistemology is essential to the development of the internally defined sense of self that is the cornerstone of self-authored reasoning and action (Baxter Magolda, 2001; Pizzolato, 2003, 2007). Understanding knowledge to be contextual, rather than either externally given and fixed or very uncertain and idiosyncratic, is the basis for people's questioning, clarifying, and then enacting their personal goals, values, and beliefs in interpersonal relationships (Baxter Magolda, 2001; Pizzolato, 2007). In self-authorship theory, this level of epistemological development is a condition for self-authorship, defined as the capacity to internally define a belief system and identity that coordinates interpersonal relations (Boes, Baxter Magolda, & Buckley, this volume).

In the ideal endpoint of epistemological development one understands that knowledge is relative, and, thus, entails multiple knowledge perspectives and necessitates construction and evaluation. These understandings are the basis for an internally driven sense of self that determines values, beliefs, and life-courses (Perry, 1970). This level of epistemological development has been found, although not broadly, in research in mostly American contexts, particularly among people with higher education (Baxter Magolda, 1998; King & Kitchener, 1994; Weinstock & Cronin, 2003).

As engagement in a certain context—formal education—seems the most important factor in epistemological development, perhaps epistemological development is not a natural, age-related development. Rather epistemologies develop consistently with the goals and values of particular cultural activities. The ideal endpoint of epistemological development described in mainstream research may not be the endpoint in cultures with different values, educational goals, and practices in which adults engage.

A Theory of Epistemological Development

The construct of epistemological development used in this chapter concerns cognition and knowledge building with a particular focus on understandings about knowledge justification, the role of interpretation in knowing, and whether knowledge admits uncertainty. As proposed by Kuhn (Kuhn, 1991; Leadbeater & Kuhn, 1989), epistemology consists of understandings concerning knowledge construction and evaluation, and has a developmental course in which knowledge is first seen as objective (absolutist), then subjective (multiplist), and then a balancing of the objective and subjective aspects of knowing (evaluativist) (Kuhn & Weinstock, 2002). This description is consistent with the trajectory and groupings of Perry's (1970) epistemological positions and King and Kitchener's (1994) elaboration of Perry's theory, as well as many of the other perspectives that focus on personal epistemological development (Hofer & Pintrich, 1997).

This orientation derives from Perry's (1970) essential finding that much of the epistemological thinking of undergraduates and changes in their epistemological positions center on the confrontation with multiple, discrepant perspectives. Consistent with the role of epistemology in self-authorship, this construct views one's epistemology as a theory-in-action, rather than a set of static beliefs, that guides thinking and sense-making about knowledge in everyday problems. Although this research orientation has focused on the intellectual dimension of student development, the theory posits that epistemological thinking is not strictly cognitive, but also is dispositional and value-laden (Kuhn, 2001; Weinstock & Cronin, 2003). Kuhn and Park (2005) found that epistemological levels are related to the valuing of engagement in difficult questions with uncertain answers. Moreover, they found cultural differences in such intellectual values as well as in the related epistemological levels. Additionally, children's epistemological understandings and intellectual values reflected that of their parents. As people's epistemologies appear to be bound up with cultural values and interactions, research on the epistemological dimension of self-authorship is not entirely separable from the intrapersonal and interpersonal dimensions.

Epistemological Development and Culture

That epistemology is related to socialized values (Kuhn & Park, 2005), and that particular educational and non-educational practices might influence its development (Baxter Magolda, 2001; Weinstock & Zviling-Beiser, in press), points to culture as a factor in epistemological development. In her review of the small body of cross-cultural epistemological research, Hofer (2008) reports that the findings from Western samples are not always replicated in other cultures. It is not simply that some cultures are more or less sophisticated in their epistemological beliefs. The "endpoint" and course of epistemological development might differ by culture. Cultural values might guide epistemological development (Hofer, 2008; Tabak & Weinstock, 2008). For instance, Chan and Elliot (2002) posit the influence of Confucian values in China and other East Asian countries.

The findings of the existent cross-cultural research indicate that the proposed construct of personal epistemology may not adequately describe the epistemologies of various cultures (Chan & Elliot, 2002; Hofer, 2008, Youn, 2000; Zhang, 1999) and that transitions in epistemological levels appear at different ages and levels of experience than might have been predicted. For instance, Karabenick and Moosa (2005) found that college students from Oman had different epistemological beliefs than their counterparts in the United States. They were more absolutist in the dimensions of the certainty and source of knowledge (see Hofer & Pintrich, 1997 for full descriptions of the dimensions).

Indications of possible culture differences in epistemology also come from research on cognitive phenomena, including causal attribution, attention, rule-learning, and the preference for dialectic or non-contradictory arguments in both formal and informal argumentation (see Nisbett, Peng, Choi, & Norenzayan, 2001). Peng and Nisbett (1999) found that when presented with contradictions in argument and social situations, American students were more likely to assert that one side had to be right and the other wrong. Chinese students were more likely to use dialectical arguments to look for a compromise position. In social situations, the Chinese students looked for ways to apportion blame evenly. Peng and Nisbett (1999; Nisbett et al., 2001) argue that the differences come from different epistemologies, with the American students having an analytic epistemology, essentially following the Greek philosophic tradition, and the Chinese students having a holistic epistemology, essentially following the Confucian tradition.

These two different conceptions of interpersonal conflict and knowledge contradictions raise questions about the phases of the development of self-authorship described by Baxter Magolda (2001). Whether contradictions provide the disequilibration necessary to engage in the struggle to develop internal foundations, whether one regards life's contradictions as a challenge to the self or a social order, and whether the resolutions to contradictions involve a more defined autonomous self or an interdependent self could well differ according to these epistemologies.

The Current Research—Epistemological Differences Between Bedouins and Jews in Israel

In the common distinction made between collectivist and individualist cultures (Triandis, 1989), collectivist cultures maintain clearly differentiated social roles, emphasizing interdependence and social goals, and individualistic cultures prize personal autonomy, personal freedoms, and the pursuit of personal goals. Although differing with Triandis' dichotomous approach, both in terms of the polarities and number of value orientations, Schwartz (1999) found differences in Arab-Israeli and Jewish-Israeli value orientations that resemble the collectivist/individualist distinction. These groups appear, respectively, to have hierarchical and mastery value orientations. Hierarchical values stress the legitimate unequal distributions of roles and power; mastery values stress self-assertion, competence, and independence.

Given different perspectives on authority, these cultural types might hold different beliefs about authority as a source of knowledge and about what is considered an authoritative method in establishing knowledge claims. An "absolutist" epistemology includes beliefs that knowledge comes from authoritative, objective, external sources, whereas "multiplist" or "evaluativist" epistemologies include beliefs that knowledge comes from personal construction and is influenced by subjective perspective. A hierarchically oriented collectivist culture might well prescribe social roles that have greater or lesser epistemic authority, whereas a mastery-oriented individualist culture would give the individual greater decision making, and presumably, epistemic authority.

Another cultural distinction concerns gender roles. Although individualist cultures are hardly immune from fostering stereotypical social roles, the emphasis of collectivist cultures on prescribed social roles and hierarchical relations, which in Arab-Israeli societies are strongly patriarchal, would enforce even greater gender-role differences. Results of American studies have been inconclusive regarding gender differences. Many have not found great gender differences in overall epistemological level (Kuhn, 1991; Kuhn, Cheney, & Weinstock, 2000; Leadbeater & Kuhn, 1989; Weinstock & Cronin, 2003). King and Kitchener (1994) found that men in half their studies had higher epistemological levels, but noted that the men also had overall higher educational attainment. Studies that focus more explicitly on gender (e.g., Baxter Magolda, 1992; Belenky, Clinchy, Goldberger, & Tarule, 1986) specify gender-specific ways of knowing within epistemological positions, yet typically confirm the overall course of development posited by Perry (1970). Hofer (2000) tested her conceptualization that epistemology consists of the four dimensions of the certainty, simplicity, source, and justification of knowledge across gender and college major. First-year college men were more likely than women to believe that knowledge is certain and unchanging and that authority is the source of knowledge. These studies, thus, suggest different patterns of growth in dimensions although not in overall epistemological level.

Cross-Cultural Research With Bedouins and Jews in Israel

In several studies, I have assessed the epistemological levels of Bedouin and Jewish adolescents in Israel. In this chapter, I report data from three preliminary studies that have served as the basis for a larger, ongoing project on epistemological understandings and argumentation norms across a variety of ethnic and religious groups in Israel. Although this research focuses on epistemological development without reference to self-authorship theory, investigations of the trajectory of epistemological development in adolescence should have bearing, given epistemology's role as a pillar of self-authorship.

Although they share geographic proximity, Israeli Bedouins and Jews live in very different worlds. They are profoundly separated by history, religion, language, lifestyle, family structure, and economic opportunity. They live in different towns and attend different schools. The schools are segregated for geographic reasons, and because the state school system maintains several tracks (secular, Jewish religious, Arab) to allow for tailored additions to the standard curriculum (Tabak & Weinstock, 2008).

The instrument (Kuhn et al., 2000) used in these studies is part of a research tradition that evokes epistemological thinking by having participants respond to questions regarding discrepant knowledge claims (e.g., Chandler, Boyes, & Ball, 1990; King & Kitchener, 1994; Kuhn & Weinstock, 2002). Such tasks were meant to distill the experience reported by the participants in Perry's (1970) open-ended interviews; life during the college years was characterized by confrontations with discrepant knowledge and values claims. The paper-and-pencil assessment used by Kuhn et al. (2000) has been found to be effective in assigning individuals to epistemological level based on similar assignment with the "Livia" task interview instrument (Kuhn et al., 2000), in which people's explanations of how historians arrive at discrepant accounts of a historical event are coded according to level of epistemological understanding.

The instrument allows assignment to absolutist, multiplist, or evaluativist epistemological level. The assessment consists of 15 items, each containing two discrepant knowledge statements. The items take the form of the following:
An indication that one must be right and the other wrong (choice 1a) is designated as an absolutist response. An indication that both are equally right

---

Dana thinks one explanation of the cause of colds is the best.
Sharon thinks another explanation of the cause of colds is the best.

1. Can only one of their views be right, or could both have some rightness?
   a. Only one could be right
   b. Both could have some rightness

2. If both could be right, could one view be better or more right than the other?
   a. One could be more right
   b. One could not be more right than the other

(choice 1b along with 2b) is designated as a multiplist response. An indication that, although both could be right to a degree, but one could be determined to be more right (choice 1b along with 2a) is designated as evaluativist.

The 15 items include three items each in five domains: taste, aesthetics, values, physical truth, and social truth. The previous example is from the physical truth domain. A taste domain example concerns whether or not a soup was spicy. An aesthetics domain item involves a disagreement about which painting was better. A values domain item concerns whether it is all right to lie. A social truth item involved a disagreement about why children do not succeed in school. The modal response to the three items in each domain was used to assign an epistemological level for that domain.

This assessment was originally written in English. It was translated into Hebrew and back-translated into English by someone unfamiliar with the English version. Only minor modifications were required to match the versions. The Arabic version was translated from the Hebrew and back-translated into Arabic by someone unfamiliar with the original Hebrew. Again only minor modifications were required to match the versions.

Review of Results

In the first study (Weinstock, 2005), data were gathered from 110 Bedouin 7th and 9th graders to compare with existing data drawn from Jewish adolescent participants in a study on epistemology and argument evaluation (Weinstock, Neuman, & Glassner, 2006). The Bedouins were students at a junior high school in a Bedouin town outside of a predominantly Jewish urban area in the south of Israel. They came from the town and smaller surrounding Bedouin settlements. The Jewish students studied at a regional school outside of the same urban area, drawing from suburban and agricultural communities. The data for comparison with the Bedouin students was drawn from the 111 7th and 9th graders in the Jewish sample. The study investigated the epistemological level of the adolescents in three of the domains, and significant associations between group and epistemological level were found (social: χ^2 (2, 258) = 46.56, p = .000; physical: χ^2 (2, 257) = 10.96, p = .004; values: χ^2 (2, 255) = 60.28, p = .000). In general, the Bedouins appeared to be more absolutist, whereas the Jews appeared to be more multiplist or evaluativist. Whereas grade differences were found among the Jews, such that the 9th graders were more multiplist than the 7th graders, no grade differences were found among the Arabs.

At first glance, this exploratory study seems to confirm the suspicion that the authority-oriented Bedouins would be more absolutist than the individualist-oriented Jews. But a further study (Weinstock, 2008), designed to capture a wider age range, showed the story to be more complex. The sample consisted of three groups of 390 seventh, ninth, and eleventh graders: 137 students (52% female) were from a combined junior and senior high school in a different Bedouin town than in the first study; 60 (64% female) were from one of the poorest Jewish towns in Israel, so there would be a Jewish group basically comparable in SES to the Bedouins (Justman & Spivak, 2004); 193 (58% female) included the 7th and 9th grade Jewish middle/upper-middle-SES sample from the first study along with 11th graders from the same school.

Most saliently, the Bedouins' responses were decidedly not multiplist (see Table 7.1). Whereas in no domain were more than 31% of the Bedouin students multiplist, in every domain each of the secular Jewish groups had at least 50% multiplists, and generally more than 65%. This finding is most striking in the taste and aesthetic domains, in which the large majority in this and other studies (e.g., Kuhn et al., 2000) tends to be multiplist, even at younger ages. The two Jewish groups were similar to one another, with significant associations between group and epistemological level in the two truth domains.

TABLE 7.1
Percentages of Students in Each Domain and Epistemological Level
Within Each Cultural Group

	Group								
Domain	Bedouins			Middle/Upper -middle-SES Jews			Low-SES Jews		
	A	M	E	A	M	E	A	M	E
Taste	33	26	42	1	92	8	6	86	9
Aesthetics	21	28	51	2	92	7	10	81	9
Values	60	18	23	11	62	27	20	63	18
Physical truth	18	31	51	14	52	38	7	69	24
Social truth	23	29	48	3	51	46	7	67	26

Note: A = Absolutist; M = Multiplist; E = Evaluativist. All chi-square tests for association were significant.

Gender differences were found only among the Bedouins. As shown in Table 7.2, more Bedouin boys than girls were absolutist and more Bedouin girls than boys were evaluativist in all domains. Grade differences were found only among the Jews. Among the middle/upper-middle-SES Jewish group, consistent with expectations, 11th graders tended to be less multiplist than the other grades in the social (χ^2 (4, 193) = 10.15, p = .038) and physical (χ^2 (4, 193) = 9.19, p = .04) truth domains, moving to be more evaluativist. The finding that more Bedouin boys were absolutist than girls supports the assumption about respect for authority in a hierarchical culture. Further, the study revealed that all the Bedouin adolescents seemed averse to the individual as the source of knowledge—which is quite characteristic of multiplist thinking—in favor of authority as the source of knowledge, either as absolutist authority or evaluative expert.

A third study (Weinstock, 2008) focused on authority as a possible factor in the cross-cultural differences. A version of the assessment described earlier (Kuhn et al. 2000) was constructed invoking authority in the item scenarios. Instead of a disagreement between two peers, one of the people became an "authority figure" (teacher, grandfather, textbook). So, in the previous example, instead of Sharon, it would read "Dana's teacher."

Ninety-seven (57% female) Bedouin and 90 (52% female) Jewish 7th graders were given this instrument alongside the original version. Again the Bedouins were particularly unlikely to be multiplist in their responses to the original instrument. No differences were found in responses between the original and authority versions among the Jews. But sign tests showed that the Bedouins were notably more absolutist and less evaluativist in the domains of taste (p = .001) and physical truth (p = .01) in response to the authority version. In taste, 38% were evaluativists and 47% were absolutists on the original assessment, compared with 18% evaluativists and 71% absolutists on the authority version. With physical truth, 55% were evaluativists and 28% were absolutists on the original assessment, compared with 38% evaluativists and 52% absolutists on the authority version. Thus, authority as a source of knowledge appears to be an important aspect of the Bedouins' epistemological thinking.

Implications for Self-Authorship Theory

The research shows different responses by Bedouins and Jews in Israel to the measure of epistemological development developed on American samples. Americans, like the Israeli Jews, have mastery-oriented cultural values

TABLE 7.2
Percentages of Each Gender in Epistemological Levels of Domains by Cultural Group

Group	Taste			Aesthetics			Values			Physical truth			Social Truth		
	A	M	E	A	M	E	A	M	E	A	M	E	A	M	E
Bedouins															
Boys	35	29	36	30	27	43	64	20	17	29	35	36	29	30	41
Girls	31	23	47	13	28	59	55	17	28	9	27	65	17	28	55
Jews 1															
Boys	1	91	7		90	10	16	54	30	17	49	35	4	53	43
Girls	0	92	8	1	94	5	6	64	27	12	50	39	2	50	48
Jews 2															
Boys	6	88	6	0	83	17	21	58	21	6	67	28	11	68	21
Girls	6	82	12	17	79	7	21	64	15	8	70	22	6	63	31

Note. A = Absolutist; M = Multiplist; E = Evaluativist; Jews 1 = middle/upper-middle-SES; Jews 2 = low-SES.

(Schwartz, 1999). The Jewish adolescents' pattern of responses conforms to the epistemological developmental trajectory that ultimately affords development into self-authorship. The responses of the Bedouins are not consistent with this trajectory. The results do not indicate a simple lag in development, with the Bedouins remaining as absolutists longer. Unlike with the Jews, and other Western samples (Kuhn et al., 2000), responses to the instrument do not show grade-related differences from early to later adolescence. Most important, there were markedly fewer multiplist responses, with an apparent preference for either absolutist or evaluativist responses. From their response patterns, it appears that their thinking is not characterized by the radically subjective relativism that is seen as critical in developing contextualized knowing or conceptual relativism (Kuhn & Weinstock, 2002; Perry, 1970).

The different response patterns may indicate that the instrument is inadequate to capture a universal epistemology among the Bedouin students; however, the patterns may also reflect underlying cultural differences in epistemological development, or that the instrument cannot capture what is essentially a different epistemology. Interviews with some of the participants in the third study regarding their responses to the instrument lend some preliminary, but not conclusive, support to these latter explanations. In the interviews, the Jewish 7th graders articulated each of the levels according to the theoretical definitions of the levels. The Bedouins did so regarding absolutist or multiplist responses. But the explanations given by those making evaluativist responses are difficult to interpret at this point in the analysis. Their expressions of the nature of knowledge and knowing do not match the theoretical outline of evaluativism. They referred to authority more than did the Jews in describing evaluativist responses, but, unlike those giving absolutist responses, they did not indicate that a knowledge claim needed to be absolute and right or wrong. More research is required to truly get a handle on this epistemological position among Bedouins and to test instruments that might best capture Bedouin epistemology.

From these studies, it is not clear whether the meaning of evaluativism, the critical phase that is the underpinning of self-authorship, is understood in the same way across cultures. Taken together, the patterns of responses and the interviews are consistent with claims in the literature reviewed that there are culture-specific ways of knowing. Western cultures might value the critical and contextual thinking of individuals in constructing and evaluating knowledge, and thus there is general development toward this, with a better chance of attaining it among the highly educated. But other cultures might have different goals in mind in training higher-order thinking. The emphasis on autonomous critical thinking—rather than the reliance on external formulas—that is necessary to start the questioning characteristic of the crossroads phase that may be a precursor to self-authorship may not be universal across cultures outside of the United States, but instead may be found among various cultures within American institutions of higher education.

Of course, self-authorship and the original theory of epistemological development concern post-secondary student development. That the trajectory of epistemological development might not hold across cultures among adolescents does not mean that the students' epistemology and potential for self-authorship do not develop in contexts of higher education regardless of cultural background. According to Kegan (1994), development toward self-authorship can occur if the context demands it and if there is sufficient support. The academic and social diversity of the environment could indeed induce the sort of epistemological development documented in studies of college students (Baxter Magolda, 1992; King & Kitchener, 1994; Perry, 1970). However, cultural constraints may not support the development toward self-authorship. Many of the Bedouin women must receive permission from fathers or husbands to study. Many Bedouin women undergraduates drop out, particularly if they get married before graduating. Whereas some of the married, graduate student women seeking careers may well be self-authoring, having the internal foundations to enact their personal goals while negotiating obstacles in the interpersonal contexts of university and culture, this is hardly the norm; there are few Bedouin graduate students. The same orientation toward external authority and a strong cultural inclination to defer to external values, beliefs, and interpersonal loyalties, which is not consistent with self-authorship (Boes et al., this volume), may influence both female and male Bedouin students' decisions through and after their college careers.

Self, Self-Authorship, and Culture

Cultural differences in epistemological understanding, and the possible social constraints of such development, raise questions about whether self-authorship would be expected or valued across cultures. Along with understanding in the epistemological realm, other aspects of self in the intrapersonal and interpersonal realms vary across cultures. Markus and Kitayama (1991) propose that the independent self, found in individualist cultures, is autonomous and self-contained, whereas the interdependent self, found in collectivist cultures, is defined by its relationship to others. The privileging of the internal over the external as the basis for decision making in the intrapersonal and personal realms in self-authorship theory (Meszaros, 2007) may be at odds with the values of different cultures. For instance, in research on motivation, interdependent Chinese displayed a high need for abasement and socially oriented achievement, with a low need for individually oriented achievement (Bond, 1986). This contrasts with typical Western views of motivation that stress high self-esteem and intrinsic motivation. According to the tellingly named Self-Determination Theory (Ryan & Deci, 2000), intrinsic motivation is contrasted most positively with extrinsic motivation. The theory stresses the satisfaction of the needs for autonomy and personal competence, as well as affiliation, as central to human fulfillment.

The degree to which one seeks internal or external bases for decisions and behavior may also differ by culture. Through the use of iconic images (e.g., the Capitol, the American Flag, Abraham Lincoln, and their Chinese counterparts), Hong, Morris, Chiu, and Benet-Martinez (2000) primed Westernized Chinese students to think like either Americans or Chinese. Those primed with the American icons were more likely to make internal attributions regarding the behavior of a fish swimming in a group and a boy on a diet, whereas those primed with the Chinese icons were more likely to make external attributions. Again, this raises the issue of how the internally defined self, the desire and effort to author one's self, is valued in different cultures.

Conclusion

The cross-cultural research on personal epistemology does not directly address the issue of how, or if, self-authorship is enacted and valued across cultures. However, as epistemology is a pillar of self-authorship, it is important to have a strong sense of the possible range of epistemological beliefs and their relationship with cultural values and conceptions of self. This focus on cultural values brings epistemological, interpersonal, and intrapersonal dimensions together in a way generally not seen in epistemological research. Findings in this and other areas of cross-cultural research should prompt consideration of the relationship between epistemology and identity, as well as how cultural values and practices do or do not serve to support the development of a contextual, evaluativist epistemology and self-authorship.

References

Baxter Magolda, M. B. (1992). *Knowing and reasoning in college: Gender-related patterns in students' intellectual development.* San Francisco: Jossey-Bass.

Baxter Magolda, M. B. (1998). Developing self-authorship in young adult life. *Journal of College Student Development, 39*(2), 143–156.

Baxter Magolda, M. B. (2001). *Making their own way: narratives for transforming higher education to promote self-development.* Sterling, VA: Stylus.

Belenky, M. F., Clinchy, B. M., Goldberger, N. R., & Tarule, J. M. (1986). *Women's ways of knowing: The development of self, voice and mind.* New York: Basic Books.

Bond, M. H. (Ed.). (1986). *The psychology of the Chinese people.* Hong Kong: Oxford University Press.

Chan, K, & Elliott, R. G. (2002). Exploratory study of Hong Kong teacher education students' epistemological beliefs: Cultural perspectives and implications on beliefs research. *Contemporary Educational Psychology, 27,* 392–414.

Chandler, M., Boyes, M., & Ball, L. (1990). Relativism and stations of epistemic doubt. *Journal of Experimental Child Psychology, 50,* 370–395.

Hofer, B. K. (2000). Dimensionality and disciplinary differences in personal epistemology. *Contemporary Educational Psychology, 25,* 378–405.

Hofer, B. K. (2008). Personal epistemology and culture. In M. S. Khine (Ed.) *Knowing, knowledge and beliefs: Epistemological studies across diverse cultures* (pp. 3–22). Netherlands: Springer.

Hofer, B. K., & Pintrich, P. R. (1997). The development of epistemological theories: Beliefs about knowledge and knowing and their relation to learning. *Review of Educational Research, 67,* 88–140.

Hong, Y., Morris, M., Chiu, C., & Benet-Martínez, V. (2000). Multicultural minds: A dynamic constructivist approach to culture and cognition. *American Psychologist, 55,* 709–720.

Justman, M. & Spivak, A. (2004). Socio-economic dynamics of local authorities in Israel: Theory and evidence. *Israel Economic Review, 2,* 1–27.

Karabenick, S. A., & Moosa, S. (2005). Culture and personal epistemology: U.S. and Middle Eastern students' beliefs about scientific knowledge and knowing. *Social Psychology of Education, 8,* 375–393.

Kegan, R. (1994). *In over our heads: The mental demands of modern life.* Cambridge, MA: Harvard University Press.

King, P. M., & Kitchener, K. S. (1994). *Developing reflective judgment: Understanding and promoting intellectual growth and critical thinking in adolescents and adults.* San Francisco: Jossey-Bass.

Kuhn, D. (1991). *The skills of argument.* New York: Cambridge University Press.

Kuhn, D. (2001). How do people know? *Psychological Science, 12,* 1–8.

Kuhn, D., Cheney, R., & Weinstock, M. (2000). The development of epistemological understanding. *Cognitive Development, 15,* 309–328.

Kuhn, D., & Park, S-H. (2005). Epistemological understanding and the development of intellectual values. *International Journal of Educational Research, 43,* 111–124.

Kuhn, D., & Weinstock, M. P. (2002). What is epistemological thinking and why does it matter? In B. K. Hofer & P. R. Pintrich (Eds.), *Personal epistemology: The psychology of beliefs about knowledge and knowing* (pp. 121–144). Mahwah, NJ: Erlbaum.

Leadbeater, B., & Kuhn, D. (1989). Interpreting discrepant narratives: Hermeneutics and adult cognition. In J. Sinnott (Ed.), *Everyday problem solving* (pp. 175–190). New York: Praeger.

Markus, H. R., & Kitayama, S. (1991). Culture and the self: Implications for cognition, emotion, and motivation. *Psychological Review, 98,* 224–253.

Meszaros, P. S. (2007). The journey of self-authorship: Why is it necessary? In P. S. Meszaros (Ed.), *Self-Authorship: Advancing students' intellectual growth, New Directions for Teaching and Learning* (Vol. 109, pp. 5–14). San Francisco: Jossey-Bass.

Nisbett, R. E., Peng, K., Choi, I., & Norenzayan, A. (2001). Culture and systems of thought: Holistic vs. analytic cognition. *Psychological Review, 108,* 291–310.

Peng, K., & Nisbett, R. E. (1999). Culture, dialecticism, and reasoning about contradiction. *American Psychologist, 54,* 741–754.

Perry, W. (1970). *Forms of intellectual and ethical development in the college years.* New York: Holt.

Pizzolato, J. E. (2003). Developing self-authorship: Exploring the experiences of high-risk college students. *Journal of College Student Development, 44*(6), 797–812.

Pizzolato, J. E. (2007). Assessing self-authorship. In P. S. Meszaros (Ed.), *Self-Authorship: Advancing students' intellectual growth, New Directions for Teaching and Learning* (Vol. 109, pp. 31–42). San Francisco: Jossey-Bass.

Ryan, R. M. & Deci, E. L. (2000). Self-determination theory and the facilitation of intrinsic motivation, social development, and well-being. *American Psychologist, 55,* 68–78.

Schwartz. S. H. (1999). A theory of cultural values and some implications for work. *Applied Psychology: An International Review, 48,* 23–47.

Tabak, I., & Weinstock, M. (2008). A sociocultural exploration of epistemological beliefs. In Khine, M. S. (Ed.), *Knowing, knowledge and beliefs: Epistemological studies across diverse cultures* (pp. 177–195). Netherlands: Springer.

Triandis, H. C. (1989). The self and social behavior in different cultural contexts. *Psychological Review, 96,* 506–520.

Weinstock, M. P. (2005, August). *Grade Level, Gender, and Ethnic Differences in Epistemological Understanding Within Domains.* Paper presented in symposium at the meeting of the European Association for Research in Learning and Instruction, Nicosia, Cyprus.

Weinstock, M. P. (March, 2008). *Cultural differences in epistemological understanding.* Paper presented at the Annual Meeting of the American Educational Research Association, New York, NY.

Weinstock, M. P., & Cronin, M. A. (2003). The everyday production of knowledge: Individual differences in epistemological understanding and juror reasoning skill. *Applied Cognitive Psychology, 17,* 161–181.

Weinstock, M. P., Neuman, Y., & Glassner, A. (2006). Identification of informal reasoning fallacies as a function of epistemological level, grade level, and cognitive ability. *Journal of Educational Psychology, 98,* 327–341.

Weinstock, M. P., & Zviling-Beiser, H. (in press). Separating academic and social experience as potential factors in epistemological development. *Learning and Instruction.*

Youn, I. (2000). The cultural specificity of epistemological beliefs about learning. *Asian Journal of Social Psychology, 3,* 87–105.

Zhang, L-F. (1999). A comparison of U.S. and Chinese university students cognitive development: The cross-cultural applicability of Perry's theory. *Journal of Psychology, 133,* 425–439.

8

PERSONAL EPISTEMOLOGY, LEARNING, AND CULTURAL CONTEXT
Japan and the United States

Barbara K. Hofer

Abstract: A comparative study of Japanese and U.S. college students' epistemic beliefs is presented as an example that could be useful in understanding ways to expand cross-cultural research on self-authorship. Issues of construct definition, comparability of meaning in terms such as "self," and the need for cross-cultural collaboration are discussed.

This chapter describes a study of cultural differences in personal epistemology, and the relation to learning strategies in the United States and Japan, as the basis for discussing the need for cultural research and culturally sensitive measures in the field of epistemology. Epistemological development has been identified by researchers in the area of self-authorship as one of the three components of the construct, which also encompasses intrapersonal and interpersonal development.

Although epistemology researchers have seldom defined their work in this broader context, the connections to these other two aspects of development within this integrative framework may provide useful theoretical connections. The consideration of culture, moreover, may be beneficial to many researchers working within both self-authorship and epistemology.

The author extends gratitude to Hirogutsu Yamouchi, Akane Zusho, Zach Hofer-Shall, Liam Aiello, and Brie Pike-Springer for assistance with this project.

Background

Individuals hold beliefs and theories about knowledge and knowing that appear to develop in patterned ways. The role of "personal epistemology" in learning and education, and its relation to intellectual development, has been a topic of study for several decades now in the United States (Hofer & Pintrich, 1997, 2002). Originating with a study of Harvard undergraduates (Perry, 1970) in the 1950s and 1960s, research on epistemological development (Baxter Magolda, 1992; King & Kitchener, 1994; Kuhn, 1991) and epistemic beliefs (Schommer, 1990) expanded widely in the decades that followed.

One important empirical and theoretical advancement beyond Perry's original scheme is the inclusion of women in research on epistemological development. Most studies included both males and females; one addressed gender-related patterns (Baxter Magolda, 1992); and one focused on women only, in order to understand "women's ways of knowing" (Belenky, Clinchy, Goldberger, & Tarule, 1986). This research was conducted at a time when developmental psychologists, and psychologists in general, were widely influenced by the work of Carol Gilligan (Gilligan, 1982), whose work challenged prevailing paradigms of moral development based on research conducted with male participants (e.g., Kohlberg, 1971). When women were excluded from the theory-building phase of research and then assessed on resulting schemes, they were found deficient. When women were included in the foundational research, advanced morality was no longer equated solely with justice, but encompassed an ethic of care. This research had a profound effect on the conduct of research in psychology, and has led to more scrutiny when results are generalized beyond the population sampled.

Culture and Personal Epistemology

In much the same way that psychology took notice of gender in an earlier era, many psychologists are increasingly aware of the need to consider culture as an important influence on human behavior, cognition, beliefs, and emotions (Heine & Norenzayan, 2006; Markus & Kitayama, 1991; Nisbett, 2003), or to recognize that mind and culture are mutually constituted (Shweder, 1991). Research in this area has proliferated, and psychological models have toppled or been expanded. For example, cultural research on the Fundamental Attribution Error, a tenet of social psychology, suggests that situational explanations may actually take precedence over personality information in many cultures (Choi & Nisbett, 1998). Similarly, the idea of self as an autonomous, bounded, rational, agentic entity appears to be congruent with the concept of an "independent self," as experienced in much of the western world. This is in marked contrast to the "interdependent self" that is relational, connected, and more context-specific, a self-construal common in many Asian countries, with differing outcomes for emotion, motivation, and cognition (Markus & Kitayama, 1991). Within psychological research, the hegemony of an independent self led to the development of theories that erroneously permitted judgment of other cultures as deficient on numerous measures. Attachment theory, for example, has been critiqued in this regard; young Japanese children, who sleep with their families and are seldom left alone or with strangers, and who are learning to be "interdependent," were typically scored as insecurely attached in the assessment paradigm that privileged autonomous behavior (Rothbaum, Weisz, Pott, Miyake, & Morelli, 2001).

Psychological research that takes culture into account appears to progress in two stages of scientific inquiry (Heine & Norenzayan, 2006). During the first stage, researchers investigate cultural differences and work toward establishing the boundaries of a phenomenon. The second stage involves the pursuit of underlying mechanisms of those cultural differences. For many constructs, considerable revision and expansion of the phenomenon take place through this process, as is evident in the constructs described previously. Epistemological research may need such reconsideration as well.

Research on personal epistemology across cultures is fairly recent, and much of the research is an expansion and replication of U.S. research into other cultural settings (Hofer, 2008), comparative work of the first stage variety. This research is extensive (Braten & Stromso, 2006; Bromme, 2003; Brownlee, 2003; Cano, 2005; Chan & Elliott, 2002; Elen & Clarebout, 2001; Karabenick & Moosa, 2005; Mason & Boscolo, 2004; Raviv, Bar-tal, Raviv, Biran, & Sela, 2003; Stoeger, 2006; Tsai, 2000; Youn, 2000; Zhang, 1999), and the cultures represented just in this sample list are highly diverse—Norway, Germany, Australia, Spain, Italy, Oman, Hong Kong, Taiwan, China, Netherlands, Israel, Korea, and others. The field is in need of more of this type of research, as well as more work on the predictive power of the construct in different contexts, and research that investigates underlying mechanisms, the stage two level of inquiry. An example of the examination of underlying mechanisms is a study of how educational practices in either general or religious schools shape the beliefs of Israeli students (Gottlieb, 2007).

Measurement Issues

As with other psychological phenomena, epistemology research presents problems of replication in other cultures. Most studies have used translated questionnaires or interviews developed within the United States. This makes it possible to compare epistemology in other cultures with the models developed by U.S. researchers, but may not provide a fair measure of how epistemology might be modeled in other environments. A growing number of studies suggest that the factor structure of epistemic beliefs, for example, as measured by a common U.S. questionnaire (Schommer, 1990), may not be similar in other cultures (Chan & Elliott, 2002; Youn, 2000). More research is needed to explore this in other contexts, as well as with other measures, and to examine the varying nature of predictive outcomes of individuals' epistemologies.

Although developmental models have been useful in charting a trajectory of epistemological understanding and in examining how such development can be viewed as an educational outcome (Baxter Magolda, 2004; Hofer, 2001; King, 1992), they typically require interviews that may be labor-intensive in terms of administration and scoring. Epistemic beliefs models, based on a premise of multi-dimensionality and possible variance among the dimensions, have typically been assessed through Likert-type scales, making larger samples easier to assess and providing potential to relate beliefs to other constructs. Most of the work that has been done in cultures other than the United States has operated from the paradigm of epistemic beliefs, although a few studies have used a written instrument of epistemological development (Mason & Scirica, 2006; Tabak & Weinstock, 2008; Weinstock, Neuman, & Glassner, 2006).

Epistemology and Learning Strategies

There is a growing body of research on the role that epistemic beliefs play in use of learning strategies and achievement. Students with more sophisticated beliefs are more likely to use productive cognitive and behavioral strategies

(Paulsen & Feldman, 2007; Schommer, Crouse, & Rhodes, 1992), and exhibit higher achievement (Hofer, 1999, 2000; Schommer, 1993) than those with less sophisticated beliefs. Recent work in European contexts suggests similarities (Braten & Stromso, 2006; Mason, 2001, 2003). We know little about whether similar relations among constructs would be expected in other cultures, notably Asian cultures, and have reason to suspect the patterns might not be universally applicable, based on differences in assumptions and beliefs about what it means to know and learn (Li, 2003; Tweed & Lehman, 2002), and differing cultural beliefs about authority (Qian & Pan, 2002).

Rationale and Need for This Study

A considerable body of work demonstrates that Japanese students outperform U.S. students on any number of standardized measures, particularly in math and science, from early elementary school through high school (Stevenson, Chen, & Lee, 1993). Researchers have investigated the teaching methods of Japanese classrooms, and ideas from elementary instruction have been of particular interest to educators in the west (Stevenson & Stigler, 1992; Stigler & Hiebert, 1999). Elementary classrooms in Japan appear to be relatively constructivist in orientation, and there have been numerous attempts to learn from the particular practices of Japanese teachers (Stigler & Hiebert, 1999). U.S. educators have been critical of secondary teaching practices in Japan, however, as they involve teaching to the test—in this case, college entrance exams. This is assumed to foster rote memorization, a practice that appears to persist in spite of recent reforms in Japanese education. This raises interesting questions about epistemic beliefs of Japanese college students and the relation to strategy use. Given that sophisticated beliefs predict higher academic performance in the United States, and that Japanese typically show higher achievement, we must ask: are the beliefs of Japanese students more sophisticated than those of students in the United States? Or might instructional practices prominent in secondary school foster a different level of beliefs than those of U.S. students? Might beliefs that are posited as "less sophisticated" in the United States be more adaptive in other environments? How these beliefs are related to learning strategies is important to understand within cultural context.

Research Questions

This exploratory study had three central research questions:

How does the factor structure of epistemic beliefs compare between Japan and the United States?

How do beliefs differ in Japan and the United States within a similar course?

Is the relation between beliefs and strategies similar between the two countries?

Method

Participants

Participants in this study were students from two highly regarded post-secondary institutions, in Japan and in the United States, all enrolled in Introductory Psychology. The participant group in Japan included 78 students (56% females), average age 19.0. The participant group in the United States included 123 students (70% females), average age 19.6.

Material

Learning Strategies   This survey instrument included items from the Motivated Strategies for Learning Questionnaire (MSLQ) (Pintrich, Smith, Garcia, & McKeachie, 1993) that consisted of four scales used in both U.S. (Pintrich & De Groot, 1990) and Japanese research (Yamauchi, Kumagai, & Kawasaki, 1999), and were previously translated for the latter study. These included *rehearsal* ("When I study for this class, I practice saying the material over and over"); *elaboration* ("When studying for this class, I often try to explain the material to a classmate or friend"); *self-regulation* ("Even when course materials are dull and uninteresting, I manage to keep working until I finish"); and a fourth factor entitled *cognitive strategies*, a composite of rehearsal, elaboration, and other study strategy items ("I ask myself questions to make sure I understand the material I have been studying in class"). Students responded on a 5-point scale (1 = "not at all true of me"; 5 = "very true of me").

Epistemic Beliefs   The epistemic beliefs questionnaire was a revised version of the instrument from an earlier study (Hofer, 2000), with 35 items representing four dimensions of personal epistemology: *certainty of knowl-*

edge ("Knowledge in this field is well-established and certain"), *simplicity of knowledge* ("Knowledge in this field is mainly made up of discrete facts"), *source of knowledge* ("In this subject, people can accept the knowledge of authorities without question"), and *justification for knowing* ("Knowledge in this subject is more a matter of opinion than fact"). Each item refers to the discipline named at the top of the questionnaire, which in this case was Psychology. Students responded on a 5-point scale (1 = agree to 5 = disagree). Scores of items were reversed, with a higher score indicating more sophisticated beliefs, for ease of analysis and interpretation.

Procedure

For the Japanese portion of the study, the epistemic beliefs measure was first translated by a native speaker of Japanese and then reviewed by a Japanese-speaking U.S. psychologist, who back-translated it into English and suggested modifications for clarity. It was then reviewed by an English-speaking Japanese psychologist for comparability of meaning and further revised to capture the nuance of the constructs. The translation of the MSLQ was obtained from a Japanese motivation researcher who had used the questionnaire in research with Japanese students (Yamauchi et al., 1999).

Student participants were recruited through introductory psychology classes and given packets to complete on their own time.

Results

The initial research question regarded factor analyses for epistemic beliefs. This was conducted through an iterative process, beginning with principal component analyses with varimax rotation of each sample independently. I eliminated items with multiple loadings in both countries and ran the analyses again with the remaining 19 items. At this point there was a discernible factor structure replicating across both cultures. Two items that lowered factor reliability were eliminated. The resulting five factors were *simplicity of knowledge, certainty of knowledge, accept authority* (an aspect of the *source of knowledge* dimension), and two factors that represented *justification*, one with criteria for *justification for knowing* and one representing *no means for justification* for what is known in this field. For factors, items, and reliabilities, see Table 8.1.

TABLE 8.1
Factor Structure of Epistemic Beliefs

Simplicity of Knowledge (overall α = .92, U.S. α = .82, Japan α = .62)

Ideas and concepts in this field are related in complex ways. (R)
Knowledge in this subject is complex. (R)
The truth in this field consists of complexly related facts and ideas. (R)
What is known in this field is complex rather than a set of simple facts. (R)

Certainty of Knowledge (overall α = .89, U.S. α = .66, Japan α = .64)

Truth is unchanging in this subject.
Knowledge in this field is well established and certain.
Principles in this field are unchanging.
What is considered truth in this subject is likely to change. (R)
Principles in this field are open to revision. (R)
The best way for people to know something in this field is for them to evaluate the evidence and come to their own conclusion. (R)

Accept Authority (overall α = .90, U.S. α = .72, Japan α = .67)

In this subject, most questions have only one right answer.
A person can just accept answers from the experts in this subject without question.
In this subject, people can accept the knowledge of authorities without question.

Justification (overall α = .58, U.S. α = .56, Japan α = .59)

Knowledge in this field is based on whether researchers consistently arrive at the same conclusions. (R)
Investigators in this field can justify their knowledge using agreed-upon methods. (R)

No means for justification (overall α = .57, U.S. α = .63, Japan α = .59)

There really is no way in this field to determine whether good answers to problems have been discovered.
There is really no way to justify what is known in this field.

Comparison of Epistemic Beliefs by Country

A second set of analyses was done to examine comparisons of epistemic beliefs by country. Results of a MANOVA indicated significant differences on all five dimensions. In all five factors, U.S. students showed more "sophistication" of epistemic beliefs (see Table 8.2). Japanese students were more likely to see knowledge as simple and certain, to rely on authority, and to see fewer grounds for justification than were U.S. students.

TABLE 8.2
Dimension of Epistemic Beliefs: Comparison by Country

Dimension	Japan Mean (SD)	U.S. Mean (SD)
Certainty of knowledge	2.06 (.55)	3.82 (.54)***
Simplicity of knowledge	2.09 (.56)	4.02 (.77)***
Accept authority	1.94 (.69)	4.10 (.71)***
Justification	3.25 (.48)	3.44 (.64)*
No means for justification	2.71 (.52)	3.26 (.51)***

Learning Strategies

The reliabilities for the four scales were low, particularly in the Japanese sample, and no significant differences were found between countries on any of these measures, although the difference in rehearsal strategies was approaching significance, with Japanese more likely to use rehearsal.

Strategies and Epistemic Beliefs

A correlation matrix of learning strategies and epistemic beliefs indicated that the more Japanese students believed that there is *no justification for knowledge*, the less likely they were to use *rehearsal* strategies (.25)* and *elaboration* (.24*). In the United States, the more students believed that they should *accept authority*, the more likely they were to use *rehearsal* strategies (-.25*). (Recall that high scores on beliefs equal greater sophistication.)

Discussion

This exploratory study surveyed Introductory Psychology students in Japan and the United States about epistemic beliefs and learning strategies. Factor analyses of epistemic beliefs suggested evidence of two factors that have consistently appeared in research on personal epistemology: certainty of knowledge and simplicity of knowledge. In addition, this measure (Hofer, 2000) was designed to assess both the source and justification of knowledge, dimensions suggested in a review of the literature (Hofer & Pintrich, 1997). Several of the items for these scales appeared as three distinct factors, suggesting aspects of justification and source of knowledge. This suggests a foundation for continued work on this measurement, and that it has some cross-cultural utility.

The comparison of beliefs between cultures, however, showed that U.S. students appeared to have "more sophisticated" beliefs about knowledge and knowing than their Japanese college counterparts, and the difference was consistent across dimensions. This may not be surprising in light of the purported differences in secondary instruction in the two countries. As noted, Japanese students prepare for high-stakes college admissions tests during high school, a process that promotes rote memorization, typically correlated with lower-level beliefs. Based on reported achievement differences between the two countries and the higher performance of Japanese students, this may be more surprising, however, as lower sophistication of beliefs typically correlates with low academic achievement. This raises questions about whether beliefs predict differently in different environments, and whether some strategies may be more effective than others in particular cultural environments. We need more research that includes achievement in different cultures and that examines—both within each country and between countries—relations among these variables.

Results of this study reflect students' epistemic beliefs about psychology. More contextual work is needed to understand the differences in how the discipline might be conveyed in these two environments. More research is necessary to understand the various influences of culture, institution, and instruction, among other factors, as well as relation to general knowledge beliefs.

Potential Contribution to the Development of Theory and Methods

Recent research on differences in cultural views of learning and knowing supports that learning needs to be considered within a cultural context (Tweed & Lehman, 2002). Underlying philosophical assumptions may influence cultural views; individuals from cultures steeped in Confucianism view learning differently than those from cultures influenced by Socratic approaches, and such beliefs may be related to epistemic perspectives. In a comparative study, U.S. students viewed learning as the acquisition of external knowledge; Chinese students viewed knowledge as indispensable to personal, social, and moral life, worth pursuing diligently (Li, 2003), another possible rationale for observed achievement differences.

As work on personal epistemology progresses in diverse cultures, researchers may wish to consider a number of issues of concern (see Hofer, 2008, for further elaboration). Foremost among these is the issue of construct definition and whether it is representative across cultures. The constructs of epistemological development and epistemic beliefs were derived in the United States, and have been exported through translation for research in other cultures, but we do not know what might be missing if these constructs were to be derived indigenously in other environments, or if cross-cultural teams were to begin anew in exploring the dimensions of epistemology. The field would benefit from a more culturally comprehensive and inclusive model.

Second, nearly all models of epistemology derived from the United States presume a similar trajectory of growth, whether that is described as moving from unsophisticated beliefs toward sophisticated ones (Schommer, 1990), or unreflective judgment to reflective (King & Kitchener, 1994), for example. We do not know if that progression is universal or is an artifact of western schooling, aligned with the goals of a liberal arts education, and whether it can be appropriately applied in other cultures. More examination of the trajectory across and within cultures is needed, from an expanded theoretical perspective. Researchers may also wish to question terminology that appears pejorative rather than descriptive of a particular stance.

The directionality of most models presumes a movement from an acceptance of authority toward a challenging, questioning approach that includes an evaluation of authoritative expertise, as well as the ability to make discerning judgments among competing authorities. The developmental assumption seems to be that only early in life would one accept authority with little further examination. This might not be likely in all cultures or all contexts, even within the United States.

A third concern for cross-cultural and cultural research on self-authorship and epistemology is that conceptions of beliefs about knowledge and knowing are presumed to reside at the individual level. That is currently how researchers conceptualize, assess, and discuss personal epistemology. Accordingly, models of epistemology and resulting research may be focused on individual knowing at the risk of ignoring socially distributed aspects of knowledge (Bromme, 2003), and cultural variation in this understanding of where knowledge resides is likely.

Fourth, issues of translation and meaning are paramount as researchers continue to expand research on personal epistemology—and, more broadly, self-authorship—into other cultures. Seldom is cross-cultural research as simple as literal translation from one language to another, and in psychology this work is particularly difficult. Considerable cross-cultural discussion is needed even to reach understanding of some of the most basic terms currently in use. Within self-authorship research, for example, it may be useful to consider cultural interpretations of the meaning of self, particularly in terms of self as independent or interdependent (Markus & Kitayama, 1991; Nisbett, 2003; Triandis, 2001). The agentic notion of "authoring" the self is most congruent with the idea of a self that is autonomous and independent, common in individualist cultures. Similarly, the intrapersonal aspect of self-authorship, grounded in studies of western college students, is likely to have been conceptualized from a similar perspective. On the other hand, the interpersonal aspect of self-authorship may be particularly salient in collectivist cultures that foster an interdependent sense of self. How the three components of self-authorship—epistemology, identity, and relationships—interrelate and the cultural patterns that exist in this regard may be of particular interest to those pursuing cross-cultural work in this area. For example, as evidenced in this study, Japanese students were far more likely to "accept authority" than were U.S. students, a pattern likely to be connected to their identity as students and their perceptions of the relationship between student and professor as more hierarchical than U.S. students might perceive it to be.

The work that lies ahead is critically important for theoretical development, research, and education. More cross-cultural collaboration is necessary in order to expand our fundamental understanding of the construct of both personal epistemology and self-authorship, as well as to address issues of measurement in multiple cultures and the interpretation of research results. Throughout our educational systems, preparing students for global citizenship and intercultural understanding and sensitivity is paramount. This involves fostering epistemological understanding, including an awareness of differing epistemic assumptions, views of authority, and the nature of what it means to know. Only by working together across cultural boundaries are we likely to make significant progress in this regard.

References

Baxter Magolda, M. B. (1992). *Knowing and reasoning in college: Gender-related patterns in students' intellectual development*. San Francisco: Jossey Bass.

Baxter Magolda, M. B. (2004). Self-authorship as the common goal of 21st-century education. In M. B. Baxter Magolda & P. M. King (Eds.), *Learning partnerships: Theory and models of practice to educate for self-authorship* (pp. 1–35). Sterling, VA: Stylus.

Belenky, M. F., Clinchy, B. M., Goldberger, N. R., & Tarule, J. M. (1986). *Women's ways of knowing: The development of self, voice, and mind.* New York: Basic Books.

Braten, I., & Stromso, H. I. (2006). Constructing meaning from multiple information sources as a function of personal epistemology: The role of text-processing strategies. *Information Design Journal, 14*(1), 56–67.

Bromme, R. (2003). Thinking and knowing about knowledge: A plea for and critical remarks on psychological research programs on epistemological beliefs. In M. H. G. Hoffman, J. Lenhard & F. Seeger (Eds.), *Activity and sign: Grounding mathematics education* (pp. 1–11). Dordrecht, Netherlands: Kluwer.

Brownlee, J. (2003). Changes in primary school teachers' beliefs about knowing: A longitudinal study. *Asia-Pacific Journal of Teacher Education, 31*, 87–98.

Cano, F. (2005). Epistemological beliefs and approaches to learning: Their change through secondary school and their influence on academic performance. *British Journal of Educational Psychology, 75*, 203–221.

Chan, K., & Elliott, R. G. (2002). Exploratory study of Hong Kong teacher education students' epistemological beliefs: Cultural perspectives and implications on beliefs research. *Contemporary Educational Psychology, 27*, 392–414.

Choi, I., & Nisbett, R. E. (1998). Situational salience and cultural differences in the correspondence bias and in the actor-observer bias. *Personality and Social Psychology Bulletin, 24*, 949–960.

Elen, J., & Clarebout, G. (2001). An invasion in the classroom: Influence of an ill-structured innovation on instructional and epistemological beliefs. *Learning Environments Research, 4*, 87–105.

Gilligan, C. (1982). *In a different voice: Psychological theory and women's development.* Cambridge, MA: Harvard University Press.

Gottlieb, E. (2007). Learning how to believe: Epistemic development in cultural context. *Journal of the Learning Sciences, 16*(1), 5–35.

Heine, S. J., & Norenzayan, A. (2006). Toward a psychological science for a cultural species. *Perspectives on Psychological Science, 1*, 251–269.

Hofer, B. K. (1999). Instructional context in the college mathematics classroom: Epistemological beliefs and student motivation. *Journal of Staff, Program, and Organizational Development, 16*(2), 73–82.

Hofer, B. K. (2000). Dimensionality and disciplinary differences in personal epistemology. *Contemporary Educational Psychology, 25*, 378–405.

Hofer, B. K. (2001). Personal epistemology research: Implications for learning and teaching. *Educational Psychology Review, 13*(4), 353–383.

Hofer, B. K. (2008). Personal epistemology and culture. In M. S. Khine (Ed.), *Knowing, knowledge and beliefs: Epistemological studies across diverse cultures* (pp. 3–22). Dordrecht, The Netherlands: Springer.

Hofer, B. K., & Pintrich, P. R. (1997). The development of epistemological theories: Beliefs about knowledge and knowing and their relation to learning. *Review of Educational Research, 67*, 88–140.

Hofer, B. K., & Pintrich, P. R. (Eds.). (2002). *Personal epistemology: The psychology of beliefs about knowledge and knowing.* Mahwah, NJ: Erlbaum.

Karabenick, S. A., & Moosa, S. (2005). Culture and personal epistemology: US and Middle Eastern students' beliefs about scientific knowledge and knowing. *Social Psychology of Education, 8*, 375–393.

King, P. M. (1992). How do we know? Why do we believe? Learning to make reflective judgments. *Liberal Education, 78*(1), 2–9.

King, P. M., & Kitchener, K. S. (1994). *Developing reflective judgment: Understanding and promoting intellectual growth and critical thinking in adolescents and adults.* San Francisco: Jossey-Bass.

Kohlberg, L. (1971). From is to ought: How to commit the naturalistic fallacy and get away with it in the study of moral development. In T. Mischel (Ed.), *Cognitive development and epistemology* (pp. 151–235). New York: Academic Press.

Kuhn, D. (1991). *The skills of argument.* Cambridge: Cambridge University Press.

Li, J. (2003). U.S. and Chinese cultural beliefs about learning. *Journal of Educational Psychology, 95*, 258–267.

Markus, H. R., & Kitayama, S. (1991). Culture and the self: Implications for cognition, emotion, and motivation. *Psychological Review, 98*, 224–253.

Mason, L. (2001). Responses to anomalous data on controversial topics and theory change. *Learning and Instruction, 11*, 453–483.

Mason, L. (2003). Personal epistemologies and intentional conceptual change. In G. M. Sinatra & P. R. Pintrich (Eds.), *Intentional conceptual change* (pp. 199–236). Mahwah, NJ: Erlbaum.

Mason, L., & Boscolo, P. (2004). Role of epistemological understanding and interest in interpreting a controversy and in topic-specific belief change. *Contemporary Educational Psychology, 29*, 103–128.

Mason, L., & Scirica, F. (2006). Prediction of students' argumentation skills about controversial topics by epistemological understanding. *Learning and Instruction, 16*(5), 492–509.

Nisbett, R. (2003). *The geography of thought: How Asians and Westerners think differently . . . and why.* New York: Free Press.

Paulsen, M. B., & Feldman, K. A. (2007). The conditional and interaction effects of epistemological beliefs on the self-regulated learning of college students: Cognitive and behavioral strategies. *Research in Higher Education, 48*, 353–401.

Perry, W. G. (1970). *Forms of intellectual and ethical development in the college years: A scheme.* New York: Holt, Rinehart and Winston.

Pintrich, P. R., & De Groot, E. V. (1990). Motivational and self-regulated learning components of classroom academic performance. *Journal of Educational Psychology, 82*(1), 33–40.

Pintrich, P. R., Smith, D. A., Garcia, T., & McKeachie, W. J. (1993). Reliability and predictive validity of the Motivated Strategies for Learning Questionnaire (MSLQ). *Educational and Psychological Measurement, 53*, 801–813.

Qian, G., & Pan, J. (2002). A comparison of epistemological beliefs and learning from science text between American and Chinese high school students. In B. K. Hofer & P. R. Pintrich (Eds.), *Personal epistemology: The psychology of beliefs about knowledge and knowing* (pp. 365–385). Mahwah, NJ: Erlbaum.

Raviv, A., Bar-tal, D., Raviv, A., Biran, B., & Sela, Z. (2003). Teachers' epistemic authority: Perceptions of students and teachers. *Social Psychology of Education, 6*, 17–42.

Rothbaum, F., Weisz, J., Pott, M., Miyake, K., & Morelli, G. (2001). Attachment and culture: Security in the United States and Japan. *American Psychologist, 55*, 1093–1104.

Schommer, M. (1990). Effects of beliefs about the nature of knowledge on comprehension. *Journal of Educational Psychology, 82*, 498–504.

Schommer, M. (1993). Epistemological development and academic performance among secondary students. *Journal of Educational Psychology, 85*(3), 406–411.

Schommer, M., Crouse, A., & Rhodes, N. (1992). Epistemological beliefs and mathematical text comprehension: Believing it is simple does not make it so. *Journal of Educational Psychology, 82*, 435–443.

Shweder, R. (1991). Cultural psychology: What is it? In R. Shweder (Ed.), *Thinking through cultures: Expeditions in cultural psychology* (pp. 73–110). Cambridge, MA: Harvard University Press.

Stevenson, H. W., Chen, C., & Lee, S.-Y. (1993). Mathematics achievement of Chinese, Japanese, and American children: Ten years later. *Science, 259* (January 1), 53–58.

Stevenson, H.W., and Stigler, J.W. (1992). *The learning gap: Why our schools are failing and what we can learn from Japanese and Chinese education.* New York: Simon and Schuster.

Stigler, J. W., & Hiebert, J. (1999). *The teaching gap: Best ideas from the world's teachers for improving education in the classroom.* New York: Free Press.

Stoeger, H. (2006). First steps toward an epistemic learner model. *High Ability Studies, 17*(1), 17–41.

Tabak, I., & Weinstock, M. (2008). A sociocultural exploration of epistemological beliefs. In M. S. Khine (Ed.), *Knowing, knowledge and beliefs: Epistemological studies across diverse cultures* (pp. 177–195). Dordrecht, The Netherlands: Springer.

Triandis, H. (2001). Individualism and collectivism: Past, present, and future. In D. Matsumoto (Ed.), *Handbook of cultural psychology* (pp. 35–50). Oxford: Oxford University Press.

Tsai, C.-C. (2000). Relationships between student scientific epistemological beliefs and perceptions of constructivist learning environments. *Educational Research, 42*, 193–205.

Tweed, R. G., & Lehman, D. R. (2002). Learning considered within a cultural context: Confucian and Socratic approaches. *American Psychologist, 57*, 89–99.

Weinstock, M., Neuman, Y., & Glassner, A. (2006). Identification of informal reasoning fallacies as a function of epistemological level, grade level, and cognitive ability. *Journal of Educational Psychology, 89*, 327–341.

Yamauchi, H., Kumagai, Y., & Kawasaki, Y. (1999). Perceived control, autonomy, and self-regulated learning strategies among Japanese high school students. *Psychological Reports, 85*(3), 779–798.

Youn, I. (2000). The cultural specificity of epistemological beliefs about learning. *Asian Journal of Social Psychology, 3*, 87–105.

Zhang, L.-F. (1999). A comparison of U.S. and Chinese university students' cognitive development: The cross-cultural applicability of Perry's theory. *Journal of Psychology, 133*, 425–439.

PART THREE

THEORETICAL AND METHODOLOGICAL CHALLENGES IN UNDERSTANDING AND ASSESSING SELF-AUTHORSHIP

E. G. Creamer

The chapters in this section build on those in the previous two sections by presenting various viewpoints about the role of culture and context in the development of self-authorship, and revisiting ways that the subject-object framework is useful in understanding major theoretical questions about development.

The contributions are distinctive in several ways. The chapters by Zaytoun, King, and Pizzolato invite a broader audience to exchanges about self-authorship by demonstrating the link to related concepts in other disciplines and bodies of literature. King's and Pizzolato's chapters each offer different viewpoints about relationships among the three dimensions of self-authorship and propose ideas about situations where one dimension may propel development in the other dimensions. Jones's and Creamer's chapters explore different approaches to measuring self-authorship, while Jones's and Berger's chapters demonstrate ways that assessment and reflective activities about self-authorship can fuel development.

This section raises a number of important theoretical questions about the movement toward and beyond self-authorship. An invitation is extended to further consider the role of culture and context in development and to frame questions about culture in terms of when it becomes possible for an individual to make culture and other elements of their context the object of reflection. Also addressed in this section are questions about the challenges and opportunities involved in developing a valid measure of self-authorship that is less time- and expertise-intensive than the in-depth one-on-one interview that has been used so fruitfully to advance the theoretical understanding of self-authorship.

9

BEYOND SELF-AUTHORSHIP
Fifth Order and the Capacity for Social Consciousness

Kelli Zaytoun

Abstract: In this chapter, I explore the relationship between Robert Kegan's fifth-order consciousness and the capacity for social consciousness and action. I examine the role of the self in coalition work in phenomenological, postcolonial, and feminist approaches, in light of Kegan's account of self-as-system.

When two violins are placed in a room, if a chord on one violin is struck the other violin will sound that note . . . this is for you . . . who know how powerful we are, who know we can sound the music and the people around us simply by playing our own strings.

Activist poet Andrea Gibson, from "Say Yes"

The conflict is potentially a reminder of our tendency to pretend to completeness when we are in fact incomplete. We may have this conflict because we need it to recover our true complexity.

Robert Kegan, on postmodern approach to conflict and fifth-order consciousness (1994, p. 319)

In the preceding quote, Kegan captures a key feature of the evolution of consciousness: as we become aware of our unavoidable and perpetual incompleteness, we are moved to greater complexity of being over the course of our lifetimes. In fifth order, or the "self-transforming self," the major movement is of self-authorship itself from subject to object. Such movement requires the transformation of one's understanding of his or her individuation, the essence of self-formation, from that which is distinct, whole, and complete, to that which is shifting, multifaceted, interdependent, and incomplete. It is the concept of interdependence, of the relationship between self and other, in fifth-order consciousness, that I engage in this essay, not only for its use-fulness to the study of individual identity development, but also to the study of collective identity and social consciousness.

Fifth-order, or "trans-systemic," consciousness is the final stage in Kegan's theory of self-evolution. In fifth order, self-authorship becomes object, or an aspect of our experience that can be reflected on and linked to something else. According to Kegan, in the transition from fourth to fifth order, "(y)ou begin to see that the life project is not about continuing to defend one formation of the self but about the ability to have the self liter-ally *be* transformative" (Kegan as cited in Debold, 2002, p. 151, emphasis hers). In the journey beyond fourth order, one begins to see that each way of making meaning has its limits, that one's identity, or self-as-form, and system for making sense of experience, are partial. In fifth order, one holds multiple systems of thinking and identifying as object, and develops a whole new capacity for seeing the relationship between those systems, and the systems of others. In fifth order the self is never complete, and a fixed truth cannot be known; one recognizes the tendency to pretend to be complete, but knows completeness cannot be achieved. According to Kegan, in fourth order "we take as prior the elements of a relationship (which then enter into relation-ship)," in fifth we take as prior "the relationship itself"; in other words, "(t)he relationship has the parts. The parts do not have the relationship" (Kegan, 1994, p. 316). Here lies the distinction between fourth and fifth orders: in fourth order, self-as-form is a priority and complete (is subject); in fifth order, the priority is the *process* of creating multiple forms; self-as(multiple)-forms becomes object.

I am interested in exploring the questions and implications that arise in consideration of what fifth-order consciousness suggests: that "it is only in relationship [with others] that we are who we are" (Love & Guthrie, 1999, p. 73). What does it mean to hold self-authorship as object and to embrace, as subject, the "interpenetration of selves" (Kegan, 1994, p. 315)? How does such a consciousness operate? What does it look like? More importantly, what is it capable of? If one's identities are understood as mutable, incomplete, and negotiated and constituted in relationship to others, might such a conscious-ness lend itself to an authentic investment in the well being of others and the social world in general? If so, how? I propose that it is within fifth-order con-sciousness that individuals find the genuine drive and quality skills to effec-tively work with others to address common social goals. This essay explores the function, potential, and philosophical basis of fifth-order consciousness, with other complementary accounts of the self as "selves-in-the-making," to ultimately offer a theory of the development of social consciousness and new directions for coalitions for social change.

I begin with a philosophical analysis of the importance of the notion of "self," or the psychological level of reality that is distinct from (but highly interrelated to) the social world, what Linda Martín Alcoff defines as "how we experience being ourselves" (2006, p. 93). I do this in order to engage phenomenological (e.g., Heidegger) and poststructural (e.g., Foucault, Der-rida) philosophical claims that call into question the existence of a "core" self, identity, and individual agency[1]. This analysis will connect contemporary philosophical responses to such accounts, and link them to Kegan's theory of fifth-order consciousness, to ultimately expand the value and utility of the notion of "self." I explore feminist phenomenological approaches, such as the "multi-voiced, multi-cultural self" of Mariana Ortega (2001), and the rela-tional self-account of Susan Brison (2002), as well as the feminist postcolo-nial approaches to self-multiplicity described by Gloria Anzaldúa (2002) and María Lugones (2006). What these theories and Kegan's fifth order have in common is the idea that the self and its identities are never complete; they are changing, situated, complex localities of consciousness constituted in association with others. This incompleteness, and the self's ability to reflect on and manipulate its own self-as-system, opens up new possibilities for understanding and acting on its relationship to the social world.

Phenomenology and the Self

Mariana Ortega describes the goal of phenomenological theories as an attempt to provide a bridge "between how we think of the world and how we live it" (2001, p. 3). She explains that phenomenology attempts to do justice

---

[1] For an historical overview and critique of philosophical approaches to self and identity, see Linda Martín Alcoff's *Visible Identities: Race, Gender, and the Self,* particularly Part One, Chapter Three. Poststructuralist accounts assert that self is constituted by discourse. Foucault and Derrida, for example, emphasized the effects of power on the self. Phenomenological accounts will be discussed in the next section.

to the social, situated experiences of human beings, and argues against the notion of self put forward by traditional Cartesian accounts of persons as autonomous, unified subjects with substantive, epistemic cores. Phenomenologists do not deny the notion of *the experience* of a self, but do reject the idea of an underlying, reflective foundational subject[2]. Being is knowing, being *is* self, a self that is continually defined, then redefined, through its prereflective activity in the social world. Individual agency, accountability, and identity are suspect under phenomenological and other nontraditional, poststructuralist lenses, and therefore, call into question major assumptions of traditional developmental psychology (i.e., progressive, structured maturation of a core self over time and experience), including cognitive structural theories such as Kegan's. The following quote from Maurice Merleau-Ponty (1964) sums up phenomenology's criticism of psychology's individuated subject or sense of self:

> What classical academic psychology calls "functions of cognition"—intelligence, perception, imaginations, etc.—when more closely examined, lead us back to an activity that is prior to cognition properly so called, a function of organizing experience that imposes on certain totalities the configurations and the kinds of equilibrium that are possible under the corporeal and social condition of the child himself. (As cited in Forrester, 2006, p. 784)

Phenomenology underscores the fundamental interrelatedness of all things; indeed, it rejects the concept of perception as "a perceiver's point of view" and asserts that the experience of perception of an object is actually property of the object; a body-subject may participate in the process of creating experience, but the subject in and of itself does not possess perspective (Forrester, 2006, p. 785). To Merleau-Ponty, experiences of the body, more specifically, prereflective, corporeal experiences intricately created with others and the world outside the body, are what constitute consciousness or self, an incarnated subjectivity. In other words, a separate consciousness does not exist outside the experience itself.

---

[2] In modern philosophy, the term "subject" was used to refer to the epistemic account of persons, which traditionally meant one's ability to reason (i.e., Descarte's "I think therefore I am"). Although some philosophers use the terms subject and self interchangeably, many make a distinction between the two, for example, those who reject the concept of "subjectivity" in its reference to the account of persons as possessing a substantial core. However, some have sought to redefine subjectivity to include alternative accounts of persons.

Given the preceding explanations of phenomenology's basic premises, it might appear that phenomenology and Kegan's subject/object theory are incompatible; what might be particularly problematic to phenomenology is Kegan's grounding in Piagetian principles that give primacy to the role of individual mental organization, or what Kegan calls "the work of the mind," in the ongoing construction of self[3] (Kegan, 1994, p. 29). However, I will explore how aspects of phenomenology resonate with Kegan's orders of consciousness, particularly fifth order, and how Kegan's subject/object approach complicates, yet appreciates and complements, goals of phenomenology. Next I will discuss how approaches inspired by phenomenology, like Ortega's "multi-voiced, multi-cultural self," are consistent with Kegan's understanding of consciousness and strengthen its validity.

Feminist Negotiations of a Phenomenological Self

Ortega (2001), influenced by Heidegger's (1962) notion of *Dasein*, or self as "being-in-the-world," and postcolonial Latina feminist writers, sought to negotiate a stance between the existence of a monolithic "core" self and its dismissal by phenomenologists, and calls for a consideration of selfhood that is complex, multiplicitous, and continually evolving, but inhabits a "togetherness or continuity" (p. 17). Although she retains phenomenology's insistence that the self is conceived through its activities in the world, she takes issue with the denial of the continuity of *a* self (vs. multiple selves). For example, she is critical of María Lugones's (1990) assertion, in her explanation of "'world' traveling,"[4] that there is no underlying "I," or that individuals become different people when they travel from one context to the next. Although she admits that this approach is appealing, in that it is truly phenomenological and avoids the problems associated with the assumptions of a unified subject, a mind/self completely distinctive from the body and others'

---

[3] Although since his earliest theorizing about psychological growth, represented in *The Evolving Self* (1982), Kegan has expanded Piaget's focus on "thinking" to include "affective, interpersonal, and intrapersonal realms," the self is constituted by its capacity for organizing experience, by what the mind does (Kegan, 1994, p. 29). Phenomenologists would argue that the mind does not exist outside of the experience itself and meaning is instead a work of the body.

[4] See María Lugones' essay, "Playfulness, 'World'-Traveling, and Loving Perception," in *Making Face, Making Soul/Haciendo Caras: Creative and Critical Perspectives by Women of Color* for a more thorough explanation of her concept of "world"-traveling.

minds and bodies, she argues that the activities of memory and the ability to identify difference require a sense of a "self," not multiple "selves." She questions how one can identify and retain a sense of "me" without continuity of some sort. She calls for a more complete exploration of "selfhood," not one that revives the traditional, transcendent subject, but one that makes it possible to explain continuity and difference in our experiences and awareness of our being.

Here is where I think phenomenology and Kegan's orders of consciousness can complement each other. Kegan offers an explanation of this complex evolution of the awareness of self, its continuity, and difference from others. The selfhood that Ortega is ultimately calling for is present in Kegan's conception of fifth-order consciousness, that which recognizes the self as having multiple forms and as constituitive only in its relationship with others; it is the part of our being that is present when we keep ourselves from becoming overwhelmed by a particular identity, set of values, or stances that may have been long in the making and held as "subject" at one time (e.g., in fourth order). What is subject in fifth order is a sense of continuity of selfhood that can hold out, reflect, and act upon all our particular, multiple selves, a sense that selfhood is not complete and is constantly being created in relationship with (also incomplete) others. Kegan's concept of subject/object, particularly as it relates to fifth order, therefore provides a means to explore Ortega's suggestion that continuity in our sense of being, and difference from others, be explored more fully than what is offered in Cartesian and phenomenological accounts.

Another account of the multiplicity and relationality of self that is compatible with Ortega and Kegan's fifth order is the compelling analysis of the impact of violence on the self of Susan Brison (2002), who supports what she calls a "feminist account of the relational self," a self that is "both autonomous and socially dependent, vulnerable enough to be undone by violence and yet resilient enough to be reconstructed with the help of empathetic others" (p. 38). Indeed, this quote exemplifies the contradiction and oppositeness present in the fifth-order dialectical (Kegan, 1994, p. 29). She supports the approach that the self is positioned, situated, and, for many, operates from a "multiple consciousness" (p. 38). She explores three aspects of the self that are revealed by the impact of trauma: an embodied self, self as narrative, and the autonomous self. Regarding the embodied self, she illustrates how her relationship to her body was transformed after being violently attacked, raped, and left for dead, and discusses that her mind and her body became "indistinguishable" (p. 44). She discovered that her physical "incapacitation by fear and anxiety," insomnia, and other PTSD symptoms, or the "bodily nature of traumatic memory," merges two aspects of self traditionally seen as separate: body and mind (p. 44). Trauma not only disrupts one's relationship to the body; it disrupts memory and concept of time as well. However, according to Brison, telling the story of trauma, the act of speech itself, can serve as a vehicle for recovery and reconstructing a voice that is silenced after the experience of violence and violation. This narrative aspect of self depends on a compassionate listener or witness to take the narrative seriously; it helps the survivor to reestablish his or her identity. Lastly, Brison discusses how a survivor's sense of autonomy, or will or control over one's responses, is called into question after trauma; for example, symptoms of PTSD can trigger an overactive startle response, and survivors may feel loss of control over what once felt like a safe environment. Brison also indicates that her trauma experience emphasized to her that autonomy is relational, or interdependent with others. Trauma can evoke a loss of connection to humanity, a loss that puts one's sense of autonomy and agency in danger. But Brison insists that recovery of the self, including the aspect of autonomy, in the aftermath of trauma is possible, but only possible in the presence of empathetic others.

One of Brison's most powerful statements related to this chapter's premise is in her criticism of the poststructuralist approach that the self is a fiction (this is *not* what she means by narrative self), in the sense that it is "freely constructed by some narrator" (2002, p. 135). She remarks, tongue-in-cheek but notably, that "no one, not even Stephen King, would voluntarily construct a self so tormented by trauma and its aftermath" (p. 135). This statement underscores the process by which lived, relational experience literally makes the self, a view consistent with phenomenological thought. But Brison, like Ortega, parts ways with phenomenology in her stance that a self (not multiple selves), even after being undermined in the aftermath of violent, debilitating trauma, can retain a sense of resiliency, autonomy, and continuity.

Through the lens of Kegan's approach, hearing a survivor say "I'm a not the same person I was before the rape" can be an indicator of how one might view the self-as-system, a means for holding a former form of the self as object, a self with which the survivor may have formerly overidentified, a self no longer subject, but part of the survivor nonetheless.[5] Kegan's fifth order provides a framework that captures the features and complexities of the self/other relationship put forth by Ortega and Brison. It retains appreciation for the lived experiences of the self and interactions with others as part of a dynamic cycle of the evolution of consciousness. Indeed, I believe that Kegan uses the language of "interpenetration of self and other" and "inter-individuation" to honor the depth and integrity of the process of interconnection and its power to transform and quite possibly merge self and other, a concept he hints at in an interview with Elizabeth Debold (2002), and an intriguing one to consider in future discussions about what lies beyond fifth order. Brison's (2002) account emphasizes the role of bodily experiences in the shaping of self, an aspect of meaning-making that Kegan does not stress but probably would not deny. Approaches like Brison's and others, rooted in phenomenology, open up possibilities for expanding Kegan's domains of knowing (i.e., cognitive, affective, and social) to include bodily forms of knowing as well.

For the purposes of this chapter, I lay out the observation that Ortega, Brison, and Kegan retain, that there is value in continuing to maintain but explore an assumption that is critical to cognitive structural approaches: the pattern of differentiation and integration in the evolution of consciousness. According to Kegan, this pattern is present "whether we are looking at mental development in infancy or the highly elaborated order of consciousness that underlies postmodernism" (1994, p. 326). He continues, "Before we can reconnect to, internalize, or integrate something with which we were originally fused, we must first distinguish ourselves from it" (p. 326). Indeed, this process of "distinguishing ourselves" is the central task in making something "object" in the subject/object relationship. This pattern is also a critical component of Marcia Baxter Magolda's (2001) work on development, in her exploration of internal vs. external foundation. Gloria Anzaldúa, in her work on consciousness (*conocimiento*) (2002), which I will discuss in more detail in the next section, also retains this pattern in describing how the self moves between settling within the body and inner psyche to reaching out and rec-

---

[5] A person operating from third- or fourth-order consciousness might also say that she is not the "same person" that she was before the rape; however, fifth order would provide a particular coping mechanism for constructing and managing the experience that third and fourth would not provide. In third order, one might become too dependent on others for healing; in fourth, one might become too dependent on oneself. In fifth order, one can appreciate how one's own autonomy is dependent on relationships with others, and find a balance between self-reliance and reliance on others.

onciling the demands from the outer world. She discussed how individuals move from the familiar, safe terrain of knowing and being until some experience pulls them into the unfamiliar, where they are required to negotiate the self within that context. Although Anzaldúa did not make reference to movement toward specific, qualitatively different perspectives on self as differentiated versus self as integrated, the alternating and negotiating of inner and integrated self is clearly a theme throughout her stages. On an interesting note, Anzaldúa's and Kegan's last stages of development similarly discuss moments of the merging of self and other. I find the latter concept intriguing and a worthy next step in understanding the evolution of consciousness, but I maintain that it is critical to emphasize and defend the existence and functions of a reflective, inner sense of self or continuity that, although highly interdependent on other beings and its environment, has distinct functions and potentials in the creation of highly functional relationships, communities, and social harmony.

I will now explore two more approaches to self from feminist postcolonial thought that call for and strengthen the possibility of the type of consciousness described by Kegan as fifth order. Looking at these theories together can help us more clearly visualize the functions of fifth order. More importantly, the following analysis will help ground the notion of a lived experience of consciousness in light of phenomenological and poststructural thought, but with the additional consideration of a lived sense of consistency of a self, a self that assumes responsibility for its own actions and its connectedness to the world.

Self and Social Consciousness and Complex Communication

Chicana writer Gloria Anzaldúa (2002), in her description of the concept of *conocimiento*, explores a cyclical journey of the self's focus back and forth between "inner work" and "public acts"[6] (p. 540). She explains the stage of "shifting realities" as one that nurtures the function of consciousness that understands that "beneath individual separateness lies a deeper interrelatedness" (p. 569). I'm particularly interested in this function as it indicates that

---

[6] For a detailed discussion of Anzaldúa's concept of *conocimiento* as a developmental theory, see Zaytoun (2005) "New Pathways toward Understanding Self-in-Relation: Anzaldúan (Re) Visions for Developmental Psychology," in Keating's *EntreMundos/Among Worlds: New Perspectives on Gloria E. Anzaldúa*.

the self is a system of relational parts and can serve to mobilize individuals to act collectively. She calls the function *la naguala*, and asserts that this form of knowing is "always with you but is displaced by the ego and its perspective," suggesting that Anzaldúa viewed the self as having a sense of continuity similar to Ortega's description. Kegan might offer that "being displaced by the ego" occurs when that way of knowing is subject. Anzaldúa describes *conocimiento* as a theory of composition, a construction of an awareness that she illustrates in the following way:

> When you watch yourself and observe your mind at work you find that behind your acts and your temporary sense of self (identities) is a state of awareness that, if you allow it, keeps you from getting completely caught up in that particular identity or emotional state. (As cited in Keating, 2000, p. 177)

Anzaldúa proposes here that a function of self exists that sees relationships between parts of the self (identities) without being consumed by them. She also suggests that this function engages and monitors interactions with others as follows:

> Orienting yourself to the environment and your relationship to it enables you to read and garner insight from whatever situation you find yourself in. This concocimiento gives you the flexibility to swing from your intense feelings to those of the other without being hijacked by either. When confronted with the other's fear, you note her emotional arousal, allow her feelings/words to enter your body, then you shift to the neutral place of *la naguala*. (Anzaldúa, 2002, p. 569)

This description can be viewed as an example of how fifth-order consciousness operates. The "neutral place of *la naguala*" may be consistent with what Kegan meant by the function of the dialectical in fifth order, that which allows for the ability to hold self-authorship, self-formation as object, and to hold as subject the contradictions and conflicts within the self and its relationships to others. What is subject in fifth order is the understanding of the self's incompleteness, malleability, multipleness, and interdependence with others; what Ortega would call a "complicated being in the making" (2001,

p. 17). It could also be argued that *la naguala* is present in fourth-order consciousness, because self-authorship allows one the ability to be influenced but
not determined by others; however, I contend that *la naguala* requires a step
beyond self-authorship, more fluidity in the understanding of self; it requires
the ability to hold one's identities (not just values and ideals) as objects; it
requires a divestment rather than investment in self-authorship. In other
words, I would argue that even in self-authorship the ego, or what is subject
in fourth order—the investment in one's differentiated values, ideals, and
identities—gets in the way, and the ego keeps one from becoming conscious
of the function of *la naguala*, which Anzaldúa sees as a gateway to understanding relatedness. But what is missing from Anzaldúa's commentary on *la
naguala* is a description of *how* the self moves its focus from the ego to a sense
of deeper interrelatedness. Here I use Lugones's work to help explore this
transformation.

In her theory of "complex communication," postcolonial philosopher
María Lugones (2006) helps to clarify the conditions under which the
shift to interrelatedness occurs. Lugones is critical of what she calls "the
logic of narrow identity"; this narrow logic, that one primarily belongs to
one fixed identity, is the basis for coalition work in the United States. She
explains that working toward social harmony cannot occur as long as we
see identities as fixed categories. She argues that complex communication
"requires a movement outward toward other affiliate groups recognized as
resistant" (p. 76). In order to make this move, it is necessary to understand
that we cannot assume the transparencies of others, nor should our goal
be to see our commonalities with them. Complex communication means
meeting others in what she calls "liminal spaces," which exist in particular times and places; liminal spaces are communicative achievements that
require reading the opacity of others, understanding their differences in
that communicative moment, and listening to their particular strategies.
According to Lugones, complex communication and coalition work
require a continual reconstruction of a self, a self conceived in liminal
space with others who may be unlike us but who are also resisting oppression. Like Anzaldúa, Lugones asserts that a change in self is essential to
achieve interrelatedness, but she qualifies that the change can only occur
in the course of understanding our own multiplicity and in reading each
other's opacity. Lugones's proposal is similar to Kegan's description that

fifth-order consciousness is interested in "the transformative *process* of our being, rather than the formative *products* of our becoming" (Kegan, 1994, p. 351, emphasis mine).

On the Functions of Fifth Order

I believe there is a link between what Lugones (2006) is calling coalitional limens, the communicative achievements made with others, and what Kegan refers to as the postmodern curriculum, navigated best by fifth-order consciousness. According to Kegan, fifth order requires transcending identification with internally fixed forms, and coming to an understanding that no system of organization or its parts is ever complete. It is understanding the self-as-system as a communicative achievement, as Lugones might say. And what can come with the knowledge that the self is a shifting process of being is the understanding that others experience this process as well, and that openness to their struggles and strategies brings depth to one's own. Such a consciousness allows one to truly hear and engage others, not for what one has in common with them, but for what their different experiences and ways of being contribute to one's own ways of thinking. I believe that this is what Lugones means by reading others' opacity. Fourth-order consciousness, where one has relationships but is not consumed by them, certainly provides a foundation for the function of reading others' opacity, but it is in fifth order that one truly appreciates the value of others' roles in the construction of their own experiences of self. Understanding the deep interrelatedness of the self requires knowing that even the act of thinking itself is not an isolated process. The activities of listening and sympathizing, for example, can be considered "relational forms of thinking" (Anzaldúa, 2002). When we truly engage in them and are open to what the experience has to offer, we and others are transformed by these acts.

Fifth-order consciousness is congruent with these functions of relationship; according to Kegan, the self-transforming self "is much more friendly to contradiction . . . to being able to hold on to multiple systems of thinking . . . (it is) more about movement through different forms of consciousness than about the defending and identifying with any one form" (DeBold, 2002, p. 154). Therefore, conflict and difference are not threatening to one's views because those views (and the self-as-form itself), having moved from subject to object, are now seen as continually open to manipulation and transformation.

Potential Contributions

> If the consciousness complexity of postmodern discourse is over our heads,
> how will it affect us? (Kegan, 1994, p. 337)

Expanding discussion of fifth order can further our understanding of our
potential as individuals and our potential for creating well-functioning
communities. Indeed, our future may depend on a shift to fifth-order consciousness, individually and collectively; a shift to a radical way of being
that honors the inextricable link between self and other. Anzaldúa,
Lugones, and others, in their work on social movements, have called for a
new sense of coalition that recognizes the fluidities of identities and inter-
sectionalities of oppression. This requires a move beyond the coalition
politics most prevalent in the United States today, one in which coalitions
are based on and divided by single identity group interests. M. Jacqui
Alexander (2005) comments that "our oppositional politic has been necessary, but it will never sustain us" (p. 282). She explains that, although
temporary gains in creating such divisions are possible, there is great risk
in living segregated lives; humans are indeed interdependent and "this is
why forced separations wreak havoc on our souls" (p. 282). I use Kegan's
theory here to strengthen this call for a more sophisticated means of
achieving social harmony. In doing so, I hope to have expanded discussion
on the functions and potential of fifth-order consciousness, and on theories of coalition building as well.

In the prologue to *In Over Our Heads*, Kegan (1994) explained that
"although the writer is the one who starts the book, the reader is the one
who finishes it" (p. 1). He further clarified that he hoped his text would
"be a context for readers' ongoing invention" (p. 2). This chapter is meant
to engage us in conversation about what happens *beyond* self-authorship,
and to encourage us to pick up where Kegan left off. Tracking the course
of fifth-order consciousness has much to offer scholars, educators, psychologists, administrators, and activists; it has the potential to reveal how
social consciousness, and other related capacities like global citizenship
develop and, therefore, how they can be cultivated and supported. Incorporating feminist and postcolonial scholars' calls for attention to shifting
identities, identities that are grounded in and inseparable from ever-
changing experiences of the body in the social world, can be a vital

contribution to exploring the capacities and possibilities of fifth order. The next steps in studying the journey beyond self-authorship will likely involve uncovering narratives of the shifting, multiplicitous, complex, resilient self, a self that is simultaneously incomplete, penetrable, and interdependent, but all the better for it. In *The Pedagogies of Crossing*, M. Jacqui Alexander (2005) sums up what I see as the major task of fifth-order consciousness in the following passage:

> When we have failed at solidarity work we often retreat, struggling to con-
> vince ourselves that this is indeed the work we have been called on to do.
> The fact of the matter is that there is no other work but the work of creat-
> ing and re-recreating ourselves within the context of community. Simply
> put, there is no other work. (p. 283)

Alexander calls for a shift in consciousness that enables the individual to see relationship as the primary source of a complex self and purpose, and means for "anchor(ing) the struggle for social justice" (p. 283). The "failures at solidarity work" to which she refers certainly could result from a variety of causes; however, I contend that they could indeed be related to our inability to move beyond self-authorship, from our investment in the hard-earned, internal, empowered sense of self, to a state in which, as Kegan says, "the self has become totally identified with the world," or, as Debold replies, "a transcendence of the limitations of the subject-object relationship itself" (Debold, 2002, p. 147). As Kegan claims, self-authorship provides a necessary foundation for the self-transforming self. As I have maintained in this chapter, the self-transforming self is necessary to recognize "the call" described previously by Alexander, the call to push through the struggles of difference, the investment in differences and identities, to work with others on common social goals and social justice concerns.

Operating in fifth-order consciousness, as individuals and as collectives, it is not so hard to see how the work of one individual could inspire a movement; it is not so hard to imagine how we ourselves can be like the violins that Andrea Gibson (2006) describes in the opening quote of this chapter, and how we might respond to her with the plea with which I close, "The world needs us more right now than it ever has before . . . pull all your strings; play every chord."

References

Alcoff, L. M. (2006). *Visible identities: Race, gender, and the self.* New York: Oxford University Press.

Alexander, M. J. (2005). *Pedagogies of crossing: Meditations on feminism, sexual politics, memory, and the sacred.* Durham, NC: Duke University Press.

Anzaldúa, G. E. (2002). Now let us shift. In G. Anzaldúa & A. Keating (Eds.), *This bridge we call home: Radical visions for transformation* (pp. 540–578). New York: Routledge.

Baxter Magolda, M. B. (2001). *Making their own way: Narratives for transforming higher education to promote self-development.* Sterling, VA: Stylus.

Brison, S. (2002). *Aftermath: Violence and the remaking of a self.* Princeton, NJ: Princeton University Press.

Debold, E. (2002). Epistemology, fourth order consciousness, and the subject-object relationship, or how the self evolves with Robert Kegan. *What is Enlightenment?* (Fall/Winter 2002): 143–154.

Derrida, J. (1984). *The margins of philosophy.* Trans. A. Bass. Chicago: University of Chicago Press.

Forrester, M. A. (2006). Projective identification and intersubjectivity. *Theory & Psychology, 16*(6) 783–802.

Foucault, M. (1983). The subject and power. In H. L. Dreyfus & P. Rabinow (Eds.). *Beyond structuralism and hermeneutics: Michel Foucault* (pp. 208–228). Chicago: University of Chicago Press.

Gibson, Andrea. (2006). Say yes. Video posted November 17, 2007 to http://www.youtube.com/watch?v=TsINiBj4pCc

Heidegger, M. (1962). *Being and time.* Trans. J. Macquarrie & E. Robinson. London: SCM Press.

Keating, A. L. (Ed.), (2000). *Gloria E. Anzaldúa: Interviews entrevistas.* New York: Routledge.

Kegan, R. (1982). *The evolving self: Problem and process in human development.* Cambridge, MA: Harvard University Press.

Kegan, R. (1994). *In over our heads: The mental demands of modern life.* Cambridge, MA: Harvard University Press.

Love, P. G., & Guthrie, V. L. (1999, Winter). Kegan's orders of consciousness. *New Directions for Student Services, 88*, 65–75.

Lugones, M. (1990). Playfulness, "world"-travelling, and loving perception, In G. Anzaldúa (Ed.), *Making face, making soul/Haciendo caras: Creative and critical perspective by women of color* (pp. 390–402). San Francisco: Aunt Lute.

Lugones, M. (2006). On complex communication. *Hypatia. 21*(3): 75–85.

Merleau-Ponty, M. (1964). The child's relations with others. In M. Merleau-Ponty (Ed.), *The primacy of perception and other essays on phenomenological psychology* (pp. 159–190). Evanston, IL: Northwestern University Press.

Ortega, M. (2001). 'New mestizas,' 'world'-travelers,' and 'Dasein': Phenomenology and the multi-voiced, multi-cultural self. *Hypatia. 16*(3): 1–29.

Zaytoun, K. (2005). New pathways toward understanding self-in-relation: Anzaldúan (re)visions for developmental psychology. In A. Keating (Ed.), *Entremundos/Among worlds: New perspectives on Gloria E. Anzaldúa* (pp. 147–159). New York: Palgrave MacMillan.

THE ROLE OF THE COGNITIVE DIMENSION OF SELF-AUTHORSHIP
An Equal Partner or the Strong Partner?

Patricia M. King

Abstract: This chapter explores the role of the cognitive dimension of Kegan's theory of self-evolution by asking whether the three dimensions serve as equal partners in the development of mature capacities, or whether the cognitive dimension serves as a strong partner (the "first among equals") in this development.

The three dimensions of Kegan's (1994) theory of the development of self-authorship (cognitive, intrapersonal, and interpersonal) add to the interpretive and explanatory richness of the literature on late adolescent and adult development by highlighting the role each dimension plays in the developing person. Further, the presentation of these dimensions as interconnected, instead of discrete and independent, adds to the conceptual richness of the theory. If more detailed explications of the theoretical and empirical relationships among the dimensions were available, scholars would have a stronger foundation on which to make theoretical claims, design studies to test these claims, and create stronger educational practices to promote self-authorship.

In this chapter, I begin the process of explicating these relationships by exploring the role of the cognitive dimension, asking whether the three dimensions serve as equal partners in the development of mature capacities, or whether the cognitive dimension serves as a strong partner (the "first among equals") in this development. This question has implications for assessment and practice as well as for theory refinement. For example, if the three dimensions are assumed to serve as equal partners, then they should be weighted equally in assessments, and educators should give equal attention to all three dimensions. However, if the cognitive dimension serves as the strong partner (e.g., if cognitive development is necessary but not sufficient for development in the other dimensions), then the cognitive dimension should be given priority in these decisions.

My aim in addressing this topic is not to argue for a particular conclusion about the relationships across dimensions at this time, but rather to provide the impetus for a conversation among scholars of human development that ultimately will lead to new data and refinements in theory-building and research on the dimensions of self-authorship. To start this conversation, I wish to point out my position and perspective. First, it is relevant to this discussion that I have devoted a considerable amount of my professional life to the study of post-adolescent and adult intellectual development based on the Reflective Judgment Model (King & Kitchener, 1994, 2004; Kitchener & King, 1981; Kitchener, King, & DeLuca, 2006). Therefore, it would not be surprising if I prioritize or privilege this dimension in my assessment of its role vis-à-vis other dimensions of development, or ascribe to it greater explanatory power than might other scholars. However, I see merit in both perspectives and have tried to develop a balanced analysis. I hope this discussion inspires others to contribute to a body of evidence that will better inform this question in the future.

First, I offer a note about terminology. After much deliberation, I have chosen to use the word "cognitive" when referring to the first dimension of Kegan's (1994) model in this chapter. I did so to be consistent with Kegan's terminology, although I find his choice problematic. The issue here is that the term "cognitive" conveys a broad set of mental activities (e.g., inductive and deductive reasoning, self-monitoring, knowledge retention), whereas the meaning-making characteristics described in the cognitive dimension are primarily related to one facet of cognition, developing epistemologies. Kitchener's (1983) analysis of related terms is informative here: she distinguished among cognition (observed reasoning strategies), metacognition (underlying assumptions about problem solving and reasoning that guide these strategies), and epistemic cognition (underlying assumptions about knowledge that structure one's metacognitions). Epistemic cognition reflects the structure of mental organization that underlies changes in meaning-making in the realm of knowing, most particularly, assumptions about knowledge (e.g., what can be known, how one comes to know). Hofer and

Pintrich (1997, 2002) subsequently coined the term "personal epistemology" to refer to this area of scholarship, which focuses on "what individuals believe about how knowing occurs, what counts as knowledge and where it resides, and how knowledge is constructed and evaluated" (Hofer, 2004, p. 1). Kegan used similar language when he referred to the inner logic of a principle of mental organization as "epistemologic" (p. 32), but did not elaborate on his definition of this term. This is unfortunate, as it both leads to questions about the focus of the "cognitive" dimension and complicates inquiries about the relationships among the dimensions. A broader definition of the cognitive dimension (the range of elements within the domain of cognitive noted previously) provides a basis for the dimension to have a stronger impact; it simply casts a broader net that encompasses more elements, and thus has a higher likelihood of playing a stronger role. A narrower definition (e.g., Kitchener's definition of epistemology noted earlier) encompasses a narrower range of elements, and observed relationships here are thus limited to that smaller set of elements. I return to this issue later with another suggestion related to the use of the "term" cognitive in this model.

Several factors complicate an analysis of the relationships across dimensions. First, development in all the dimensions is associated with increased cognitive complexity. For example, if complexity in understanding oneself reflects cognitive complexity applied to intrapersonal questions, then this would be an argument for the cognitive dimension as the strong partner. However, if development of intrapersonal complexity were substantively different from development of cognitive or interpersonal complexity (not the application of cognitive skills in this domain), then such evidence would support the equal partners perspective.

Second, meaning-making is at the heart of all three dimensions in Kegan's (1994) theory, and meaning-making itself is arguably a cognitive function. Kegan (1982) describes meaning-making as "that most human of 'regions' *between* an event and a reaction to it—the place where the event is privately composed, made sense of, the place where it actually *becomes* an event for that person" (p. 2, italics in original). That is, discerning meaning from experiences (e.g., interpreting experiences and communicating reactions and interpretations with others) often involves—and may require—thought; explaining this to others requires cognitive capacities such as thinking and constructing ideas, in addition to verbalizing them. Indeed, development across the orders of consciousness shows how individuals develop the capacity to make different structures of *thinking* object across the developmental continuum. I am not suggesting that meaning-making involves only thoughts to the exclusion of other sources of awareness (e.g., emotions or intuitions), but rather that meaning-making is closely associated with thinking processes ("sense-making"), and thus the cognitive dimension may be more active or at least more visible than the other two dimensions because of the demands of the meaning-making process.

Third, many research studies of self-authorship report only an overall developmental assessment, without reporting data separately for each dimension. (See the Creamer chapter in this volume for a related discussion of this point.) Further, interview assessments are heavily dependent on the articulation of meaning-making, and because articulation requires putting thoughts into words (another arguably cognitive task), such evidence of meaning-making may emphasize the cognitive dimension. A similar argument could be made about the cognitive demands of responding to survey items, which requires respondents to report how they *think* about the items, which also emphasizes the cognitive demands.

These are the considerations that both informed and motivated my interest in this topic. I turn now to a consideration of each perspective.

The Equal Partners Perspective

Framing one's perspectives with increasingly abstract and inclusive categories is a key feature of Kegan's (1994) model of the development of orders of consciousness, and applies equally to all three dimensions. Although cognitive development plays an important role in Kegan's (1994) theory, it is neither the sole nor the primary focus of the model, as it shares the stage with the other two dimensions that are portrayed as equal partners in the development of mature capacities. It is important to point out that Kegan does not discuss the three dimensions separately in detail; rather, he intertwines the dimensions in his examples, but does list them separately in his summary tables and figures.

By "equal partners," I intend to convey that all three dimensions play equally important roles in the development of self-authorship. Each dimension encompasses developmental issues in its respective domain, but development in all three is necessary for movement to self-authorship. By merit of being of equal developmental importance, it would be consistent to hypothesize relationships between dimensions as mutual or even synergistic, with development in one dimension spurring or mediating development in another dimension.

Being of equal importance does not imply that development across dimensions necessarily unfolds uniformly and evenly. An example of uneven development is reflected in Kroll's (1992) observation that students reveal a "leading edge of development" (p. 13), such as an area of learning in which they show receptiveness to evaluating existing perspectives and learning new ones. Similarly, among those who are very interpersonally astute, awareness may first enter their consciousness through an interpersonal interaction, later leading to insights that reflect a new cognitive or intrapersonal awareness; here, the interpersonal dimension serves as a leading edge. Thus, forward movement could be initiated by development in any dimension. Which dimension is in the lead could likely vary at different times in an individual's life, and which dimension leads more often would vary for different people. Whatever the roles the dimensions play at a given time in a given circumstance, all three are involved in the individual's development.

Several studies of young adult and adult development provide evidence that supports the equal partners perspective; I highlight four for this purpose. The first of these is Baxter Magolda's (2001) 22-year longitudinal study of a group of college students who are now in their forties. She reports that although her study initially focused on the epistemological dimension during their college years, the participants themselves increasingly introduced topics that related to the intrapersonal and interpersonal dimensions. She notes:

> It seemed that they could not address the epistemological dimension, or the "how you know" question, without working with the other two dimensions. Stories from their twenties convey that adopting contextual assumptions about the nature of knowledge was necessary but insufficient for contextual knowing. In order to know and make decisions contextually they also needed to construct an internal self-definition that enabled them to choose what to believe and mediate their relations with the external world . . . Their collective stories . . . extend our understanding of the three dimensions, how they interweave during the journey through the twenties, and what contexts aid in the transformation to self-authorship. (p. 23)

Among the many rich examples in *Making Their Own Way* (2001) that illustrate how the dimensions are intertwined, the story of Dawn's journey (what she calls "a self-discovery of powers," p. 152) is particularly insightful. Dawn was an actress who discovered herself in part through the characters she played:

> Acting has been the one thing that I discovered myself that I could do and wanted to do, not something that someone said, "You should be a doctor because of whatever reason." It's been the one thing that I could latch onto and make my very own. That's a great feeling. I think that's probably why I'm so passionate about it, because it's like, "This is all mine. Nobody can do this for me; nobody can give me the answers. It's all mine to do and to create and be." So that's so exciting and makes it all worth it. . . . It's one continual process—discovering myself helps my acting and by doing acting I discover myself. (p. 152)

As Baxter Magolda points out, Dawn's discovery of self led to her discovery of herself as a knower. For Dawn in this example, the intrapersonal dimension seems to represent the leading edge of development.

Baxter Magolda (personal communication, February 29, 2008) has used the metaphor of strands of a rope to illustrate how the dimensions of development are woven together. For example, it is not until one looks closely at a rope that the three intertwined strands are visible. Further, strength in one strand can keep a rope useful after one or both of the others have begun to fray. For example, a gay man who experiences workplace harassment based on his sexual orientation can draw strength from his understanding of power and privilege (the cognitive dimension), and from the fact that he has healthy professional relationships with other colleagues (the interpersonal dimension), and thus be bolstered in his resistance to the assault on his sense of self (the intrapersonal dimension) in this context.

A second example of research that supports the equal partners perspective is Torres' four-year longitudinal study of Latino/a college student identity development. Torres and Baxter Magolda (2004) reported strong links between cognitive and intrapersonal development:

> Cognitive dissonance and the construction of more complex ways of thinking was key to decreasing susceptibility to stereotype vulnerability and creating positive images of their ethnicity. Cognitive movement points seemed

to enable complementary shifts in intrapersonal and interpersonal developmental dimensions. In the case of these participants, ethnic identity reconstruction was intricately interwoven with cognitive and relationship reconstruction. (p. 345)

This finding of the interwoven relationships among dimensions illustrates the rope metaphor introduced previously.

Torres and Hernandez (2007) analyzed data from Torres' longitudinal study using Kegan's holistic framework. One of the patterns they observed is particularly relevant to the current discussion: "Although students progressed at different rates among the dimensions, no student ever progressed more than one phase without development in the other dimensions moving forward" (p. 570). This strongly suggests that the dimensions are interrelated, and that development in all dimensions is required for advancement to the next developmental level. They also creatively illustrated this in a table of identity-related tasks organized by dimension and self-authorship level. This matrix clearly illustrates the coherence of each dimension across levels and the structural similarities within developmental level across dimensions, and led to their suggestion of a synergistic relationship among dimensions.

A third study illustrating the "equal partners" perspective is the work of Abes, Jones, and McEwen (2007). In a departure from theories of identity development that focus on a selected aspect of identity (e.g., gender, race, ethnicity, religion), Jones and McEwen (2000) proposed a model of multiple dimensions of identity (based on Jones, 1997) that offered a way of conceptualizing relationships among social identities and between one's personal and social identity. The 2007 work (Abes et al.) is a reconceptualization of that model, informed by the work of Abes and Jones (2004). Here, their focus on multiple identities is augmented by the inclusion of contextual influences (e.g., peers, family, sociopolitical conditions) and a meaning-making filter (e.g., one's order of consciousness). This conceptualization illustrates how one's meaning-making filter mediates the influence of the contextual factors on one's sense of identity, thus integrating intrapersonal development with cognitive and interpersonal domains.

The evidence noted in the preceding paragraphs suggests that all three dimensions develop in relationship to each other, that development in one dimension may be beneficial to development in one or both of the other dimensions, and that development across strands is not necessarily uniform.

For example, addressing interpersonal issues may provide a salient context for and motivation to reconsider one's sense of self. In this way, the interpersonal domain may provide a leading edge for development among college students operating within Kegan's (1994) third order who place great importance on, and invest a great deal of effort in, their relationships with peers, especially when they experience dissonance associated with trying to keep others happy at their own expense. Such experiences may provide what Pizzolato (2005) calls a "provocative moment" that spurs development.

Little is known about the mechanisms involved with a leading edge of development, though it seems to be a useful construct, and one that educators readily recognize. Several studies offer examples of individuals who appear to be more open to developmental challenges in one dimension over another or have a higher degree of readiness to address the challenges posed through a given dimension. Developing maturity in this dimension may serve to "pave the way" for development in the other dimensions. Alternatively, recognizing that one's capacities in one dimension lag behind the others may be a source of dissonance that motivates a person to work harder in this dimension and give it special attention (thus making object the recognition of these internal imbalances). These mechanisms remain largely unexplored.

The Strong Partner Role of the Cognitive Dimension

A rich array of theories of cognitive development in late adolescence and adulthood, and a large body of research, are available to inform our understanding of the cognitive dimension of self-authorship. The depth of scholarship in this area is one reason this dimension may be seen as the strong partner: we simply have more data to inform our understanding of development in this domain. In addition, much of the research suggests that meaning-making is a cognitive activity, as it requires one to engage in tasks variously described as thinking about, making sense of, and figuring out, all of which require expending cognitive effort.

Perry's (1970) seminal work inspired or contributed to each of the following models of intellectual development (listed here in chronological order): Fischer (1980); Kitchener and King (1981); King and Kitchener (1994); Belenky, Clinchy, Goldberger, and Tarule (1986); Baxter Magolda (1992); and Kegan (1994). (See Love & Guthrie, 1999, for short descriptions of each of these models and an excellent integrative analysis.) Because several of these theories share common historical roots and fall within the constructive developmental tradition, it is perhaps not surprising that despite differences in focus, emphasis, and samples, they share common features. One such feature is that each describes ways in which people's thinking becomes more complex over time and as they face challenging questions and situations, resulting in models that illustrate increasing complexity in thinking across developmental levels. In each of these models, successive levels of development are associated with more inclusive ways of understanding relationships between and among elements. (Fischer's model portrays this most clearly).

Development of Complexity in the Cognitive Dimension

In the developmental models previously noted, individuals who reason at early developmental levels tend to rely on single sources or perspectives when solving problems, whereas those who reason at more advanced developmental levels tend to take into account information from multiple sources. Another underlying feature of this family of models is that one's capacity to frame a problem using multiple lenses reflects more advanced levels of development than does framing a problem using only one perspective; doing so also reflects (or requires) greater cognitive complexity. For example, identifying similarities between conflicting views calls for analyzing two perspectives at the same time and in relation to each, which requires greater complexity than does examining them one at a time.

The Reflective Judgment Model (RJM; King & Kitchener, 1994) describes another relevant feature in detail—developmentally ordered differences in the ways people justify their beliefs. I will use this model to illustrate how the development of cognitive complexity provides a foundation for the strong partner claim. Based on Dewey's (1933) concept of reflective thinking, the RJM describes changes in assumptions about knowledge and what can be known, how knowledge is gained, how beliefs are justified, and the certainty with which one can know and make knowledge claims. Seven developmental stages are organized into three levels, prereflective, quasi-reflective and reflective thinking. Each successive level is associated with developing assumptions about the nature of knowledge: at the prereflective level, knowledge is assumed to exist absolutely and concretely; at the quasi-reflective level, knowledge is assumed to be uncertain and idiosyncratic to the knower; and at the reflective thinking level, knowledge is described as the outcome of a process of reasonable inquiry. The type of increasing structural complexity across RJ stages is similar to that described in Fischer's (1980) skill theory. (For an introduction to skill theory in a higher education context, see King & VanHecke, 2006.) For example, each successive RJ stage shows increasing complexity as individuals learn to relate elements, use these to form more inclusive wholes, break new wholes into new subparts, and discern new relationships at more abstract levels. These changes in mental organization show how people learn to draw from multiple frames of reference and to make reflective judgments (King & Kitchener, 1994; Kitchener & Fischer, 1990). Given the salience in many contexts of capacities such as learning to expand one's frame of reference, using relevant evidence in the support of interpretations, and understanding the limitations of one's ability to know, it is reasonable to suggest that the cognitive dimension has the most influence on development of the three dimensions.

Development of Complexity in the Intrapersonal Dimension

Complexity is also apparent in the developmental changes that occur within the intrapersonal dimension of Kegan's (1994) model, which focuses on developing the capacities for constructing self-understanding. Development within this dimension evolves across the orders of consciousness from enduring predispositions (needs, preferences, self-concept) in order 2, to inner states (subjectivity, self-consciousness) in order 3, to self-authorship (self-regulation, self-formation, identity, autonomy, individuation) in order 4, and to self-transformation (interpenetration of selves, inter-individuation) in order 5. This illustrates how successive developmental positions encompass prior sets of assumptions. Thus, this dimension maps out developmental changes in the ways people learn to make meaning around issues of personal identity, with each order of development reflecting increased awareness and cognitive complexity. (It also provides a developmental interpretation of Descartes' famous assertion, "I think, therefore I am.") Baxter Magolda (2001) offers an insightful analysis of the intrapersonal dimension and its focus on how individuals constructed their identities, offering many examples of the evolution of complexity in this dimension over time.

Development of Complexity in the Interpersonal Dimension

In describing development within the interpersonal dimension, Kegan (1982) drew from seminal theorists of human development (Piaget, Kohlberg, Loevinger, Maslow, McClelland, Murray, and Erikson), all of whom documented changes over time in the complexity with which individuals come to balance their own needs and values with those of others as they mature. This can be complicated, especially as an individual is cognizant of others' expectations for one's behaviors, and as s/he realizes that different contexts may call for different ways of expressing the balance and responding to such expectations. Thus, in this dimension as well, understanding interpersonal relations in a nuanced way requires a complex view of interpersonal phenomena. (For an example of the role of cognitive complexity in understanding multicultural interactions, see King & Shuford, 1996).

The Development of Complexity as Necessary but Not Sufficient

Given that cognitive complexity is a thread that runs through all three dimensions, is development in the cognitive dimension necessary but not sufficient for development in the other dimensions? If so, the cognitive dimension would provide a foundation without which development in the other domains is restricted. For example, one would have to be able to think complexly before being able to think complexly about identity and/or interpersonal or social issues. Evidence of such a relationship would support the strong partner position.

King and Kitchener (1994) discussed this question in regard to the relationship between reflective judgment and moral development. In a chapter devoted to this topic, we asked whether the ability to make reflective judgments enables one to make better moral decisions, framing the question as follows:

> Is a person who accepts uncertainty in the intellectual domain more likely to accept uncertainty in the moral domain? Is a person who is aware that evidence about an issue is open to different perceptions and interpretations in the intellectual domain similarly aware when dealing with moral issues? . . . The structural similarities [in models of development across domains] suggest that there may be mechanisms underlying development in both domains (as suggested by Fischer, 1980) that may affect how the individual operates on both sets of tasks. (p. 207)

Data from our 10-year longitudinal study of reflective judgment informs this relationship. The Time 1 sample of this study consisted of 20 16-year old high school students and 40 21-year old college students who were matched by gender and aptitude to a sample of 20 advanced graduate students whose . average age was 28. (For details on the methods, see King & Kitchener, 1994; see Wood, 1990, 1997 for a discussion of these relationships.) Follow-up assessments were conducted two years, six years, and ten years later. Correlations between the Reflective Judgment Interview (RJI; Kitchener & King, 1981) and the Defining Issues Test (Rest, 1979) were moderate (.46–.58) at all four testings, and lower when the effects of age and number of years of higher education were statistically controlled. Differences in RJI scores by group (i.e., the three educational levels) and time (i.e., the four times of testing) remained significant when the effects of moral judgment scores were statistically removed, but the converse did not hold: both group and time differences in moral judgment became nonsignificant when the RJI scores were covaried out. These findings supported the conclusion that development of reflective judgment is necessary but not sufficient for development in moral judgment.

More specifically, it may be that a given level of cognitive development (such as Abstract Level 1 in Fischer's (1980) model or Stage 4 in the RJM) is necessary for advancement to the more advanced levels of development. Guthrie (1996; Guthrie, King, & Palmer, 2000) tested 48 undergraduate and graduate students on Reflective Judgment and two measures of tolerance (defined as low levels of prejudice toward African Americans and homosexuals). Virtually all who scored below average on the tolerance measures scored below Stage 4 of the RJM. Among those who scored above average on the tolerance measures, twice as many scored above Stage 4 as below Stage 4, and cognitive development accounted for 44% of the variance in tolerance. These findings support the proposition that a given level of cognitive complexity (here, RJM Stage 4 reasoning) is necessary but not sufficient for advanced levels of tolerance.

These quantitative findings may inform the question raised earlier about the cognitive demands associated with using an interview for assessment purposes (e.g., articulating meaning-making). That is, the instruments used in these studies to measure moral judgment and tolerance were surveys that were recognition tasks (King, 1990), as was the RJM measure in the Guthrie study. As such, these avoided the methodological confounding of different task demands (recognizing a response as similar to one's own versus producing and verbalizing one's own response) when judging the role of the cognition dimension on other dimensions of development.

Taken together, this body of scholarship supports the perspective that the cognitive dimension is the strong partner because cognitive complexity is at the foundation of all three dimensions. That is, cognitive complexity seems to undergird intrapersonal and interpersonal development: without cognitive complexity, one does not have a cognitive frame of reference that would accommodate integrating several aspects of self or seeing multiple possibilities and choices about the kinds of friendships one constructs.

Enabling Effects of Cognitive Dissonance and Cognitive Awareness

In the first part of this chapter, I used the Torres study (Torres & Baxter Magolda, 2004) of the influence of cognitive development on the development of ethnic identity among Latino/a students to illustrate the "equal partner" perspective, drawing from their discussion of the integration among dimensions. However, an argument can also be made for using this study as an example of the strong partner role of the cognitive dimension. That is, in this analysis, they reported examples of students who experienced cognitive dissonance and as a result, shifted cognitive perspectives in ways they navigated issues related to their ethnic identity. This shift of perspective, or reframing the way they defined the issue, seemed to allow—if not promote—identity development. For example, in a discussion of Angelica's development over time, they report how Angelica's exposure to the idea of knowledge being socially constructed and how socialization affected how people construct knowledge led her to talk with her family about her own socialization in her family.

> Her evolving awareness and acceptance of uncertainty and multiple perspectives led to movement away from authority's knowledge claims to personal processes for adopting knowledge claims—a shift in the cognitive dimension of development. Similarly, her critique of her own family socialization and attempts to examine her ethnic identity reveal her evolving awareness of her own values and sense of identity distinct from external others' perceptions. (p. 344)

Although her two experiences are described as parallel processes, the sequential order of events implies that reliance on authorities decreased first in the cognitive domain, and was subsequently used in the ethnic identity domain. This suggests that the development in the cognitive domain enabled Angelica to "reframe" the way she thought about her ethnic identity in ways that enabled her to ask questions, assimilate the information from multiple sources, and arrive at a more complex understanding of herself.

A second example of the cognitive dimension playing the strong partner role may be seen in their description of Angelica's fourth-year interview, in which she acknowledged the need to take responsibility for her beliefs, identity, and relationships.

> She is cognitively aware of the need to construct an internal belief system and an internally generated sense of self to take into authentic relationships with others. Although she has yet to construct herself along these dimensions, her cognitive awareness of the need to allows her to articulate her future plans. (Torres & Baxter Magolda, 2004, p. 345)

This suggests that cognitive awareness may enable (or at least precede) aspects of intrapersonal (identity) development, consistent with the strong partner perspective.

In summary, the cognitive dimension may be seen as the strong partner for several reasons. The first is that development in all domains strongly reflects—and arguably requires—cognitive complexity. Related to this, development of increasingly abstract systems is a common thread across dimensions of development, a thread that reflects or requires cognitive development. Further, another element in the cognitive domain, cognitive dissonance (Festinger, 1957), or the Piagetian construct of cognitive disequilibrium (Piaget, 1970), is widely recognized as stimulating development, as exemplified in the Torres study (Torres & Baxter Magolda, 2004), where it appeared to promote identity resolution.

Discussion and Conclusion

Having examined the relationships across dimensions, and whether the cognitive dimension is an equal partner or a strong partner, I now return to some of the broader questions raised previously about the role of the cognitive dimension as it relates to the other two dimensions of development. Here, I offer a few additional reflections and a possible resolution.

First, I encourage scholars to find new and creative ways to systematically examine patterns of relationships across dimensions. For example, just as evidence was presented earlier for cognitive development (specifically, epistemic assumptions) being necessary but not sufficient for moral development, scholars should also study whether the development of intrapersonal or interpersonal capacities is necessary but not sufficient for development in the cognitive dimension. That is, could a similar argument be made in the other direction, asking whether one needs skills of social discernment in order to access and utilize one's critical thinking skills in regard to interpersonal issues? Studies that focus on any dimension in a way that illuminates its role might yield findings distinctive to the targeted dimension; all would contribute to our understanding of this phenomenon. To my knowledge, studies exploring such relationships across self-authorship dimensions that could help answer this question have not been conducted.

In order for future research to be helpful in analyzing relationships across dimensions, coding of self-authorship levels will need to go beyond an overall assessment to include assessments of all three dimensions. This is currently being done in the analysis of interviews conducted for the Wabash National Study of Liberal Arts Education (Baxter Magolda & King, 2007). Similarly, although development in the cognitive, intrapersonal, and interpersonal dimensions may follow similar developmental pathways, different experiences may affect the progression along each pathway. Whether one is using qualitative or quantitative assessment methods, being able to identify such differential effects will also require assessments of all three dimensions.

Last, I return to the question of the role of cognitive complexity, which I have shown is a common characteristic across dimensions at the level of self-authorship. One answer to the question about the role of the cognitive dimension is that cognitive complexity develops within each dimension, and is thus applied within different developmental arenas. For example, in the cognitive dimension, cognitive complexity is evident when people explain the basis for their carefully reasoned judgments about a range of topics and issues in the intellectual domain, such as evaluating proposals to reduce greenhouse gases, or calculating the effects of financial aid on college retention rates. In the intrapersonal dimension, cognitive complexity is evident when individuals employ a complex view of self that embraces possible contradictions, such as weaknesses *and* strengths, areas of moral clarity *and* moral blind spots, among other considerations. In the interpersonal domain, cognitive complexity is evident when people make moral choices that are justice-based *and* care-based, discerning *and* compassionate, are aware of the sources of their own and others' moral principles, and can effectively construct and repair mutual relationships with others. Each of these examples illustrates cognitive complexity as applied to the three dimensions: in each dimension, increasingly complex ways of making meaning (about knowledge, self, and relationships) are the object of one's reflection.

Considering complexity of understanding within dimensions leads to a different issue of terminology that in turn, suggests a possible resolution to the alternatives discussed here. Part of the confusion of the role of the cognitive dimension may stem from locating "complexity" in that dimension, as in "cognitive complexity." Rather, locating it elsewhere might resolve this quandary. One such possibility is to locate cognitive complexity as a foundation that underlies all dimensions; in this foundational role, cognitive complexity is necessary but not sufficient for self-authored meaning-making.

In this foundational role, a shift in focus and language from cognitive complexity to "connective complexity" may better capture this element that underlies development across dimensions. Here, in addition to being able to take divergent elements into consideration as one makes meaning of experiences (attributes of cognitive complexity), connective complexity reflects one's capacity to make connections between and among these elements, forming and reforming the connections to allow for more inclusive wholes as one's understanding of the relationships among elements becomes more complex. This idea is drawn in part from Fischer's (1980) skill theory, where he organizes levels of skills into increasingly complex structures of thought. Thus, the ability to make more complex connections illustrates development both within and across dimensions without relying on an attribute that is located within the cognitive dimension.

I organized this discussion as a contrast of alternative explanations of the role of the cognitive dimension of self-authorship, each with different implications for assessment and educational practice, and concluded that at this time, good evidence exists to support of both views, but not enough to endorse one over the other. I also concluded that the dilemma raised in this chapter could be addressed by repositioning the role of complexity and clarifying its focus. This chapter illustrates the need to propose and test more detailed conceptual frameworks about self-authorship, including its defining features and how the three dimensions of development are related to each other. I ask others to participate in this extended conversation about our collective assumptions about how this rich explanatory model "works," and to do so in ways that lead to theory refinement, testing of new frameworks, the refinement of assessment strategies, and to educational strategies based on this research. This brings us full circle: more detailed explications could lead to more detailed theoretical claims, to more sophisticated assessments and research designs, and ultimately to a stronger foundation for educational practices designed to promote self-authorship. This process starts with looking deeply at theoretical descriptions and explanations and candidly exchanging questions and ideas about self-evolution. These are the kinds of exchanges that lead to provocative insights about the mysteries of human development.

References

Abes, E. S. & Jones, S. R. (2004). Meaning-making capacity and the dynamics of lesbian college students' multiple dimensions of identity. *Journal of College Student Development, 45*(6), 612–632.

Abes, E. S., Jones, S. R., & McEwen, M. K. (2007). Reconceptualizing the model of multiple dimensions of identity: The role of meaning-making capacity in the construction of multiple identities. *Journal of College Student Development, 48*(1), 1–22.

Baxter Magolda, M. B. (1992). *Knowing and reasoning in college: Gender-related patterns in students' intellectual development.* San Francisco: Jossey-Bass.

Baxter Magolda, M. B. (2001). *Making their own way: Narratives for transforming higher education to promote self-development.* Sterling, VA: Stylus Publishing.

Baxter Magolda, M. B., & King, P. M. (2007). Interview strategies for assessing self-authorship: Constructing conversations to assess meaning making. *Journal of College Student Development, 48*(5), 491–508.

Belenky, M. F., Clinchy, B. M., Goldberger, N. R., & Tarule, J. M. (1986). *Women's ways of knowing: The development of self, voice and mind.* New York: Basic Books.

Dewey, J. (1933). *How we think: A restatement of the relation of reflective thinking to the educative process.* Lexington, MA: Heath.

Festinger, L. (1957). *A theory of cognitive dissonance.* Stanford, CA: Stanford University Press.

Fischer, K. (1980). A theory of cognitive development: The control and construction of hierarchies of skills. *Psychological Review, 87,* 477–531.

Guthrie, V. L., (1996). *The relationship of intellectual development and tolerance for diversity among college students.* Unpublished doctoral dissertation, Bowling Green State University.

Guthrie, V. L., King, P. M., & Palmer, C. J. (2000). Higher education and reducing prejudice: Research on cognitive capabilities underlying tolerance. *Diversity Digest, 4*(3), 10–11, 23.

Hofer, B. (2004). Epistemological understanding as a metacognitive process: Thinking aloud during online searching. *Educational Psychologist, 39*(1), 43–55.

Hofer, B., & Pintrich, P. (1997). The development of epistemological theories: Beliefs about knowledge and knowing and their relations to learning. *Review of Educational Research, 67,* 88–140.

Hofer, B., & Pintrich, P. (2002). *Personal epistemology: The psychology of beliefs about knowledge and knowing.* Mahway, NJ: Lawrence Erlbaum Associates, Inc.

Jones, S. R. (1997). Voices of identity and difference: A qualitative exploration of the multiple dimensions of identity development in women college students. *Journal of College Student Development, 39,* 376–386.

Jones, S. R., & McEwen, M. K. (2000). A conceptual model of multiple dimensions of identity. *Journal of College Student Development, 41,* 405–414.

Kegan, R. (1982). *The evolving self.* Cambridge, MA: Harvard University Press.

Kegan, R. (1994). *In over our heads: The mental demands of modern life.* Cambridge, MA: Harvard University Press.

King, P. M. (1990). Assessing development from a cognitive developmental perspective. In D. Creamer and Associates, *College student development: Theory and practice for the 1990s* (pp. 81–98). Alexandria, VA: ACPA Media.

King, P. M., & Kitchener, K. S. (1994). *Developing reflective judgment: Understanding and promoting intellectual growth and critical thinking in adolescents and adults.* San Francisco: Jossey-Bass Publishers.

King, P. M., & Kitchener, K. S. (2004). Reflective judgment: Theory and research on the development of epistemic assumptions through adulthood. *Educational Psychologist, 39*(1), 5–18.

King, P. M., & Shuford, B. (1996). A multicultural view is a more cognitively complex view. *American Behavioral Scientist, 40*(2), 153–164.

King, P. M., & VanHecke, J. R. (2006). Making connections: Using skill theory to recognize how students build—then rebuild—understanding. *About Campus, 11*(1), 10–16.

Kitchener, K. S. (1983). Cognition, metacognition, and epistemic cognition. *Human Development, 26,* 222–232.

Kitchener, K. S., & Fischer, K. W. (1990). A skill approach to the development of reflective thinking. In D. Kuhn (Ed.) *Contributions to human development:*

Vol. 21. Developmental perspectives on teaching and learning thinking skills, (pp. 48–62). New York: S. Karger.

Kitchener, K. S., & King, P. M. (1981). Reflective Judgment: Concepts of justification and their relationship to age and education. *Journal of Applied Developmental Psychology, 2,* 89–116.

Kitchener, K. S, King, P. M., & De Luca, S. (2006). The development of reflective judgment in adulthood. In C. Hoare (Ed.), *Handbook of adult development and learning* (pp. 73–98). New York: Oxford University Press.

Kroll, B. (1992). Reflective inquiry in a college English class. *Liberal Education, 78*(1), 10–13.

Love, P. G., & Guthrie, V. L. (1999) (Eds.). *Understanding and applying cognitive development theory.* New Directions for Student Services, No. 88. San Francisco: Jossey-Bass.

Perry, W. G., Jr. (1970). *Intellectual and ethical development in the college years: A scheme.* Austin, TX: Holt, Rinehart, and Winston.

Piaget, J. (1970). Piaget's theory. In P. H. Mussen (Ed.), *Carmichael's manual of child psychology.* Vol. 1. New York: Wiley.

Pizzolato, J. (2005). Creating crossroads for self-authorship: Investigating the provocative moment. *Journal of College Student Development, 46*(6), 624–641.

Rest, J. R. (1979). *Development in judging moral issues.* Minneapolis, MN: University of Minnesota Press.

Torres, V., & Baxter Magolda, M. B. (2004). Reconstructing Latino identity: The influence of cognitive development on the ethnic identity process of Latino students. *Journal of College Student Development, 45*(3), 333–347.

Torres, V., & Hernandez, E. (2007). The influence of ethnic identity on self-authorship: A longitudinal study of Latino/a college students. *Journal of College Student Development, 48*(5), 558–573.

Wood, P. K. (1990). Construct validity and theories of adult development: Testing for necessary but not sufficient relationships. In M. Commons, C. Armon, L. Kohlberg, F. A. Richards, T. A. Grotzer, & J. Sinnott (Eds.), *Adult development 2: Models and methods in the study of adolescent and adult thought* (pp. 113–130). New York: Praeger.

Wood, P. K. (1997). A secondary analysis of claims regarding the Reflective Judgment Interview: Internal consistency, sequentiality, and intra-individual differences in ill-structured problem solving. In John S. Smart (Ed.), *Higher Education: Handbook of theory and research* (pp. 245–314). Edison, NJ: Agathon.

11

WHAT IS SELF-AUTHORSHIP?
A Theoretical Exploration
of the Construct

Jane Elizabeth Pizzolato

Abstract: This chapter uses past research and literature from both college student development and cultural psychology to propose a new, potentially more culturally relevant model for understanding self-authorship.

Many reasons lie behind the research choices I have made, but one that is most interesting to me is that I am studying self-authorship at all. My choice was partially a result of my interest in understanding the student athletes I was working with, and partly because my mentor for my fellowship expressed disinterest in the topic I first proposed. But most importantly, I chose self-authorship because I was not sure what it was. It seemed so big, and seemed to beg questions of how it was different from self-actualization, self-efficacy, purpose, and the like. I continue to find the question of what self-authorship is an interesting one. Over time my answer to the question of "What is self-authorship?" has shifted as new information has emerged from examining data from diverse samples, and from interactions with others who study self-authorship through different lenses than the ones I bring to my research.

In this chapter I reexamine this question of "What is self-authorship?" The approach I take here is a retelling of my past work and a foreshadowing of my future work. Through mixing this narrative work with a theoretical exploration of the literature, I hope to highlight the ways I am shifting my understanding of self-authorship. In the end I propose a revised relationship between the dimensions of self-authorship, as well as implications for future research.

Separate Dimensions?

If I step back enough to examine my own bias, a number of issues are worth noting. First, I went to graduate school because I was introduced to epistemological development research as a college sophomore, and was so intrigued that I changed my career plans so I could research how people made meaning and understood the nature of knowledge. In my second year of graduate school, a professor challenged me to integrate my academic understanding of identity development with my own identity. My response to this possibility was a combination of terror and bemusement. At the time I thought of meaning-making as separate from identity.

My dissertation data forced me to recognize the false dichotomy between meaning-making and identity. Who my participants were deeply influenced how they knew. The pieces I've published on this data reflect this connection, in that I consider how being classified as high-risk created dissonance between students' self-perceptions and the ways in which others perceived them (Pizzolato, 2003, 2004, 2006). Dion talked about how hard it was when you "couldn't never get over the top," and how when he was able to reflect on his effort and outcomes and those of his more privileged peers, he saw that although he might never "get above them, he could be better than them." Cosette talked about how dissonance around her multiracial identity helped her change the way she thought about her responsibility in shaping her own identity.

> It's just really hard, because . . . I don't look Hispanic, because I have white skin, and people see me as White, and I don't fit into their little categories. . . . I think of myself as Hispanic, but other people don't, and they don't want me to think of myself that way. . . . I guess another step is processing and identifying myself, because after you take away high school and all of those norms, who are you? What do you *really* want? And I thought I had that figured out, but I guess I still have a long way to go. Now I have to really spend some time really processing what's going on here. (Pizzolato, 2004, 431–432)

Originally I focused on understanding how multiple perspectives on who these participants were created dissonance for them, and how students' meaning-making in these and similar situations reflected the cognitive move toward self-authorship (Pizzolato, 2003, 2004). In other words, my focus was on understanding how students' meaning-making about their identities influenced the way they answered the who-am-I question of the intrapersonal dimension.

At the time I focused on this because the data seemed to suggest that, as my participants struggled with defining who they were, they were compelled to develop more complex meaning-making strategies that then could be reapplied to the who-am-I question in ways that allowed for increasingly more nuanced conceptions of self. In other words, self-authorship emerged as students' dissonance in one dimension (intrapersonal) led to a compulsion for further development along another dimension (cognitive or epistemological[1]), and this development rippled across the other dimensions. This particular way of understanding self-authorship is not unlike that which Torres and colleagues (Torres, 2003; Torres & Baxter Magolda, 2004; Torres & Hernandez, 2007) proposed as a result of Torres' study of ethnic identity development among Latino and Latina college students.

Rereading my work now, I am struck by the fact that, although I gesture toward the ways in which identity and cognitive change are related, and that these changes happen through new relationships, I don't explicitly address the interpersonal dimension. Instead, things interpersonal are confined to mention of context at home or at school, or to specific relationships. The interpersonal is not described as developing within or in relationship to the student. Rather the context is described as acting on the student. At this point I see this as a major flaw. Omission of explicit discussion of what the interpersonal dimensional is, and what development on this dimension looks like, could be indicative of a failure to thoughtfully consider how culture plays into both meaning-making and identity development.

I could believe that I am accounting for culture in my samples (Chaudhari & Pizzolato, 2008; Pizzolato, 2003, 2004, 2006; Pizzolato, Chaudhari, Murrell, Podobnik, & Schaeffer, 2008; Pizzolato & Ozaki, 2007). I have consistently aimed to include diverse or traditionally marginalized participants in my samples. This inclusion has allowed for investigation into the transferability of theory generated from data from White college students at selective institutions in the Midwest and on the East Coast. Despite the benefits of this

---

[1] Both terms are used here to signify that both have been used interchangeably in the literature. Later discussion in this chapter will propose the use of only "cognitive" to describe the meaning-making dimension of self-authorship.

research for clarifying both self-authorship development and the experiences of students from traditionally marginalized groups, this research is culturally shortsighted. Having culturally diverse participants is useful in providing rich description of meaning-making and identity patterns to compare to White participants. Even claims about comparison, however, are marred by the cultural insensitivity of the research design. Merely including diverse participants, or being a researcher of color, does not negate the fact that existing research on diverse populations has largely failed to examine whether it is even appropriate to use existing constructs, measures, or methods to understand culturally diverse students (c.f., Abes & Kasch, 2007).

Cultural Considerations, the Self, and Self-Authorship

What I failed to consider when I came to UCLA for data collection was the racial composition of the university. I should have anticipated a predominantly Asian sample; over 90% of the participants in my sample were Asian. In response to our participants' descriptions of meaning-making, my team and I began asking more questions about family and culture. Once the data were transcribed and analyses were underway, we hit a snag. How do we use the self-authorship framework to understand our participants? Namely, how do we factor their largely collectivist cultural orientation into our assessment of their progress toward self-authorship, when the language of self-authorship is so individual?

When considering self-authorship, it is impossible to ignore the prominence of the term "self." Beyond the name of the construct, the self is given importance through one of the three dimensions of self-authorship (the intrapersonal dimension; Baxter Magolda, 2001a). Here the self is specified as a statement or understanding of who a participant considers her or himself to be. Consequently the mere notion of a self is not the whole of the intrapersonal dimension; rather this dimension includes how the self defines itself. The interaction between self and knowing is also reflected in the descriptions of epistemological development theories. Belenky, Clinchy, Goldberger, and Tarule (1986) termed their ways of knowing, "the development of self, voice, and mind." And across theories the self becomes important because in order to understand individuals' conceptions of the nature of knowledge, what is being assessed is not just a cognitive manifestation of what counts as knowledge, but also a perception of one's relationship to knowledge. Cognition is always embodied—meaning-making is situated in people with pasts, cultures, and relationships that influence how meaning is made.

This connection between self and cognition is illustrated through examination of positions participants may inhabit along the epistemological development trajectory. Movement toward self-authorship is bound up in development of the self. In order to know in complex ways, students must sense that they can act autonomously—to the extent that they must be able to disagree with others, and they must have a sense of how they will bring personal values, beliefs, and goals to bear on the knowledge construction process. In other words, in order to know in epistemologically complex ways, it is assumed that knowers have (a) an autonomous sense of self, and (b) a set of values, beliefs, and goals they are able to use in their evaluation of options. As young adults move toward seeing knowledge construction as neither absolute nor exclusively subjective, but instead based on the norms of the context (i.e., contextual knowing), they are developing methods for using the autonomous sense of self, in conjunction with community standards. Culminating the development process, young adults develop internally defined sets of beliefs, values, and goals that they integrate into their contextual knowing—understanding that knowledge is socially constructed in nature.

Development of this last type—self-authorship—emerges through experiences that catalyze reflection on the viability of current meaning-making strategies, sense of self, and current relationships (Baxter Magolda, 2001a; Pizzolato, 2005). Research on the types of events that catalyze self-authorship development suggests that they require people to figure out what to believe or do without an external formula. Specifics regarding the composition of these events highlight the self by calling into question participants' answers to the who-am-I question. Sometimes the questions come from others' comments that clash with participants' perceptions of themselves, whereas at other times participants begin to feel uncomfortable with who they are, and at other points, transitional moments (e.g., marriage), prompt participants to begin to ask themselves questions about who gets to determine who they are (Baxter Magolda, 2001a; Chaudhari & Pizzolato, 2008; Pizzolato, 2003, 2006; Pizzolato & Ozaki, 2007). In other words, epistemological development seems coupled with continued development of a sense of self as separate from stereotypes and others' expectations.

Despite the consistent discussion of self and its role in promoting self-authorship development, this notion is at odds with research on such development of Asian and Asian American students (Chan & Elliott, 2002, 2004; Nisbett et al., 2001; Pizzolato, Nguyen, & Chaudhari, 2008; Zhang, 1999). In fact, Zhang provided evidence from Chinese university students that epistemological development goes in the reverse direction of that supported by data from research on White American students. This finding implied that the self and independent thinking about issues became less important as these Chinese students developed epistemologically. Conversely, however, Creamer, Lee, and Laughlin (2006) have used the self-authorship framework to explore development among South Korean females, and have not yet reported evidence of unexpected developmental directions. Adding to complexity of the apparent contradiction is the term "Asian," which is sometimes used to describe a racial group regardless of whether the participants are Asians in Asia or Asians in America. Here I use "Asian" to refer to the broad racial group; most of the research focuses on Asians in Asia. "Asian American" is used when the participants were Asians in North America.

Asian and Asian American "Selfways" and Their Implications for Epistemological Development

Effectively examining the connection between epistemological development and sense of self requires examination of the notion of self (see Shweder, Goodnow, Hatano, LeVine, Markus, & Miller, 1998). Self and cultural context are inextricably related, as the cultural context shapes individuals' conceptions of and importance ascribed to the self (Goodnow, 1990; Heine, Lehman, Markus, & Kitayama, 1999; Hoshino-Browne, Zanna, Spencer, Zanna, & Kitayama, 2005; Shweder et al., 1998). Markus, Mullaly, and Kitayama (1997) called this "selfways," and claimed that the community's idea of what it means to be a person in terms of a culturally shaped notion of how to be in relationships and in habits is key to understanding how people understand the concept of self. The selfway is the socialization of individual selves toward the culturally agreed-upon ways of being and knowing.

Research on Asian and Asian American cultures revealed a distinctly different selfway than that in Western culture, where the selfway focuses on the development of autonomy. In Asian cultures selfways send messages of interdependence and the value of relationships. The self in Asian cultures is thus seen not as autonomous but as developed through, valued in, and inextricably tied to relationships with others (Heine et al., 1999; Hoshino-Browne et al., 2005; Markus & Kitayama, 1991; Pizzolato et al., 2008; Shweder et al., 1998; Zhang, 1999). Consequently the goal in Asian and many Asian American cultures is to develop and maintain the equilibrium of relationships through appropriate control of individual desires that have the potential to disrupt the relationship. So strong is this tie that comparative research has demonstrated that East Asians and North Americans are differentially affected by and attuned to relationships, in that East Asians used ways of knowing that focused on context, and sought to make decisions and reduce dissonance through focus on the good of the relationship over the individual self (Heine & Lehman, 1997; Hoshino-Browne et al., 2005; Kitayama, Conner Snibbe, Markus, & Suzuki, 2004; Nisbett et al., 2001).

The consistent focus of Asian students on the contextual factors is important to note here, as it points toward differential influences in motivation and meaning-making. Being epistemologically attuned to the context and concern for the collective, Asian students may be less likely to experience the extreme subjectivism that is a midpoint on all epistemological development trajectories. Furthermore, if Asian selfways encourage regard for the context and for collective good over autonomy and individual gain, as Asian students become more adept at meaning-making in ways consistent with their cultural community, they use collective goals and values to inform their meaning-making. This focus on context over individual may explain Zhang's (1999) findings that Chinese university students' epistemological development is the inverse of North American college students' development. Alternatively, it seems plausible that autonomy may not be important to Asian students, and so Asian students may not need self-authorship.

Figuring self-authorship as potentially culturally based seems interesting given the literature on cultural experiences of dissonance. According to Baxter Magolda (2001a), her participants were propelled toward self-authorship as they encountered situations where contextual knowing was not sufficient. This dissatisfaction stemmed from participants' need to personally justify their decisions. In an attempt to make sense of their dissatisfaction, participants engaged in self-reflection that Baxter Magolda called "becoming the author of one's life." Participants developed and defended their growing set of internally defined beliefs, values, and goals, which then entered their meaning-making process in ways that helped them make sense of the possibilities emerging from contextual knowing. Experiences of dissonance led participants to engage in self-authorship in order to reduce experienced dissonance and to justify their choices.

In their experimental research, however, Heine and Lehman (1997) were able to demonstrate differences in experiences of dissonance between Asian American and European American students. When placed in situations where they could choose from any number of options, Asian American students did not experience dissonance in making choices that were not ideal for themselves, whereas European American students experienced dissonance if they had to make a choice that was not ideal for themselves. Here ideal refers to choices that require subjugation of personal goals or preferences. Based on these results, Heine and Lehman suggested that the dissonance experienced seemed positively related to the degree to which students saw the self as independent. Other researchers have found further evidence to support this relation. They have also noted that the degree to which Asian students not residing in Asia see themselves as Asian versus the dominant culture of their residential community similarly influences the degree to which they experience free choice dissonance; more Asian identifying students experience little dissonance, whereas biculturally identifying and Western identifying students experience respectively more dissonance (Hong, Morris, Chiu, & Benet-Martinez, 2000). This finding has implications for epistemological development, as development is predicated on the notion of dissonance as the catalyst for development, and dissonance is typically assessed through processing of situations with free choice. Research has suggested that Asian students respond with belief change to interpersonal dissonance, but that this response requires specification of contextual factors such as who the audience is, who will be affected by the decision, and/or preferences and beliefs of key others involved in or affected by a choice or decision (Kitayama et al., 2004; Markus & Kitayama, 1991). Given this difference in type of dissonance and the factors that go into eliciting belief change and student ability to engage in a free choice task, existing measures of epistemological development may not effectively target this form of dissonance, leaving open the possibility of error in assessment and understanding of self-authorship development.

Although it initially appears that cultural messages may impede self-authorship development for Asian students, a return to Kegan's (1994) description of the interpersonal dimension suggests otherwise. According to Kegan, the interpersonal dimension encompasses not just one-on-one relationships, but the broader societal context. If the interpersonal dimension is this broad, then it means that cultural messages and norms—including selfways—are all a part of the interpersonal dimension. For example, among the "mental demands" of early self-authorship (i.e., fourth order self-authorship) are to "be able to *look at* and evaluate the values and beliefs of our psychological and cultural inheritance" (Kegan, p. 302), and to "examine ourselves, our culture, and our milieu" (p. 303). It is important to acknowledge this definition of the interpersonal dimension, because it means that culture, not just relationships between people, must be considered in the interpersonal dimension.

Existing research tends to describe the interpersonal dimension within the confines of a specific relationship (e.g., romantic relationship, parent-child, or peer-peer (Baxter Magolda, 2001a; Chaudhari & Pizzolato, 2008; King & Baxter Magolda, 2005; Pizzolato, 2003, 2004; Pizzolato & Ozaki, 2007; Torres, 2003). Focusing on discrete relationships allowed for investigation into the key question for the interpersonal dimension that Baxter Magolda found in her longitudinal data—what kind of relationship do I want to be in? On the surface, this question does not seem to fit with the key questions of the other two dimensions. The other questions are phrased in the present, but the interpersonal question is a future question; a projection of how one wants to be rather than how one is. Also seemingly problematic is the way the question appears not to align with Kegan's claim that the interpersonal dimension was about one's relationship to relationships, rather than oneself in relationships.

Considering the sample for Baxter Magolda's (2001a) study, however, provides an alternative view. Because her participants were themselves perseverating on this question and typically maintained a focus on a specific relationship, the apparent misfit of the verb tense of the question is telling of her participants' socialization toward relationships. Relationships were things one could move into and out of, things in which one could lose one's autonomy or support achievement of one's goals. Though compromise and interdependence were considered part of any relationship, subjugation of self was considered ideally unnecessary in any healthy relationship. Consequently in their development, Baxter Magolda's participants, as well as demographically similar participants in other studies, emphasized the autonomous self across dimensions, even in the interpersonal dimension. Collectively this similarity is telling of their relationship to relationships, and implies what the cultural messages and norms are around relationships. Selves are brought into relationship with each other rather than a more Eastern notion that selves are defined through relationships.

In terms of a model of self-authorship then, it seems that it may be necessary to place more emphasis on the nature of the interpersonal dimension. The specific interpersonal dimension Baxter Magolda (2001a) has identified for her participants is just as she has consistently stated—specific. These participants are not without cultural influence; rather it is their cultural influence of independence that creates language that obscures the power of culture in shaping the goal of individuality, and value of choice and autonomy. In investigating where the self is in self-authorship, it appears that the self could be in constant relationship with the interpersonal dimension. The intrapersonal question—who am I?—and the interpersonal question are intertwined and reciprocal. No matter how elementary or complex a participant's answer to the who-am-I question, the answer is informed by the way they answer the interpersonal dimension question of what-kind-of-relationship-do-I-want-to-be-in, and vice-versa.

Cognition or Epistemology?

Based on the previous discussion then, it seems that the intra- and interpersonal dimensions are inextricably related. The next task then seems to be figuring out how the third, and inconsistently named, dimension fits with these other two dimensions. Before moving forward, it is necessary to clarify some terminology. The central question of the dimension most specifically focused on meaning-making is: "How do I know?" I believe this dimension should be called the cognitive dimension rather than the epistemological dimension, as does Patricia King in another chapter in this volume. Henceforth I use the term "cognitive dimension" to make this argument. The intellectual history of the naming of this dimension illustrates confusion and/or dissension over the nature and scope of the dimension. Kegan (1994) called this dimension "cognitive." Torres has consistently called it "cognitive" (Torres, 2003; Torres & Baxter Magolda, 2004; Torres & Hernandez, 2007), as do King and Baxter Magolda (2005). Baxter Magolda used cognitive in her early writing about self-authorship (1999), but more recently uses epistemological (Baxter Magolda, 2001a, 2004; Baxter Magolda & King, 2007). I have consistently chosen to use the term "cognitive" rather than "epistemological," because I see epistemology as addressing assumptions about meaning-making and the nature of knowledge, but not the specific processes of how people know.

I view self-authorship itself as a point on the epistemological trajectory; it is an epistemological position or orientation. In this section I explore what counts as cognition, and why cognitive is a better term than epistemological for the third dimension of self-authorship. Then I move to discussion of why self-authorship must be an epistemology itself, rather than a wholly other type of construct.

Cognition as a construct encompasses a wide array of meaning-making practices, from sensation and perception—what is seen or noticed in seeing or experiencing a situation—to organizing and evaluating information, to practices of information gathering and storage, to meta-cognition. Collectively these pieces of the meaning-making process form a response to the central question of, "How do I know?" It is important to note, however, that cognition itself is not just a construct, but also an entire area of study that includes various theoretical frameworks for studying and bounding what counts as cognition. One such theory—situated cognition— seems particularly appropriate for the type of meaning-making included in the cognitive dimension. Situated cognition asserts that meaning-making occurs through social interaction with people and the environment. How people think is complex, individual, and yet inextricably bound by the opportunities and values presented in social interaction (Greeno, 1998; Lave & Wenger, 1991).

Reviewing what was used as evidence of how one knows suggests that situated cognition and the term "cognitive" may be more appropriate than "epistemological." As participants moved along the self-authorship continuum, their progress was marked by different relationships with people in the knowledge construction process. As they experienced situations that called into question their meaning-making strategies about knowledge construction, understanding of self and/or relationships, they used new ways of meaning-making. Their cognitive strategies shifted as environmental and relationship demands and stressors shifted. Cognitive changes were tied to the opportunities and values presented in participants' social interactions.

In the case of existing college student development literature, cognition has been primarily studied with samples of White students at selective institutions (Abes & Kasch, 2007; Baxter Magolda, 1999, 2001a; Baxter Magolda & King, 2007; Belenky et al., 1986; King & Kitchener, 1994; King & Baxter Magolda, 2005; Perry, 1968). And in those samples that have included more diverse or non-White participants, the study of these students' cognition has still been framed by the patterns of knowledge construction and meaning-making constructed through study of the less diverse and over-whelmingly White samples. Consequently, the norm for understanding cognition in college students seems to be based on socially shaped information regarding how one organizes and solves problems, and the degree to which these practices are individual.

Looking at a representative student from my Asian American study, cognition is less individual, but still deeply situated. Jessie explained her take on individualism and collectivism.

> Individualism is something that you kind of take together and make the best out of, and so it will always come from the collective idea first, and then [I] pick out the one thing that sums it all up . . . and I think that most people think of it as the other way, where I have my own thing that I'm good at, and I'm going to contribute it to the bigger collective.

She approached making choices about and for herself by starting with the collective, and then making choices and meaning out of her own situations based on the values and needs of the collective. Because of this approach to meaning-making, her process for trying to figure out her post-graduation plans was laced with understanding and regard for the collective.

> I don't want to say, "They're [my family] all I have," but a lot of things I do, I do for them. . . . I felt like what I choose to do would affect everybody else, so this is sort of related to what I want to do when I graduate . . . because I'm hoping the sooner that I get a job, the more well off like my parents, then my parents can stop what they're doing and have me take care of them. . . . I feel like I can do, go to medical school, so why not, . . . but not really because I think that if I were to become a doctor, it'd be a really

selfish thing to do, because first of all I'd be putting myself through debt, and then, my parents would have to wait much longer because I want to be a doctor.

Although Jessie recognized that this was "my time to be selfish," and become a doctor if that is what she wanted to do, she also recognized that if she stepped back and looked not just at what her college friends were thinking, but considered how her decision would affect others, she had to see the ways in which this choice did not fit with broader goals. Because Jessie moves between the Western, individualistic culture of her university and the Eastern, collectivist culture of her family, she juggles the ways in which she sees meaning constructed. Her meaning-making is informed by a balancing of both frameworks for meaning-making.

Defining cognition as situative is useful in that it both continues to fit existing indications of cognition in self-authorship theory, while also being inclusive of both cultural differences and development before achieving self-authorship. This articulation of cognition is flexible, allowing for knowing and knowing processes to account for differences between Asian American and White students, as well as other cultural groups. Perhaps more important, however, is the way this notion of cognition enhances understanding of the three dimensions of self-authorship before the development of self-authorship. Taking cognition as always situated in the cultural context, and sense of self as also inherently relational and tied to context, would suggest that these two dimensions might separate before self-authorship, but always stay connected to the interpersonal dimension. Is the interpersonal dimension the link between the dimensions across the developmental trajectory? I propose here that the answer is no, and that instead the dimensions are always connected. What changes is not the coming together of separate dimensions, but rather that it is at the point of self-authorship that participants become aware of their ability to control the ways in which the three dimensions interact.

Figure 11.1 illustrates this model of perpetual connection. Here the interpersonal dimension remains inextricably tied to the questions of "Who am I?" and "How do I know?" In turn, these two questions have also been collapsed into a single embodied cognition circle. Comprising the functions of both the original intrapersonal and cognitive dimensions, this combination here attempts to illustrate the relatedness of these two dimensions as described in the literature.

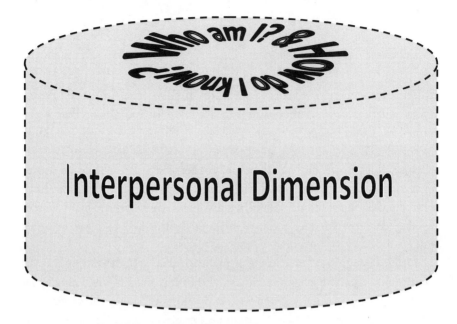

Figure 11.1. A Revised Model of Self-Authorship

It is through cues from the interpersonal dimension that participants are compelled to question who they are and how they know. The interpersonal dimension exerts force on participants' developing responses to "Who am I?" and "How do I know?," and participants' developing response with regard to these two questions determined not just whether, but how participants respond to these external forces (Abes, Jones, & McEwen, 2007). Additionally, because the interpersonal dimension includes relationships, participants not only respond to external forces and cues through filtering—deciding what to attend to (Abes, Jones, & McEwen)—and interpreting external forces, or even balancing them, but rather renegotiate relationships with others in ways that represent healthy compromise. Because of this interaction between the original three dimensions of self-authorship, Figure 11.1 shows no overlapping of the dimensions that illustrate the location of self-authorship. Rather self-authorship is the emergence of the ability to consciously control the three dimensions. Self-authorship represents that space where participants can get the three dimensions to interact with each other rather than merely respond to, enhance, or constrain each other. Consequently, Figure 11.1 includes no shaded space that illustrates self-authorship. Instead I propose that self-authorship, like other orientations, occurs in the spaces between the dotted lines of the three dimensional constructs.

Implications for Research Design

This proposed model necessarily leads to implications for future research. First and foremost, it seems important to test this model empirically with a diverse sample. Without substantial descriptive and measurement work, however, testing the model will be exceptionally challenging.

Quantitatively, the first challenge that arises is that no reliable quantitative measure of self-authorship that works across students at different institutional types and degrees of religious fundamentalism yet exists. Additionally, the quantitative measures in existence (Creamer, this volume; Pizzolato, 2007) have been constructed based on the original understanding of self-authorship. Also, these measures are Likert-type scales. Such a measurement design assumes that the self-authorship development trajectory is linear and that a self-authored person would generate the highest scores possible. In reality, however, people who are staunch independent knowers—an earlier, highly subjective way of knowing—may score the highest. This possibility arises because, in order to understand if participants are self-reliant, autonomous thinkers (identifying characteristics of self-authorship), items such as "I tend to think authorities like teachers have better ideas than I do" are used. If a participant says this statement is not true of her/him, it is more likely she or he is self-authored than a participant who says the statement is true for her/him. Still, the relationship between the trueness of this statement and the likelihood of self-authorship is not a purely inverse one. Rather, a staunchly independent knower may strongly disagree with the statement, thinking "All ideas are equal. Mine are from my experience and teachers cannot negate that. What's a good idea for me, may or may not be a good idea for you and vice versa." A self-authored knower, however, may only disagree with the statement, figuring that although her/his ideas are important to consider in knowledge construction, it is also important to consider others' ideas—especially those with related experience in knowledge construction.

Given the situation on the quantitative front, qualitative methods may seem like the best option for self-authorship research. It is important to note, however, that how qualitative research is conducted matters. The first way the how matters is in terms of how interview questions or short response items are constructed. Just in comparing two methods of epistemological development assessment—the Measure of Epistemological Reflection (MER) (Baxter Magolda, 2001b; Baxter Magolda & Porterfield, 1985), using the constructivist coding scheme; and a semi-structured interview that was more aligned with Baxter Magolda's (2001a; Baxter Magolda & King, 2008) interviews, and thus not as focused on academic contexts as the MER—showed large differences in classifying individual participants along the epistemological development trajectory (Pizzolato, 2007). Building on this concern, the model proposed in this chapter suggests that what interviewers ask is important.

In order to account for differences in the etiology of dissonance by context or culture, it seems prudent to devise interview questions that elicit participant discussion of dissonance from diverse origins. Beyond openness in stem questions, following up on participants' initial responses with probes is crucial to beginning to describe the self-authorship development process cross-culturally. Without probes to understand what participants mean when they describe family honor or compliance, for example, participant meaning may not be captured, rather reversion to traditional coding schemes that might relegate such comments to early stages of epistemological development may occur. Careful follow-up questions must be constructed in order to differentiate between passivity and true interdependence on the part of the participant. Following this line of thinking, what I propose here is an emphasis on and expansion of Baxter Magolda's (2001b) discussion of how to code the MER. Across a five-phase coding process, she suggested the importance of examining not just how participants fit into existing positions along the epistemological trajectory, but also keeping an eye out for new possibilities. It is the latter that seems particularly important here. By identifying new possibilities or anomalies, and then examining the patterns across participants that lead to the emergence of these new possibilities or anomalies, it seems possible to expand the cultural relevance of self-authorship and collective understanding of the developmental process.

Zooming out, the model proposed here pushes researchers to follow up on propositions Taylor (2008) made regarding the context in which self-authorship development occurs. In order to investigate the adequacy of the model proposed here, significantly more attention must be paid to the interpersonal dimension in its broadest sense—the culture(s) in which participants are situated, in addition to the individual relationships of participants. Here paying attention to these aspects means not just identifying what they are, but the meaning participants make of the relationships and contexts. Understanding the context at various levels should aid in understanding group differences in the self-authorship process, as well as just how the interpersonal dimension fits into the picture.

Future Directions

I am now moving into a collaborative project aimed at developing an appropriate survey method of assessing this nonlinear development trajectory of self-authorship. On a more qualitative front, I am leading two distinct projects into how cultural selfways interact with self-authorship development. The first is a longitudinal study of Asian American college students. The second is a longitudinal study of a cohort of 13-year-olds living in a low-income, predominantly African American neighborhood in Washington, DC. In this latter study, data are being collected from students, the schools, and students' families. From these projects I hope to be able to comment on the adequacy of the model proposed here for this population, as well as unveil a coding scheme designed to include more possibilities for dissonance and meaning-making that are inclusive of the diversity of cultural selfways.

References

Abes, E. S., Jones, S. R., & McEwen, M. K. (2007). Reconceptualizing the model of multiple dimensions of identity: The role of meaning-making capacity in the construction of multiple identities. *Journal of College Student Development, 48*(1), 1–22.

Abes, E. S., & Kasch, D. (2007). Using queer theory to explore lesbian college students' multiple dimensions of identity. *Journal of College Student Development, 48*(6), 619–636.

Baxter Magolda, M. B. (1999). *Creating contexts for self-authorship: A constructive-developmental pedagogy.* Nashville, TN: Vanderbilt University Press.

Baxter Magolda, M. B. (2001a). *Making their own way: Narratives for transforming higher education to promote self-development.* Sterling, VA: Stylus.

Baxter Magolda, M. B. (2001b). A constructivist revision of the Measure of Epistemological Development. *Journal of College Student Development, 42*(6), 520–534.

Baxter Magolda, M. B. (2004). Self-authorship as the common goal of 21st–century education. In M. B. Baxter Magolda & P. King (Eds.) *Learning partnerships: Theory and models of practice to educate for self-authorship* (pp. 1–36). Sterling, VA: Stylus.

Baxter Magolda, M. B., & King, P. (2007). Interview strategies for assessing self-authorship: Constructing conversations to assess meaning making. *Journal of College Student Development, 48*(5), 491–508.

Baxter Magolda, M. B., & Porterfield, W. D. (1985). A new approach to assess intellectual development on the Perry scheme. *Journal of College Student Personnel, 26,* 343–351.

Belenky, M. F., Clinchy, B. M., Goldberger, N. R., & Tarule, J. M. (1986). *Women's ways of knowing: The development of self, voice, and mind.* New York: Basic Books.

Chan, K-W., & Elliott, R. G. (2002). Exploratory study of Hong Kong teacher education students' epistemological beliefs: Cultural perspectives and implications on beliefs research. *Contemporary Educational Psychology, 27,* 392–414.

Chan, K-W., & Elliott, R. G. (2004). Epistemological beliefs across cultures: Critique and analysis of beliefs structure studies. *Educational Psychology, 24*(2), 123–142.

Chaudhari, P., & Pizzolato, J. E. (2008). Understanding the epistemology of ethnic identity development in multiethnic college students. *Journal of College Student Development, 49*(5), 443–458.

Creamer, E. G., Lee, S., & Laughlin, A. (2006). Self-authorship as a framework for understanding life decision making among college women in Korea. *The Korean American Journal of Career Education Research, 19*(3), 59–72

Goodnow, J. (1990). The socialization of cognition: What's involved? In J. W. Stigler, R. A. Shweder, & G. Herdt (Eds.), *Cultural psychology: Essays on comparative human development* (pp. 259–286). New York: Cambridge University Press.

Greeno, J. G. (1998). The situativity of knowing, learning, and research. *American Psychologist, 53*(1), 5–26.

Heine, S. J., & Lehman, D. R. (1997). Culture, dissonance, and self-affirmation. *Personality and Social Psychology Bulletin, 23,* 389–400.

Heine, S. J., Lehman, D. R., Markus, H. R., & Kitayama, S. (1999). Is there a universal need for positive self-regard? *Psychological Review, 106*(4), 766–794.

Hong, Y-Y., Morris, M. W., Chui, C-Y., & Benet-Martinez, V. (2000). Multicultural minds: A dynamic constructivist approach to culture and cognition. *American Psychologist, 55,* 709–720.

Hoshino-Browne, E., Zanna, A. S., Spencer, S. J., Zanna, M. P., & Kitayama, S. (2005). On the cultural guises of cognitive dissonance: The case of easterners and westerners. *Journal of Personality and Social Psychology, 89*(3), 294–310.

Kegan, R. (1994). *In over our heads: The mental demands of modern life.* Cambridge, MA: Harvard University Press.

King, P. M., & Baxter Magolda, M. B. (2005). A developmental model of intercultural maturity. *Journal of College Student Development, 46*(6), 571–592.

King, P. M., & Kitchener, K. S. (1994). *Developing reflective judgment.* San Francisco: Jossey Bass.

Kitayama, S., Conner Snibbe, A., Markus, H. R., & Suzuki, T. (2004). Is there any free choice? Self and dissonance in two cultures. *Psychological Science, 15,* 527–533.

Lave, J., & Wenger, E. (1991). *Situated learning: Legitimate peripheral participation.* Cambridge, UK: Cambridge University Press.

Markus, H. R., & Kitayama, S. (1991). Culture and the self: Implications for cognition, emotion, and motivation. *Psychological Review, 98,* 224–253.

Markus, H. R., Mullaly, P., & Kitayama, S. (1997). Selfways: Diversity in modes of cultural participation. In U. Neisser & D. Jopling (Eds.), *The conceptual self in context: Culture, experience, self-understanding* (pp. 89–130). Cambridge, UK: Cambridge University Press.

Nisbett, R. E., Peng, K., Choi, I., & Norenzayan, A. (2001). Culture and systems of thought: Holistic versus analytic cognition. *Psychological Review, 108*(2), 291–310.

Perry, W. P. (1968). *Forms of intellectual and ethical development.* New York: W. W. Norton & Co.

Pizzolato, J. E. (2003). Developing self-authorship: Exploring the experiences of high-risk college students. *Journal of College Student Development, 44*(6), 797–812.

Pizzolato, J. E. (2004). Coping with conflict: Self-authorship, coping, and adaptation to college. *Journal of College Student Development, 45*(4), 425–442.

Pizzolato, J. E. (2005). Creating crossroads for self-authorship: Investigating the provocative moment. *Journal of College Student Development, 46*(6), 624–641.

Pizzolato, J. E. (2006). Achieving college student possible selves: Navigating the space between commitment and achievement of long-term identity goals. *Cultural Diversity & Ethnic Minority Psychology, 12*(1), 57–69.

Pizzolato, J. E. (2007). Assessing self-authorship. In P. Meszaros (Ed.), *New Directions in Student Services: Advancing students' intellectual growth through the lens of self-authorship* (pp. 31–42). San Francisco: Jossey Bass.

Pizzolato, J. E., Nguyen, T-L. K., & Chaudhari, P. (2008, November). Cultural selfways and self-authorship: The case of Asian American students. Paper presented at the annual meeting of the Association for the Study of Higher Education, Jacksonville, FL.

Pizzolato, J. E., & Ozaki, C. C. (2007). Moving toward self-authorship: Outcomes of learning partnerships. *Journal of College Student Development, 48*(2), 196–214.

Pizzolato, J. E., Chaudhari, P., Murrell, E., Podobnik, S., & Schaeffer, Z. (2008). Ethnic identity, epistemological development, and achievement among students from disadvantaged backgrounds. *Journal of College Student Development, 49*(4), 301–318.

Shweder, R. A., Goodnow, J., Hatano, G., LeVine, R. A., Markus, H. R., & Miller, P. (1998). The cultural psychology of development: One mind, many mentalities. In R. M. Lerner (Ed.), *Handbook of child psychology: Vol. 1 Theoretical models of human development* (5th ed., pp. 865–937). New York: Wiley.

Taylor, K. (2008). Mapping the intricacies of young adults' development journey from socially prescribed to internally defined relationships, and beliefs. *Journal of College Student Development, 49*(3), 215–234.

Torres, V. (2003). Influences on ethnic development of Latino college students in the first two years of college. *Journal of College Student Development, 44*(4), 532–547.

Torres, V., & Baxter Magolda, M. B. (2004). Reconstructing Latino identity: The influence of cognitive development on the ethnic identity process of Latino students. *Journal of College Student Development, 45*(3), 333–347.

Torres, V., & Hernandez, E. (2007). The influence of ethnic identity on self-authorship: A longitudinal study of Latino/a college students. *Journal of College Student Development, 48*(5), 558–573.

Zhang, L-F. (1999). A comparison of U.S. and Chinese university students' cognitive development: The cross-cultural applicability of Perry's theory. *The Journal of Psychology, 133*(4), 425–439.

12

DEMONSTRATING THE LINK BETWEEN REASONING AND ACTION IN THE EARLY STAGES OF SELF-AUTHORSHIP

Elizabeth G. Creamer

Abstract: A quantitative measure of self-authorship is used to test the link between reasoning and action. Results confirm a statistically significant link between the intrapersonal dimension, openness to input, and the frequency of interacting with others during the process of career decision making for a sample of college students.

A good deal of evidence indicates that higher education in the United States is not effective in promoting the type of complex thinking that empowers individuals to make informed decisions by weighing diverse viewpoints and bringing to the forefront options that are congruent with personal values and conceptions of self. Baxter Magolda, author of a longitudinal study of holistic development that has spanned more than 20 years (2002), concludes that only about 16% of college seniors progress beyond the point of unquestioning reliance on external authority, which is an early step in the developmental journey toward self-authorship. Lack of exposure to educational contexts that promote self-authorship is one explanation for why many college students find themselves ill prepared to make important life decisions, like career choice.

A link between reasoning and action is embedded in the definition of self-authorship. One of the ways that Baxter Magolda has defined self-authorship is as "the ability to collect, interpret, and analyze information and reflect on one's own beliefs in order to form judgments" (1998, p. 143).

Pizzolato offered a slightly broader definition of self-authorship that explicitly links self-authorship and action, taking the position that self-authorship involves reasoning and "action congruent with such reasoning" (2007, p. 36). Pizzolato argued that it is important to assess both reasoning and action to get a full sense of development.

The process used to make an important life decision offers a rich context to assess self-authorship because it involves reasoning about options and also taking action (Pizzolato, 2007). The link between reasoning and action has important ramifications for the career decision-making process, particularly in efforts to expand the career options students consider. Self-authorship is linked to career decision making because it influences how individuals make meaning of the advice they receive from others, and the extent that the reasoning they employ reflects an internally grounded sense of self (Baxter Magolda, 1998; 1999; 2001). Prior to the development of self-authorship, individuals rely on meaning-making structures that have them looking to others as a source of direction for important life decisions. They are not in a position to deconstruct gender and racial stereotypes (Torres & Hernandez, 2007), such as those that apply to careers. Whereas input of significant others is an appropriate consideration in any major life decision, overreliance on the views of others without independent reflection can lead to consideration of a narrow range of career choices that may be divorced from values, interests, and skills. These are among the reasons why the development of self-authorship is so germane to the career decision making process and the women's interests in nontraditional fields in science, engineering, and technology (SET) (Creamer & Wakefield, in press).

The lack of a robust, quantitative measure of self-authorship has limited the ability to provide empirical support to document a link between self-authored reasoning and action. Chandler, Hallett, and Sokol (2002) called for such research when they argued that what is needed is not more research about "fine grained differences" in development, but serious efforts to "demonstrate that changes in peoples' tacit epistemologies actually impact on the ways in which they run their lives" (p. 164). Providing empirically grounded evidence of the link between reasoning and action has the potential to advance theory about self-authorship and to illustrate its application to the process of career decision making.

This chapter adds to the theoretical understanding of self-authorship by exploring the link between self-authorship and different elements of the process of career decision making. It compares a theoretically grounded model that depicts the relationship among the three dimensions of self-authorship and a measure of interacting with others during the process of career decision making, with results confirmed through a statistical procedure and a quantitative measure of self-authorship developed from a section of the Career Decision Making Survey (CDMS, 2006). Similarities between the two models provide preliminary evidence of the construct validity of the CDMS measure of self-authorship.

The research presented in this chapter is based on analysis of one section of the CDMS, a questionnaire designed by members of an interdisciplinary research team (with external funding from the National Science Foundation (NSF)) to identify factors that predict women's interest in careers in information technology (IT). During an early phase of the research project, similar questionnaire items were grouped in scales or factors to measure key elements of the career decision-making process, including openness to input and the credibility of different information sources (Creamer, Lee, & Meszaros, 2007).[1] Prior to 2008, the team struggled to use questionnaire items from the CDMS to produce a statistically robust and theoretically meaningful measure of self-authorship simply using confirmatory factor analysis. In spring 2008, Jessica Yue, a doctoral student at Virginia Tech, used some of the data from the project and Item Response Theory for a class project and produced a moderately reliable measure to assess the three dimensions and first three phases of the developmental journey toward achieving "self-authorship" (Creamer, Baxter Magolda, & Yue, 2009 in press). Her analysis led to a substantive revision to the chapter first presented at the RIVA conference in May 2008. This chapter presents the results from an analysis of 18 items from the CDMS designed to measure self-authorship, as distinct from a construct we referred to as "Decision Orientation" in previous publications.

---

[1] In addition to myself, Dr. Peggy S. Meszaros, Professor of Human Development and Director of the Center for Technology Impacts and a Co-PI on the project, along with then doctoral students Anne Laughlin in the Higher Education Program and Soyoung Lee from Human Development, made substantive contributions to this project. Jessica Yue, now a doctoral student in Educational Research, provided statistical expertise in the stage of the project described in this chapter. All were affiliated with Virginia Tech during the project.

Related Literature

Some exciting theoretical questions have emerged as the community of scholars exploring self-authorship has grown and the populations studied have become more heterogeneous. Theoretical questions persist about situations where reasoning and action may not be congruent and whether the dimensions of self-authorship are interrelated at all points of the developmental continuum.

The link between reasoning and action was in the foreground of a study conducted by Pizzolato (2005, 2007). Pizzolato questioned her own earlier definition of self-authorship when she later found only a moderate correlation between two pen and paper instruments designed to "assess skills underlying each dimension necessary for self-authored reasoning and action" (2007, p. 37). The first instrument, the Self-Authorship Survey (SAS), is a 29-item paper and pencil questionnaire designed to assess recognition of statements reflecting different types of meaning-making. The second instrument, the Experience Survey (ES), aspires to assess optimal ways of knowing by asking respondents to write an essay in which they describe the process they used to make two important decisions, including the decision to apply to college. Narratives were scored on a scale of one to four on three domains that overlap with the subscales on the SAS (decision making, problem solving, and autonomy). Pizzolato saw the two instruments together as providing a measure of self-authorship.

Pizzolato speculated that once self-authorship is developed, the expression of it might be situational (2007). She demonstrated that situations exist in which reasoning and action are not always consistent. Some participants reasoned in a self-authored way, as measured by responses to questionnaire items, but in an essay did not describe their actions in ways that reflected self-authorship. Pizzolato cautioned that it is easy to misidentify a reasoning-action split. She observed: "Students who show signs of self-authored reasoning but chose to act in ways seemingly inconsistent with their reasoning may in fact be making a decision that shows self-authorship in an arena larger than the immediate decision" (pp. 38–39).

Interesting questions about the differences between reasoning and action arose during the first phase of a mixed-methods research project designed to identify the role of self-authorship in the process used to consider information about career options (Creamer, Lee, & Meszaros,

2007[2]). Analysis of transcripts from one-on-one interviews with 119 first- and second-year college women about their approach to decision making led to the insight that participants were making a subtle distinction between "listening to" and "hearing" career advice (Creamer & Laughlin, 2005; Laughlin & Creamer, 2007). Participants distinguished between listening politely and actually engaging or reflecting on what they heard during interactions about career options. Not only were participants reluctant to pursue career information from those they did not trust to have their best interests in mind, they often said that they "would not listen" if the guidance conflicted with what they had been told by important others. Later research, matching questionnaire with interview data from the same individuals, confirmed our suspicion that most of our participants were probably operating from the first step of the developmental continuum known as external formulas. We interpreted the difficulty some individuals encounter in "hearing" career advice, particularly when it is at odds with the recommendations of trusted others, as a reflection of early developmental reasoning. Many first- and second-year college students have little experience with decision making, and lack the epistemological sophistication to judge the credibility of information, to consider their own values, to recognize stereotypes, or to navigate diverse opinions and viewpoints.

Methods

The analysis presented in this chapter derives from 183 respondents who completed the CDMS in 2006–2007. Respondents in this phase of the project were older than those in previous phases of data collection. Because of the nature of our external funding, respondents were juniors and seniors enrolled in one of several research universities in the mid-Atlantic region of the United States who expressed an interest in or were actually enrolled in a major leading to a career in IT. The majority of respondents are male (n = 121 or 68% male; n = 57 or 32% female) and were 21 years or older at the time they completed the survey (n = 138, 69.8%). The sample is relatively

---

[2] Many publications were produced from this project. The Creamer, Lee, and Meszaros (1997) article is the only publication cited because it provides a good overview of the development of the model and constructs until 2007.

diverse in that about one-fourth of the respondents self-identified as being from an underrepresented group (African American, Asian American, Hispanic, multiracial, and other (n = 49, 27.2%).

Instrument

CDMS is a pen and paper 119-item instrument that takes about 20 minutes to complete. In addition to demographic information, the instrument contains questions organized in 11 sections, four of which are used in the analysis presented in this chapter. A 4-point response option was used for all questions (1 = disagree, 2 = somewhat disagree, 3 = somewhat agree, 4 = strongly agree). All questions were coded so that the higher the value, the more positive the response. During 2007, Baxter Magolda provided advice about weighting each questionnaire response option from 1 to 3, with 1 reflecting external formulas; 2, crossroads; and 3, self-authorship.

For the purpose of statistical analysis, scales are latent variables that contain multiple questionnaire items whose relationship is established by theory and demonstrated through factor analysis with at least moderate reliability. The following section provides a brief description for each scale used in the analysis, along with the title of the section in the questionnaire, a definition, and the response options. A complete list of the items used to measure the dimensions of self-authorship, by phase, appears in Appendix A.

Credibility (credibility of information sources) contains ten items about the likelihood of considering career advice from different individuals, with response options from very unlikely (= 1) to very likely (= 4).

Receptivity (response to input) contains five items about the value or importance given to input from others in the process of making a career decision, with response options from disagree (= 1) to strongly agree (= 4).

Information Sources (sources of career information) contains ten items about how often respondents reported that they spoke to groups of people about career options from never (= 1) to many times (= 4). Groups included parents, teachers, counselors or advisors, family members, friends, and others.

Self-Authorship–Intrapersonal contains four items that assess agreement or disagreement with statements about the role of self in career choice, with response options from disagree (=1) to strongly agree (=4).

Self-Authorship–Interpersonal contains six items that assess agreement or disagreement with statements reflecting expectations of counselors/advisors during the process of career decision making, with response options from disagree (=1) to strongly agree (=4).

Self-Authorship–Epistemology contains eight items about the nature of knowledge and expertise and what type and source of information is considered important to choosing a career, with response options from disagree (=1) to strongly agree (=4).

The analysis was conducted in two steps. In the first step, a confirmatory factor analysis was conducted to refine a set of scales to represent the constructs in the model. In the second step, path analysis was used to determine the relationship among the factors.

Results of a confirmatory factor analysis using the 28 original questionnaire items developed to measure self-authorship and varimax rotation confirmed the presence of the three distinct dimensions. Items were deleted from each scale that reduced its overall reliability, leaving a total of 18 items. The removal of items during this process explains why the final measure of each dimension does not contain an equal number of questions. For purposes of the analysis, the three dimensions related to self-authorship were treated as separate factors in the path analysis. An advantage of treating the dimensions of self-authorship as separate factors in the path analysis is that it allows an examination of their unique contribution.

Path analysis was used to test the relationships among the variables. Path analysis is a unidirectional flow model where arrows depict direct relationships between dependent and independent variables that are considered to be causal (Maruyama, 1998). The direction of the arrows is determined by theory. Path analysis is useful to articulate the underlying logic of a theoretical model. Path analysis is a special case of structural equation modeling that is accomplished by running separate regression equations for each of the relationships depicted in a model (Fassinger, 1987).

Results

Following a review of descriptive information and reliability information about each of the scales, two models depicting the relationship between elements of the career decision making process are presented. The first model (Figure 12.1) shows the relationships that would be hypothesized from a theoretical perspective. The second model (Figure 12.2) shows the relationships that were confirmed from a series of hierarchical regressions conducted among the scales.

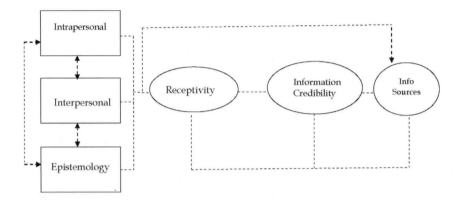

Figure 12.1. Theoretical Model of the Relationships Among Three Dimensions of Self-Authorship, Receptivity to Input, Judgment About the Credibility of Different Information Sources, and Number of Sources Contacted for Career Information

Descriptive Information About the Scales

Reliability of all of the scales in the model is in the moderate range, including the scales developed to measure the three dimensions and three stages in the development of self-authorship, which are all in the moderate range. The Cronbach alphas range from a low of .58 to a high of .71. These are explained in greater detail elsewhere (Creamer, Baxter Magolda, & Yue, 2009 in press).

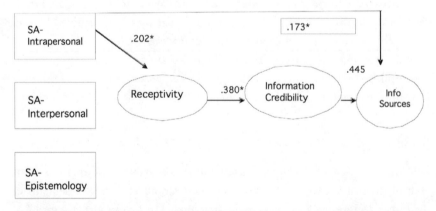

Figure 12.2. Statistical Relationships Among Dimensions of Self-Authorship, Receptivity to Input, Judgment About the Credibility of Information Sources, and Amount of Interaction ($p < .05$). Numbers are standardized Beta Coefficients. Only statistically significant paths are shown.

Means and standard deviations of the variables and scales are presented in Table 12.1. The following section interprets the meaning of the statistical information provided in Table 12.1.

Each questionnaire item was keyed to one dimension and one phase in the movement toward self-authorship. For example, the item "To make a good choice about a career, I think that experts are in the best position to advise me about a good choice" is keyed to the dimension, epistemology, and the stage, external formulas. The means on the scales measuring the dimensions of self-authorship range from a low of 2.28 for the interpersonal to a high of 3.37 for the epistemological dimension of self-authorship (see Table 12.1).

The means are consistent with the crossroads. For the epistemological and intrapersonal dimensions, respondents largely agreed with questions reflecting reasoning employed by individuals both in external formulas and crossroads, but not with those reflecting self-authorship. Levels of agreement to the higher order questions were lower for the interpersonal dimension than for the other dimension.

A mean of 3.82 on the five-item receptivity scale means that most respondents agreed somewhat or strongly to questions about how much they valued the input of others when making an important personal decision. With a response option of 1 for very unlikely to 4 for very likely on ten items, the mean of 29.23 on the information credibility scale means that not all of the groups of individuals listed on the questionnaire were considered a

TABLE 12.1
Range, Mean, and Standard Deviation of the Variables and Scales (*n* = 183)

Variable or Scale (Number of Items)	Range	Mean	Standard Deviation
Age (1 item)	19–43	21.647	2.25
Intrapersonal (4 items)	1–4	2.96	.75
Interpersonal (6 items)	1–4	2.28	.65
Epistemology (8 items)	1–4	3.37	.63
Receptivity (5 items)	1–4	3.28	.65
Information Credibility (10 items)	13.00–40.00	29.23	4.74
Information Sources (10 items)	1.00–30.00	17.73	5.59

credible source of career information. The mean of 17.73 (out of a possible score of 40) on the information sources construct means that on average the respondents did not interact with all the individuals they evaluated to be credible as a source of career information.

The means on the scales are consistent with the conclusion that the three-dimensional self-authorship scores reflect meaning-making that is characteristic of the crossroads. That is because respondents showed some discrimination in their choice of credible sources of career information and, unlike those firmly grounded in reasoning that characterizes external formulas, placed less emphasis on family and friends as valid sources of career information.

The Theoretical Model That Links Reasoning and Action

Figure 12.1 provides a visual depiction of the theoretical relationship between the key constructs in the study, including the relationship between a measure of each of the three dimensions of self-authorship and value awarded to input (receptivity), what types of individuals are judged to be credible sources of career information (credibility), and the measure of action (information sources), which is the frequency of interaction with ten groups of individuals about career options. Dotted lines are used in this figure to demonstrate that the relationships are hypothesized.

Figure 12.1 depicts a link between reasoning employed and a measure of action. It demonstrates that the three dimensions used to measure progress toward self-authorship are conceptualized as being interrelated and engaged during the process of decision making. An important theoretical assumption is that the sequence of steps in the model would be expected to be the same, but the reasoning employed would vary between those operating from external formulas, crossroads, and self-authorship.

The strongest evidence of an emergence of self-authorship is reasoning that reflects an internally defined sense of self, which is a reflection of the intrapersonal dimension. The intrapersonal dimension would not be strong when self-authorship is not present, in part because, before this developmental position, individuals cannot make their values the object of reflection. There would be some evidence of the emergence of self-authorship if the intrapersonal dimension was more strongly related than the other two dimensions to other constructs in the theoretical model. On the other hand, a stronger role played by the interpersonal dimension would point to being more strongly influenced by others, a characteristic of reasoning that reflects external formulas. A stronger role of the epistemological than for any of the other dimensions might signal individuals in transition, because they might be reasoning at a higher level than they are actually employing.

Statistical Confirmation for Elements of the Original Model

The second model (Figure 12.2) depicts the statistical results of the path analysis. Results confirmed a number of the expected relationships predicted theoretically by demonstrating a direct, causal link between one dimension of the CDMS measure of self-authorship and aspects of the process of weighing career information. However, in a number of ways, results did not match what was predicted theoretically. The failure to find a statistically significant link between the three dimensions of self-authorship is of greatest concern.

Figure 12.2 provides a summary of the results of the path analysis confirming a statistically significant link among the intrapersonal dimension of self-authorship, openness to input, and the number of sources actually contacted for career information. The paths in the model are shown with solid, rather than dotted, lines, as were used in the previous figure. The solid lines indicate a statistically significant, direct link between the constructs. The numbers associated with the lines in the figure are standardized Beta coefficients that are a measure of the strength of the relationship between the constructs, when the effects of other constructs are controlled. All the lines in Figure 12.2 represent a statistically significant positive relationship.

The model depicted in Figure 12.2 confirms a direct, causal link between some aspects of reasoning and action. The measure of the intrapersonal dimension of self-authorship had a significant direct effect on openness to input and how often others had been consulted about career options. This presents a considerably more positive view of the decision-making process than was seen in this research project with younger samples of high school and college students (Creamer, Lee, & Meszaros, 2007). Fitting with the assessment that the majority of students agreed with statements reflecting crossroads or the middle point of three steps in the developmental continuum, this sample of students responded to questionnaire items in a way that suggests that they engaged an internally defined sense of self in the decision-making process. The model captures a different process than one that simply reflects "going through the motions" directed by others, where a significant link between the interpersonal dimension and the constructs in the center of the model would be expected. The results confirm the theoretical proposition that one dimension can play a stronger role at certain points in the development journey.

The theoretical model depicted in Figure 12.1 and the results of statistical analysis presented in Figure 12.2 exhibit some noteworthy inconsistencies. Results do not demonstrate that the three dimensions of self-authorship are statistically interrelated. This is a clear indication that the participants are not yet self-authored. It also would be expected that both the interpersonal and cognitive dimensions of self-authorship would have a significant direct effect on the other elements of the model. Views about the nature of knowledge and authority would be expected to have a direct impact on the value awarded to diverse viewpoints and to whose advice is valued during the process of career decision making. In most circumstances, the value given to input (receptivity) should have a direct impact on how frequently others are engaged (information sources) during the process of career decision making.

Setting aside questions related to measurement issues, a number of conceptual explanations are possible for why some of the expected relationships are absent from the model depicted in Figure 12.2. The heart of the issue may lie in context and the nature of the sample. Because data collection was part of the NSF project designed to predict interest in a career in IT, the sample consisted largely of male students who were third- or fourth-year college students enrolled in upper-level courses in a single technical, applied major where exposure to a liberal arts curriculum is limited. This is a group of respondents who were at a point in their college experience when they were likely to be quite certain of their career interests. At the time they responded to the questionnaire, they were not in the process of making the choice; the choice had been made. The absence of a significant role of the interpersonal dimension could reflect that, in the context of career choice as a group, they were no longer dependent on external validation for their choice of major. The epistemological dimension may not be significant because they were no longer in the process of weighing options and, thus, were not engaging questions about authority and expertise on this particular topic. This explanation contextualizes the quantitative data, which was collected from a nonrandom sample. It may be simpler, however, to assume that anomalies in the results are the product of measurement and sampling issues. The explanation just provided for the differences between the hypothesized and actual model introduces a new specter that questions the theoretical assumption that meaning-making structures operate similarly regardless of the context or nature of the decision.

Discussion

Results of the path analysis shown in Figure 12.2 address two key theoretical questions about self-authorship. The first is the question about the link between reasoning and action, and the second is a question about the relationship between the dimensions of self-authorship.

Within the limits of the available measures and the sample of respondents, results provide statistical confirmation for a link between reasoning and action during the process of weighing career options. Data from questionnaire respondents provide evidence of the construct validity of the CDMS-SA measure of self-authorship by demonstrating the theoretical assumption that there is a causal link between phase of development of self-authorship and openness to input. The reasoning-action connection is supported by the finding of a statistically significant path between a scale measuring judgments about the credibility of information sources and self-reported behavior of frequency of interacting with others about career options.

From a theoretical perspective, reasoning, not action, is the most salient issue. Results only address a portion of the reasoning-action split, as the point most germane to self-authorship is not if an individual interacts with others about career options but how they process information once they get it. There is no way to know from the available evidence about the quality, depth, or content of these interactions or whether these interactions had any impact on career choice.

The finding that statistical analysis only confirmed a significant role for a single dimension of self-authorship during the elements of the decision-making process depicted in the model adds fuel to the debate about whether the dimensions of self-authorship are always in synchrony. I have speculated that rather than disequilibrium that would mark a developmental transition, the statistical model captures a group of individuals who have internalized a commitment to a career choice. This is a point in the process of career choice when the intrapersonal dimension provided the tool to negotiate diverse viewpoints. From Kegan's theoretical framework that would mean that they were in a position of being able to make their values the object of thought. The viewpoints of others and the interpersonal dimension would likely have been more prominent with a group of students who were at an earlier point in the career decision-making process when the respondents were weighing choices with an eye on the opinions of influential others.

Conclusion

My suggestion of a contextual framework for interpreting the statistical results of the path analysis utilizing a measure of self-authorship raises a number of issues that are particularly germane to efforts to measure self-authorship in ways others than the Subject Object Interview (SOI; Lahey, Souvaine, Kegan, Goodman, & Felix, 1988). I have speculated that some decisions may engage different dimensions of self-authorship to a greater extent than others, if for no other reason than they affect whose input is valued relative to the question at hand. Choice of a life partner, for example, may bring forward a stronger interpersonal dimension than decisions with less long-term personal implications or a decision that can be navigated largely with the epistemological dimension at the forefront. Similarly, the dimensions of self-authorship that are most salient in the recounting of any important personal decision probably depend to some extent on whether the recounting occurs while in the process of decision making or in a retroactive construction of the decision, when enough distance from it has been achieved that it has become possible to make the decision an object of thought. The context of the decision, and the point of time of reflection about it, may explain differences in conclusions authors have reached about which dimension of self-authorship leads, and under what circumstances. A richer way to shape future dialogue about dimensions is not whether one dimension of self-authorship leads development, but under what circumstance it may lead.

The applicability of the CDMS measure of self-authorship is limited because the questions are framed in the specific context of career decision making. Although the CDMS could be revised to be less context-specific, what is really needed at this point is the convening of a diverse panel of experts to construct a multi-method instrument to assess self-authorship. This will invite further testing of important theoretical questions, but also open the door to the construction of an instrument that would be useful to practitioners in the assessment of interventions designed to promote self-authorship.

Researchers from diverse disciplinary backgrounds have acknowledged the challenges of developing a quantitative measure of self-authorship and other multidimensional constructs related to epistemological development (Baxter Magolda, 2001; Baxter Magolda & King, 2007; Schraw, Bendixen, & Dunkle, 2002; Wood, Kitchener, & Jensen, 2002). One reason for this is the difficulty in assessing underlying meaning-making structures that are used across contexts and that distinguish between stages of reasoning that are recognized or articulated from those that are actually employed. I share a healthy skepticism about the ability to develop a delicately nuanced quantitative measure of self-authorship from a brief questionnaire that simultaneously provides a straightforward way to isolate the types of interactions and experiences that promote more complex thinking and how these vary by stage. Finding a measure that can pinpoint contextual supports that accelerate the development of self-authorship and how this operates across diverse populations remains a pressing task in furthering the theoretical understanding of self-authorship and its implications for practice.

References

Baxter Magolda, M. B. (1998). Developing self-authorship in young adult life. *Journal of College Student Development, 39*(2), 143–156.

Baxter Magolda, M. (1999). *Creating contexts for learning and self-authorship.* Nashville, TN: Vanderbilt University Press.

Baxter Magolda, M. (2001). A constructivist revision of the measure of epistemological reflection. *Journal of College Student Development, 42*(6), 520–534.

Baxter Magolda, M. (2002). Epistemological reflection: The evolution of epistemological assumptions from age 18 to 30. In B. K. Hofer & P. R. Pintrich (Eds.), *Personal epistemology: The psychology of beliefs about knowledge and knowing* (pp. 89–102). Mahwah, NJ: Lawrence Erlbaum Associates.

Baxter Magolda, M. B., & King, P. M. (2007). Interview strategies for assessing self-authorship: Constructing conversations to assess meaning making. *Journal of College Student Development, 48*(5), 491–508.

Career Decision Making Questionnaire (CDMS) (2006). http://www.wit.clahs.vt.edu/survey-o6.pdf

Chandler, M. J., Hallett, D., & Sokol, B. W. (2002). Competing claims about competing knowledge claims. In B. K. Hofer and P. R. Pintrich (Eds.), *Personal epistemology: The psychology of beliefs about knowledge and knowing* (pp. 145–168). Mahwah, NJ: Lawrence Erlbaum Associates.

Creamer, E. G., Baxter Magolda, M. B., & Yue, J. in Press (2009). Preliminary evidence of the reliability and validity of a quantitative measure of self-authorship. Manuscript submitted for publication.

Creamer, E. G., & Laughlin, A. (2005). Self-authorship and women's career decision making. *Journal of College Student Development*, 46(1), 13–27.

Creamer, E. G., Lee, S., & Meszaros, P. S. (2007). Predicting women's interest and choice in a career in information technology: A statistical model. In C. J. Burger, E. G. Creamer, & P. S. Meszaros (Eds.), *Reconfiguring the firewall: Recruiting women across continents and cultures* (pp. 15–38). Wellesley, MA: AK Peters.

Creamer, E. G., & Wakefield, K. (in press). Self-authorship and its role in STEM and engineering education. AWE-CASEE Literature Suites.

Fassinger, R. E. (1987). Use of structural equation modeling in counseling psychology research. *Journal of Counseling Psychology, 34*(4), 425–436.

Laughlin, A., & Creamer, E. G. (2007). Engaging differences: Self-authorship and the decision-making process. In P. S. Meszaros (Ed.), *Self-authorship: Advancing student's intellectual growth through the lens of self-authorship* (pp. 43–52). *New Directions for Teaching and Learning*. Number 109. San Francisco, CA: Jossey-Bass.

Lahey, L. L., Souvaine, E., Kegan, R., Goodman, R., & Felix, S. (1988). *A guide to the Subject-Object Interview: Its administration and interpretation*: Available from: Subject-Object Research Group, 201 Nichols House, HGSE, Cambridge, MA 02138.

Maruyama, G. M. (1988). *Basics of structural equation modeling*. Thousand Oaks, CA: Sage.

Pizzolato, J. E. (2005). *Assessing self-authorship*. Paper presented at the annual meeting of the American Educational Research Association, Montreal, Canada.

Pizzolato, J. E. (2007). Assessing self-authorship. In P. S. Meszaros (Ed.), *Self-authorship: Advancing students' intellectual growth* (pp. 31–42). *New Directions for Teaching and Learning*, No. 109. San Francisco, CA: Jossey-Bass.

Schraw, G., Bendixen, L. D., & Dunkle, M. E. (2002). In B. K. Hofer & P. R. Pintrich (Eds.), *Personal epistemology: The psychology of beliefs about knowledge and knowing* (pp. 261–275). Mahwah, NJ: Lawrence Erlbaum Associates.

Torres, V., & Hernandez, E. (2007). The influence of ethnic identity on self-authorship: A longitudinal study of Latino/a college students. *Journal of College Student Development, 48*(5), 558–573.

Wood, P., Kitchener, K., & Jensen, L. (2002). Considerations in the design and evaluation of a paper-and-pencil measure of epistemic cognition. In B. K. Hofer and P. R. Pintrich (Eds.), *Personal epistemology: The psychology of beliefs about knowledge and knowing* (pp. 277–294). Mahwah, NJ: Lawrence Erlbaum Associates.

13

GETTING TO THE COMPLEXITIES OF IDENTITY
The Contributions of an Autoethnographic and Intersectional Approach

Susan R. Jones

Abstract: This chapter explores multiple social identities and self-authorship using an intersectional framework and autoethnographic methodology. Drawing from the results of an autoethnographic study, the chapter explores the contributions of an autoethnographic approach to the study of self-authorship and extends discussion of the applicability of self-authorship to diverse populations.

One's being in the world is always marked, molded, formed, and transformed in and through encounters with others and with a world . . . identity is never simply a question of self-authorship. . . . Identity, one could argue, is already always haunted by the other, by that which is not "I." Or to put it another way, identity is social, unstable, continually in process, and to some extent, is both necessary and impossible.

Sullivan, 2003, p. 149

Nikki Sullivan's observation about identity complicates both the construct of identity and self-authorship and hints at the importance of multiple and intersecting identities and the sociocultural contexts in which identities

I would like to acknowledge the other participants in the autoethnographic research project presented here. Although I served as sole author of this chapter, several participants read drafts of this chapter to assure that it stayed true to both our process and results. Particular thanks to Kristan Cilente and José Riera.

are constructed and negotiated. It also intimates the influence of one's espoused epistemological and methodological framework in understanding identity and self-authorship. Sullivan's ideas are rooted in a postructural and queer theoretical approach, whereas most other research on self-authorship is situated in the constructivist-developmental domain. What difference does the epistemology and methodological approach make to the study and understanding of self-authorship?

The purpose of this chapter is to take up this question and to explore the framework of intersectionality and the methodology of autoethnography as new approaches to studying self-authorship. Autoethnography is a unique methodological approach that utilizes narrative writing to illuminate both the individual lived experience and the larger sociocultural conditions in which these stories are nested. With an explicit focus on methodology, autoethnography is discussed in relation to both potential contributions and challenges in the study of self-authorship. To provide an example of the advantages and limitations of autoethnography, the results of an autoethnographic study on multiple identities and intersectionality are summarized in relation to the question of how the theory of self-authorship might be informed by both an intersectional analysis and an autoethnographic approach.

Studying Self-Authorship

In a wonderfully revelatory article tracing her own epistemological evolution, Baxter Magolda (2004) chronicled her movement from a positivist and objectivist lens to a constructivist framework that better portrayed her underlying phenomenon of interest: epistemological reflection and self-authorship. She noted:

> I found the assumptions of the constructivist paradigm—realities are multiple, context-bound, and mutually shaped by interaction of the knower and known (Lincoln & Guba, 2000)—a better fit with constructive-developmental theory than were the positivist assumptions (e.g., objective reality, context-free, researcher objectivity) I had superimposed on it. . . . The constructivist assumptions that knowledge is context-bound resonated with participants' unique experiences and varied stories. The assumption that entities shape each other was also evident in the participants' narratives. (pp. 35–36)

Indeed, many other researchers interested in studying self-authorship followed in the intellectual and methodological footsteps of Baxter Magolda (e.g., Abes & Jones, 2004; Pizzolato, 2003; Torres & Hernandez, 2007), finding that a constructivist approach holds greater potential for illuminating the phenomenon of self-authorship and for understanding how research participants make meaning of their lives.

When studying self-authorship, a constructivist epistemological lens is often then paired with grounded theory methodology or narrative inquiry, presumably because of the interest in generating theory about self-authorship that is grounded in the data itself and in telling the identity stories of self-authoring individuals from their own perspectives. Typically, these studies focused on a particular population of students, so the grounded theory addresses, by way of example, self-authorship for high-risk students (Pizzolato, 2003; 2005), Latino/a students (Torres, 2003), or lesbian students (Abes & Jones, 2004). More specifically, Pizzolato (2003) justified her use of grounded theory with this statement: "Through the use of grounded theory I could move beyond the description of the students' individual stories toward generation of a theory rooted in data that brought together the voices of participants with my interpretations of their collective experiences, as developed through constant comparative analyses" (p. 800). Likewise, Abes and Jones provided the rationale for a constructivist narrative inquiry as "well-suited to identity studies because stories offer revealing glimpses into inner selves . . . and revealed the complexity of participants' thinking and the meaning they made of their identities" (p. 615).

Some of the recent scholarship on self-authorship (foremost the examples provided previously), building on the work of Baxter Magolda, includes participants from marginalized groups and begins to explore the influence of race, ethnicity, sexual orientation, and social class in relation to self-authorship. This work not only, and importantly, expands the sample to include a more diverse group of participants, but also begins to suggest that the process of self-authorship may look different for different individuals depending on factors such as race, sexual orientation, and ethnicity.

However, some identity scholars view this as an "additive approach" (e.g., Bowleg, 2008; Sullivan, 2003) to understanding a complex phenomenon such as the intersections of social identities with self-authorship, and argue against the tendency to advance "categories of containment" (Lather, 2006, p. 47). Instead, as Lather suggested, in order to work against such categories, researchers must begin "by saying yes to the messiness, to that which interrupts and exceeds tidy categories" (p. 48) and resist the "epistemological sovereignty" (Lather, 2004, p. 19) of using one approach to study a particular phenomenon. The chapter now turns to two approaches, one theoretical (intersectionality) and the other methodological (autoethnography), which break out of the more typical strategies for exploring self-authorship.

Intersectionality

Intersectionality is an analytic lens that emerged from and draws upon feminist theory and the scholarship of women of color. A central tenet of intersectionality is that it centers social identities such as race, class, and gender in analysis, and constructs identity as multiple, layered, and entangled within systems of both oppression and privilege (Dill, McLaughlin, & Nieves, 2007). Intersectionality foregrounds identity as the subject of inquiry and engages both the individual lived experience of identity and the power dynamics at work in the structures and systems in which individuals move. Indeed, as Dill et al. suggested, "To a large extent, intersectional work is about identity" (p. 630). What intersectionality contributes to the theory of self-authorship is the insistence on connecting individual identities to the larger categories of analysis (Dill, et al.), and focusing on "the relationships among multiple dimensions and modalities of social relations and subject formations" (McCall, 2005, p. 1771). As a heuristic for exploring the relationships between social identities and larger social systems of inequality, intersectionality illuminates the complexities of the lived experience (Jones, 2009), including what it means to be self-authored and to express one's core sense of self (Baxter Magolda, 2008; Jones, 1997) or "authentic sense of self" (Shields, 2008, p. 301).

Scholarly interest in intersectionality has "grown directly out of the way multiple identities are experienced" (Shields, 2008, p. 304) and in recognition that identities can be defined and understood only in relation to one another and to systems of power and privilege. Indeed, as Risman (2004) captured, "there is now considerable consensus growing that one must always take into consideration multiple axes of oppression; to do otherwise presumes the whiteness of women, the maleness of people of color, and the heterosexuality of everyone" (p. 422). In her examination of gender and intersectionality, Shields offered a comprehensive definition of intersectionality:

The specific definition of *intersectionality* varies by research context, but a consistent thread across definitions is that social identities which serve as organizing features of social relations, mutually constitute, reinforce, and naturalize one another. By *mutually constitute* I mean that one category of identity, such as gender, takes its meaning as a category in relation to another category. By *reinforce* I mean that the formation and maintenance of identity categories is a dynamic process in which the individual herself or himself is actively engaged. . . . By *naturalize* I mean that identities in one category come to be seen as self-evident or "basic" through the lens of another category. (p. 302)

Emergent interest in intersectionality from a research perspective generated attention to methodology and the attendant issues and complexities (e.g., Bowleg, 2008; McCall, 2005), primarily how to get at intersecting and mutually constitutive dimensions of identity, rather than looking at discrete variables, as is more common in the additive approach. When extending the definition of intersectionality to intersectional research, the following set of core characteristics emerge from the work of Collins (2007) and Dill (2002) are emphasized: (a) a primary focus and centering on the lived experiences of individuals; (b) an exploration of identity salience as influenced by systems of power and privilege and the interacting nature of such systems; and (c) a larger purpose of contributing to a more socially just society.

Drawing on the overlapping constructs and characteristics of intersectionality and self-authorship offers the potential for new developmental understandings that integrate power and privilege with self-authorship. Both frameworks foreground identity and the lived experience of one's full sense of an authentic self. However, unlike much of the work on self-authorship that delineates distinct developmental tasks for those who are privileged and those who experience oppression, intersectionality acknowledges that individuals simultaneously inhabit both privileged and oppressed identities (Dill, et al., 2007). Thus, identity emerges as a phenomenon that is at once stable, and fluid and constantly negotiated. Conceptually joining intersectionality, which situates identity within larger structures of inequality, with self-authorship and its emphasis on holistic development, provides a way into these complexities. In order to fully understand these complexities, an appropriate methodological approach is needed.

Autoethnography

What autoethnography offers to the study of self-authorship is an emphasis on the construction of personal narratives that link the narrator with larger sociocultural structures. As Ellis and Bochner (2000) described, "Back and forth autoethnographers gaze, first through an ethnographic wide-angle lens, focusing outward on social and cultural aspects of their personal experience; then, they look inward, exposing a vulnerable self that is moved by and may move through, refract, and resist cultural interpretations" (p. 739). Through this constantly shifting gaze, autoethnographers construct narratives that connect individuals to their social worlds and back again.

Autoethnography is defined as an "autobiographical genre of writing and research that displays multiple layers of consciousness, connecting the personal to the cultural" (Ellis & Bochner, 2000, p. 739). Integrating personal narratives with sociocultural analysis, autoethnographies are presented as "a self-narrative that critiques the situatedness of self with others in social contexts" (Spry, 2001, p. 710) and results in the creation of "evocative stories" (Ellis & Bochner, p. 744). As such, "autoethnographic research blurs the boundaries characteristic of post-positivist inquiry of researcher-participant-text and surfaces multivocal and unique perspectives illuminating lived experience" (Jones, 2009). Specific characteristics of autoethnographic work include: (a) participation as reciprocity; (b) partiality and reflexivity as strategies for dialogue; (c) dialogue as a space for debate and negotiation; (d) personal narrative and storytelling as an obligation to critique; (e) evocation and emotion as incitements to action; and (f) engaged embodiment as a condition for change (Holman Jones, 2005, p. 773).

Much of what is written about autoethnography is portrayed autoethnographically, which provides the reader with methodological exemplars, but lacks the sometimes desired set of rules and procedures typical in describing methodological approaches. For example, Holman Jones (2005) wrote her way into a definition, before settling on the idea that there is no one way to capture the essence of autoethnography. She mused:

Autoethnography is:

Setting a scene, telling a story, weaving intricate connections among life and art, experience and theory, evocation and explanation . . . and then letting go, hoping for readers who will bring the same careful attention to your words in the context of their own lives.

Making a text present. Demanding attention and participation. Implicating all involved. Refusing closure or categorization.

Believing that words matter and writing toward the moment when the point of creating autoethnographic text *is* to change the world. (p. 765)

The use of personal autobiographical narratives is not new either to educational research in general or to the exploration of identities, in particular. Much of the theorizing on multiple and intersecting identities—the precursor to intersectionality—developed from scholarship in the disciplines of Women's Studies and Black Studies. Through narrative approaches, the voices and lived experiences of marginalized people are illuminated and acknowledged. What distinguishes autoethnography from more traditional narrative approaches is the insistence on making the connection between personal lived experiences and sociocultural analysis. Drawing upon the results of an autoethnographic study brings to life the characteristics, challenges, limitations, and potential contribution of autoethnographic research in relation to the study of self-authorship.

Findings From an Autoethnographic Study

To highlight the potential of autoethnography as a methodological approach to advance the understanding of self-authorship, I summarize several findings from a research project designed to explore the complexities of identity development using an intersectional framework. A full discussion of the research may be found elsewhere (Jones, 2009). This study drew upon theories of self-authorship and multiple identities and, in particular, a view of identities as socially constructed, which results in the necessity to consider identities in relation to the dynamics of power, privilege and sociocultural histories of particular groups (Collins, 1990; Jones, 2009). Several scholars suggested that this is a missing piece in the theory of self-authorship (Abes, 2009; Abes & Kasch, 2007; Jones, 2009; Torres, 2008; Torres & Hernandez, 2007). Although self-authorship is holistic in its integration of cognitive, intrapersonal, and interpersonal domains of development, it does not necessarily or explicitly focus on the dimensions of race, gender, social class, ethnicity, or sexual orientation, for example, in either an additive or intersectional approach. Although these dimensions relate to all individuals, they are not typically foregrounded in self-authorship research nor investigated for their influence on the self-authorship process or as central to an internal sense of self (Baxter Magolda, 2001).

One compelling example, illustrating both the significance of a methodological approach and shifting results with an explicit focus on social identities, is found in Abes and Kasch (2007). Using queer theory to reanalyze data gathered in the more typical constructivist-developmental approach, Abes and Kasch *queered* self-authorship, finding that "self-authorship alone is an incomplete theoretical framework to describe the experiences of lesbian college students" (p. 630). They found that development may not be linear as lesbian students learn to resist a heteronormative society and live in multiple developmental locations simultaneously. They concluded that when queering self-authorship, "the developmental process looks different for lesbian college students, an observation suggesting that the nature of the developmental process might also be reexamined for other dimensions of identity, such as social class, race, and ethnicity" (p. 630).

In an effort to address the complexities of identity construction and the self-authoring process when social identities are explicitly considered, the questions that guided our research included: (a) what is the lived experience of identity construction and negotiation when multiple identities are considered?; (b) how is identity experienced at the intersections?; (c) what are the sociocultural contexts and structures of power and privilege that influence and shape identity?; and (d) what implications for an understanding of the self-authoring process might be found in an intersectional analysis of multiple identities? (Jones, 2009).

Participants engaged in this autoethnographic research included eight individuals (one participant withdrew in the later stages of the research due to time constraints; however, his narrative is used in our analysis), recruited from a doctoral program in a college of education. All individuals met sampling criteria, which included an interest in the project, prior consideration of their social identities, and diversity in social identities. Consistent with autoethnographic research, as the primary investigator, I too was a participant. Demographically we represented five women and three men; four participants of color (one Korean American, one Latino, two African Americans) and four White; ages ranging from 28–52; three participants who self-identified as LGBT; three participants with children; and diversity in the social class status of our families of origin.

Data were collected in three phases: (1) writing our individual autobiographical narratives focused on our lived experience of multiple and intersecting identities; (2) reading aloud our narratives and beginning the process of connecting the personal to the cultural; and (3) engaging in ten focus group discussions and analysis of our narratives. The focus groups served as both strategies for data collection and analysis, as the discussions represented our collective effort to understand multiple and intersecting identities, the identity construction process, and the influence of sociocultural contexts (e.g., structures of privilege and oppression) to those constructions. The data analysis process then included concrete description of what was going on in the data, more abstract analysis and conceptualizations, and interpretations using the frameworks of intersectionality and self-authorship. Seven participants were involved in every stage of the data collection and analysis process. The research process took place over the course of a full year.

Summary of Results

The emphasis of this summary of results is on what contribution an autoethnographic methodological approach and intersectional analysis might make to the understanding of self-authorship. I offer three of the themes that emerged in this study to illuminate the strengths and limitations of an autoethnographic approach.

Managing Perceptions and Negotiating Identities   Prior research on self-authorship illuminates the process of moving from external formulas to internal foundations, which involves developing greater skill in managing external contexts. Thus, as one becomes more self-authored, one is better able to resist and negotiate external definitions so as to rely on internal meaning-making. Our results complicate this trajectory by suggesting that two processes are simultaneously and persistently at work: managing perceptions and negotiating identities. Julie captures this interplay well:

> There are two different things going on—one is managing perceptions—
> and I was the one who wrote down like managing perceptions different
> from identity negotiations, 'cause [managing perceptions is] externally
> focused whereas identity negotiations are more internally focused—and
> how you personally make meaning for your own self about things . . . we'd
> talk about them in the same breath, but I think they are different things.
> (Jones, 2009 p.298)

Although this dual process of managing how we view ourselves and how we think others view us resembles the self-authorship process, we found the relationship between the internal process (identity negotiation) and the external (managing perceptions) to be ongoing, complex, fluid, and contingent. Our findings suggest that external influences, particularly for those from marginalized identities, continue to exert significant authority on the individual. Stacey illuminates this dynamic and the ongoing role of the external:

> A mother, a wife, a woman, a daughter, a sister, an aunt, a niece, a professional, a student, I am who you want me to be in different environments in different places at different times, but it does not stop there. I am Christian, I am Black, I am from the south, I am middle class, I am African American, which is the first identity seen by others when I walk down the street, or enter a room. So to answer the question, who am I as a person, I am all of the above to different people in different settings at different times. (Jones, 2009 p. 293)

To further complicate the process, we also found reflected in both our autoethnographic narratives and discussions, as the above quotation testifies, that the need to manage others' perceptions was a persistent one for participants of color. Yet, the opportunity to negotiate one's identity, reflected in an internal process, was the privilege of the White participants. This suggests that the self-authoring process may look different for those from marginalized identities and underrepresented groups. This was further nuanced by the visibility or invisibility of one's marginalized identity (e.g., a White gay man still had the privilege to pass and negotiate his identity, rather than constantly manage perceptions).

Tensions Between Privileged and Oppressed Identities   What our autoethnographic narratives and focused dialogues pointed to was a relationship (and tension) between privileged and oppressed identities. How does one inhabit both locations simultaneously? José described the tension:

> But this idea . . . this tension between . . . [long pause] . . . all of us possess both dominant and, marginalized, you know, identities. And so, how those interact? . . . not all identities are the same, so you can't talk about them as the same. . . . I feel like, well, there's these categories but they're weighted . . . [laughs]. Because, some of them have kind of more, maybe pervasive characteristics about them throughout your life because they are marginalized. And somehow that is different than those that are privileged. And then there's the context of what we can show or not show. (Jones, 2009 p. 295)

Identifying the tensions in belonging to both privileged and marginalized groups brought a realization through the autoethnographic process that self-definitions cannot be considered outside this dynamic tension between privileged and oppressed identities. An intersectional analysis brought us to a recognition that we were more likely gazing toward our oppressed locations (e.g., our own and others), with much less awareness and scrutiny of our privileged identities. And this was a consistent finding regardless of whether or not our primary identifications were with privileged or oppressed identities (e.g., White, Black, woman, gay, straight, Latino, Asian American). I provided an example in my narrative of this tension in discussing the connection between social class and sexual orientation:

> Social class paved the way for me. The privileges of social class made the awareness of race (we lived in an all-white neighborhood and I attended nearly all white schools) and sexual orientation (kids from upper class families are not gay, and if they are, we certainly don't talk about it) invisible and thus, protected from scrutiny. This is how the system is perpetuated. (Jones, 2009 p. 297)

Troubling Authenticity   As our dialogues centered on identity negotiation and perception management, the experience of difference, navigating oppressed and privileged identities, and the influence of contexts, we came to the question of authenticity. What is the "core" sense of self, and is this the same as authenticity? Is leading a self-authored life an authentic one? Similarly, often considered a goal of holistic development, to lead an authentic life, we wondered if authenticity was possible, given the shifting terrain of identity negotiations and the external constraints to authenticity, which are influenced by context and the structures of power, privilege, and oppression. We found, as Marybeth stated, "The authentic self is a really challenging concept."

What made authenticity troubling was the influence of different contexts, some of which were supportive of one's whole self, but others were not, and this resulted in decision making about how (and who) to present oneself in these different contexts. "Is this an authentic way to be?" mused several participants. Is self-authorship possible when contexts shift and we protect what is core by not showing it? José described his thinking about resolving the tension: "I do it in a way that I feel like I could live with myself and be authentic with myself without giving myself away. . . . Okay, yeah. I feel good about downplaying this part of my identity for the sake of this context but not downplaying too much." Similarly Julie queried, "Is authenticity only there if we're completely internally self-defined? 'Cause it seems, yeah, how can we remove ourselves from the effects of external contexts?" Kristan then responded to this deliberation:

> I'm sensing that there's the overarching feeling we have to be internally defined to be authentic, that there had to be just this internal; and why can't it be a both/and, why can't we recognize the power of the environment and our internal sense of identity and the role we play in shaping the environments in which we're in and that sort of comfortable tension in acknowledging those pushes and pulls, because we won't ever be devoid of context.

The theme of authenticity, or living authentically, was omnipresent through our dialogues and most fully revealed in discussions about what lives as one's core sense of self. It seemed to us that a focus on intersectionality and social identities complicates the discussion of authenticity and self-authorship.

Contributions and Limitations of Autoethnography

> As a reader and a writer, I look to text, written or spoken, to find connections between myself and others, in a way to lessen my own sense of otherness. . . . Really, at the most basic, fundamental level, isn't that what we're doing with this autoethnography project? Seeking to find meaning in the interweaving of our stories that is deeper and more substantial than what we'd find on our own? (Julie; Jones, 2009 p. 299)

As the summary of results highlights, autoethnography as a methodological approach to investigating multiple identities and self-authorship brings new questions and considerations to light. Richly descriptive and powerful in illuminating multiple voices and social locations, autoethnography is also somewhat (and characteristically) elusive in an effort to capture much complexity. In the next section I explore some of the advantages and potential contributions as well as the limitations and disadvantages to the use of autoethnography in exploring self-authorship.

Advantages and Contributions

Getting Closer to the Complexities of Lived Experience   The primary contribution and advantage of autoethnographic research is the foregrounding of lived experience in a narrative that gets at the complexity of this lived experience and at the relationship between individual identity and larger social systems. Intersectional and autoethnographic research and analysis break from traditional student development research by situating individuals within structures of power and oppression that influence the lived experience. The writing and rewriting of these narratives enables participants to work through the shifting terrain of identity when both individual lived experience and larger systems of inequality are considered simultaneously.

Whereas much of the research on student development treats social identities as distinct (or absent), an autoethnographic approach enables participants to write themselves into a greater sense of wholeness by integrating multiple identities. More specifically, autoethnographic research holds the potential to become a self-authoring opportunity and an empowering process for those involved because of the self-reflection and self-knowledge that are central to the research methodology itself. In autoethnographic research, one tells one's own story, rather than relying on someone else's telling, which as Lincoln (1997) suggested, always runs the risk of telling the story that will "buttress some point of my own interpretation, not necessarily a point of theirs" (p. 43). The story told by an autoethnographer is necessarily incomplete as it continues to unfold; however, the story is truly narrated in one's own voice.

Handling Complex Questions   This point is not meant to suggest that research on self-authorship using different methodological approaches is less complex; after all, self-authorship itself is a complex phenomenon. However, the use of written narratives as a methodological strategy, as Julie's words evoked, yielded "data" that interviews likely could not. Beginning the research process with each participant's written stories, we waded into the complexities of self-perceived identities from the very start. This richness and depth in data would take even the most skilled interviewer much time to approach and accomplish.

Further, both intersectionality as a theoretical framework and autoethnography as a methodological approach create space for the complexity that comes with an analysis of multiple and intersecting identities. More typically, complexity is "managed" by "analysis of a social location at the intersection of single dimensions of multiple categories, rather than at the intersection of the full range of dimensions of a full range of categories" (e.g., exploring the experiences of Black women) (McCall, 2005, p. 1781). However, the autoethnographic approach relies less on "managing" complexity and more so on bringing the complexity out into the open as a greater reflection of the realities of lived experience. Autoethnography also demands the inclusion of social identities in a study of self-authorship; the individual cannot be fully understood outside the structures of privilege and oppression because these structures construct and pattern individual identities in specific and significant ways. Autoethnographic research illuminates within-group differences, rather than relying on singular articulations of same group identity experiences and explores social locations as both identity and system of privilege and/or oppression. This is consistent with Lather's (2006) urging researchers not to "revert to romantic 'too easy' ideas about 'authenticity' in negotiating the tensions between both honoring the 'voices' of participants and the demand for interpretive work on the part of the inquirer" (p. 50).

Broadening the Analysis   Because the emphasis in autoethnography is on connecting the personal and individual with the sociocultural, analytic possibilities are expanded to more fully address significant contextual influences. For example, although much of the research on identity suggests that "identity is emphasized as a quality that enables the expression of the individual's authentic sense of self" (Shields, 2008, p. 301), an autoethnographic analysis of authenticity raises significant questions about the possibility of authenticity or how authenticity might "look" different when external contextual influences are considered. Further, when marginalized identities are more thoroughly foregrounded, other dynamics come in to play in the self-authoring process. For example, in our study, different tensions emerged in relation to the question (and possibilities) of negotiating identities and managing perceptions.

Role of "the Researcher"   The role of researcher in autoethnographic studies is that of full participant in the research project, and as such, provides a unique set of circumstances, benefits, and challenges. Although all qualitative inquiry situates the researcher in a more direct relationship with participants, autoethnography requires an intimacy and vulnerability on the part of the researcher that can be avoided in other methodological approaches. Describing qualitative research, Demerath (2006) suggested that all researchers must ask themselves the questions "what is required to do research with people as they live their lives, and what happens (empirically, as well as ethically and politically) as the lives of qualitative researchers and their participants inevitably get intertwined" (p. 101). In the context of autoethnography, Ellis (2007) described one response as the need for "relational ethics." She further explained: "Relational ethics requires researchers to act from our hearts and minds, to acknowledge our interpersonal bonds to others, and initiate and maintain conversations. As part of relational ethics, we seek to deal with the reality and practice of changing relationships with our research participants over time" (p. 4).

Overlap clearly exists in the quality of the researcher-participant relationship in autoethnographic and constructivist methodological approaches, particularly those that are longitudinal in design. What is distinct about autoethnography is the intent for a purely collaborative research process in which no one person is considered the primary investigator. To accomplish this is challenging, but deeply rewarding. Rarely does a researcher have an opportunity to experience firsthand the role participants are in when they agree to participate in a study. This alone may bring about otherwise untapped insights on the research process. In our study, each of us found that considerable risk was required as conversations were held that crossed boundaries rarely traversed in our everyday lives. As Bochner and Ellis (2006) conveyed: "Autoethnographies show people in the process of figuring out what to do, how to live, and what their struggles mean" (p. 111). To engage in such a process with intimate others (Ellis, 2007) is a transformative experience for all participants.

Challenges and Limitations

"Measuring" complexity   Many of strengths and contributions of autoethnography also pose potential challenges. Designing autoethnographic and intersectional research that captures the inhabiting of multiple locations simultaneously is difficult because of "the complexity that arises when the subject of analysis expands to include multiple dimensions of social life and categories of analysis" (McCall, 2005, p. 1772). How is it that you *measure* something so complex and shifting? The goal of autoethnography is not necessarily to *grasp* complexity, but more so to expose it as central to everyday lived experience. Regardless of approach, getting at the complexities of intersectionality and multiple identities is challenging.

Two issues seem particularly vexing to the question of how complexity is measured: designing interview protocols that approach the complexity (in our case, the intersections), and then knowing how to analyze the data one "collects," which in an autoethnographic approach such as this project relied on a dialogic process and thus was ongoing and increasingly revealing. Clearly, in all research projects, the data a researcher collects are directly tied to the way in which questions are asked. This is the case regardless of whether the researcher is designing survey items or in-depth interview questions. What makes an autoethnographic and intersectional approach so complicated is the absence of language that resists the more common additive approach to studies on identity. This challenge is further heightened in autoethnography because typically the researcher begins with one guiding question that is explored through a written narrative. The author/researcher is then at great liberty to take that narrative in the direction that is most compelling, without the intrusion of an interviewer who can bring the participant back to a primary focus. Although this is the purpose of intersectionality and autoethnography, it nonetheless poses challenges, particularly related to analysis and interpretation.

The Story Continues: Analyzing and Interpreting Data   Several challenges and potential limitations exist related to the question of how to make sense of data collected using an autoethnographic approach to studying self-authorship. First, data are collected in an ongoing process such that new data emerge through the narrative and dialogic approach. If the narratives were written at the end of the autoethnographic process, they would most likely be different, informed by the growth and awareness cultivated by the dialogic process. This then gives rise to a second challenge. How does the researcher studying self-authorship know when the research is "completed"? This is a different dynamic than longitudinal research, which is critical when studying ongoing development. When using autoethnography to study self-authorship, the emphasis is less on chronicling a process than capturing a personal narrative story about a particular phenomenon in a moment in time. The purpose of an autoethnographic account is to create "evocative stories" that "long to be used rather than analyzed; to be told and retold rather than theorized and settled; to offer lessons for further conversation rather than undebatable conclusions; and to substitute the companionship of intimate detail for the loneliness of abstracted facts" (Ellis & Bochner, 2000, p. 744). What this means for the study of self-authorship using autoethnography is the foregrounding of personal narrative over analysis; that is, creating the space through the writing process for the story of self-authorship to emerge rather than hearing a story and analyzing it using self-authorship as an analytic lens.

Interpreting autoethnographic and intersectional research can also be challenging as a result of the role of the researcher as both inquirer and participant. The potential benefit of other qualitative approaches is the primary investigator, who presumably can be fully present during data collection but then achieve the distance needed for interpretation. In autoethnography, the phenomenon of researcher as participant raises the question of the importance of this "bird's eye view," to use the phrase used by one of the participants in our study. It may be difficult then to know when, and if, it is appropriate to step back to take another view of the data. Further, because the researcher is both in and of the data, a critique of autoethnography may be that this limits the depth and breadth of interpretive and analytic perspective available to the researcher. For example, if a researcher is working on building an internal foundation or perhaps represents primarily dominant identities, will he/she recognize the characteristics of someone more secure in internal commitments (Baxter Magolda, 2008) or the nuanced experiences of one from marginalized, intersecting identities? The intersectional framework used in this study pushed us to examine such questions, but this was challenging to us and created difficult dialogues.

Related, the participatory nature of autoethnography also complicates more traditional strategies to assure trustworthiness of findings. For example, member checking is often used to assure that a primary researcher is interpreting and representing participants' perspectives in ways that participants recognize as their own. When participants and researchers are one and the same, member checking takes on a different look. What ought the criteria for trustworthiness look like for autoethnographic research?

Heightened Vulnerability   Autoethnographic research is time intensive, intellectually and emotionally demanding, and depends upon the presence of a self willing to be vulnerable. Further, an intersectional analysis adds to this vulnerability because of the integral focus on "ordinary people who live at the crux of structural inequality based on intersections of race, class, sex, gender, sexual orientation, and disability" (Bowleg, 2008, p. 323). As such, autoethnography is more difficult for some participants than others; and it is not always obvious when some participants were holding back or why and how to interpret silences. Autoethnographic research requires trust and openness as well as a willingness to experience discomfort as personal topics were brought forward and discussed.

This heightened vulnerability also brings with it ethical implications and complexities. Indeed as Ellis (2007) noted, "autoethnography itself is an ethical practice" (p. 26). Of particular challenge is the issue of confidentiality and anonymity. Despite the obvious feature of autoethnography as written about the self, by the self, and the presumption that all our names would be used in published material and presentations, when it came time to actually committing to this practice we had long discussions about the potential risks involved. Many of us shared with the group dimensions of our selves (and others in our lives) that few others knew. We would clearly be recognizable to those who knew us and were not sure about how we felt about making ourselves so transparent. Although challenging to sort through, this phenomenon might also be considered a limitation to autoethnography as it suggests very good reasons why participants would hold back on sharing of themselves.

Concluding Thoughts

Through my participation in this autoethnographic project, I appreciate the unique perspective that autoethnography and intersectionality, as theoretical and methodological approaches, provide to the study and understanding of self-authorship. Similar to Baxter Magolda's (2004) methodological move from positivist to constructivist grounded theory resulting in a different set of results and understanding of self-authorship, so too does the shift from constructivism to intersectionality and autoethnography tell a different story. An intersectional and autoethnographic approach to the study of self-authorship continues to foreground personal narratives, but also centers contextual influences including structures of privilege and oppression. As such, the analysis becomes not only telling individual stories, but connecting individuals to groups and society and exploring the relational and mutually constitutive nature of these relationships. We found that this emphasis took us to a depth of intercultural conversations not typical of our daily lives.

As our results demonstrated, autoethnography illuminated the contextualized and problematized nature of constructs central to self-authorship such as "core sense of self," "essence," "internal foundation," and "authenticity." As a participant, I wondered, what is at my core? Is the core a meaningful construct? Is the core contextual in relation to social identities? What constitutes an authentic sense of self when I bump up against larger sociocultural influences that challenge who I am? My own investment in the autoethnographic process caused me to question anew the self-authoring process, particularly when the self I was authoring was not always the self I knew myself to be. This reminded me of Lather's (1991) notion of "the profound uncertainty about what constitutes an adequate depiction of social reality" (p. 21).

What is now clearer to me is that the study of self-authorship, like other complex phenomena, benefits from examination using multiple interpretive lenses. I am also more assured of the importance of explicitly examining the lived experience of those who occupy both privileged and marginalized social identities, rather than focusing primarily on one group, or the other. Intersectionality and autoethnography provided a vehicle for this and illuminated the complexities of self-authorship as a result. For example, many of us involved in this project, myself included, grew up with a pain, loss, shame, or confusion related to some aspect of our identities. I wrote in my own narrative about "carrying around this secret about myself for a long time" and as a result learning "how to move through very different environments and like a chameleon, blend[ing] in to the setting." These types of experiences carry much weight in relation to the self-authoring process and have everything to do with the individuals we become.

I conclude with a quote from one of the autoethnographic narratives in the study highlighted in this chapter. It poignantly illuminates the power of voice in autoethnography and in the telling of evocative stories, linking the narrator's journey to structures of inequality:

> I write and rewrite my story to counter the stories I have heard, stories that told me that my voice didn't matter, that I shouldn't rock the boat, that this country does not belong to me, that I don't belong here. I write to claim my voice and my space and my self. (Jones, 2009 p.303)

References

Abes, E. S. (2009). Theoretical borderlands: Using multiple theoretical perspectives to challenge inequitable power structures in student development theory. *Journal of College Student Development, 50*(2), 141–156.

Abes, E. S., & Kasch, D. (2007). Using Queer Theory to explore lesbian college students' multiple dimensions of identity. *Journal of College Student Development, 48*(6), 619–636.

Abes, E. S., & Jones, S. R. (2004). Meaning-making capacity and the dynamics of lesbian college students multiple dimensions of identity. *Journal of College Student Development, 45*(6), 612–632.

Baxter Magolda, M. B. (2001). *Making their own way: Narratives for transforming higher education to promote self-development.* Sterling, VA: Stylus.

Baxter Magolda, M. B. (2004). Evolution of a constructivist conceptualization of epistemological reflection. *Educational Psychologist, 39*(1), 31–42.

Baxter Magolda, M. B. (2008). Three elements of self-authorship. *Journal of College Student Development, 49*(4), 269–284.

Bochner, A. P., & Ellis, C. (2006). Communication as autoethnography. In G. Shepherd, J. St. John, & T. Striphas (Eds.), *Communication as . . . : Perspectives on theory* (pp. 110–122). Thousand Oaks, CA: Sage.

Bowleg, L. (2008). When Black + lesbian + woman ≠ Black lesbian woman: The methodological challenges of qualitative and quantitative intersectionality research. *Sex Roles, 59*, 312–325.

Collins, P. H. (1990). *Black feminist thought: Knowledge, consciousness, and the politics of empowerment.* New York: Routledge.

Collins, P. H. (2007). Pushing the boundaries or business as usual? Race, class, and gender studies and sociological inquiry. In C. J. Calhoun (Ed.), *Sociology in America: A history* (pp. 572–604). Chicago: University of Chicago.

Demerath, P. (2006). The science of context: Modes of response for qualitative researchers in education. *International Journal of Qualitative Studies, 19*(1), 97–113.

Dill, B. T. (2002, Fall). Work at the intersections of race, gender, ethnicity, and other dimensions of difference in higher education. *Connections: Newsletter of the Consortium on Race, Gender, and Ethnicity,* 5–7.

Dill, B. T., McLaughlin, A. E., & Nieves, A. D. (2007). Future directions of feminist research: Intersectionality. In S. N. Hesse-Biber (Ed.), *Handbook of feminist research* (pp. 629–637). Thousand Oaks, CA: Sage.

Ellis, C. (2007). Telling secrets, revealing lives: Relational ethics in research with intimate others. *Qualitative Inquiry, 13*, 3–29.

Ellis, C., & Bochner, A. P. (2000). Autoethnography, personal narrative, reflexivity: Researcher as subject. In N. K. Denzin & Y. S. Lincoln (Eds.), *The handbook of qualitative research* (2nd ed., pp. 733–768). Thousand Oaks, CA: Sage.

Holman Jones, S. (2005). Autoethnography: Making the personal political. In N. K. Denzin & Y. S. Lincoln (Eds.), *The Sage handbook of qualitative research* (3rd ed., pp. 763–791). Thousand Oaks, CA: Sage.

Jones, S. R. (1997). Voices of identity and difference: A qualitative exploration of the multiple dimensions of identity development in women college students. *Journal of College Student Development, 38*, 376–386.

Jones, S. R. (2009). Constructing identities at the intersections: An autoethnographic exploration of multiple dimensions of identity. *Journal of College Student Development, 50*(3), 287–304.

Lather, P. (1991). *Getting smart: Feminist research and pedagogy with/in the postmodern.* New York: Routledge.

Lather, P. (2004). This IS your father's paradigm: Government intrusion and the case of qualitative research in education. *Qualitative Inquiry, 10*(1), 15–34.

Lather, P. (2006). Paradigm proliferation as a good thing to think with: Teaching research in education as wild profusion. *International Journal of Qualitative Studies, 19*(1), 35–57.

Lincoln, Y. (1997). Self, subject, audience, text: Living at the edge, writing in the margins. In W. G. Tierney & Y. S. Lincoln (Eds.), *Representation and the text: Reframing the narrative voice* (pp. 37–55). Albany: SUNY Press.

Lincoln, Y. S., & Guba, E. G. (2000). Paradigmatic controversies, contradictions, and emerging confluences. In N. K. Denzin and Y. S. Lincoln (Eds.), *Handbook of qualitative research* (2nd ed., pp. 163–188). Thousand Oaks, CA: Sage.

McCall, L. (2005). The complexity of intersectionality. *Signs: Journal of Women in Culture and Society, 30,* 1771–1800.

Pizzolato, J. E. (2003). Developing self-authorship: Exploring the experiences of high-risk students. *Journal of College Student Development, 44*(6), 797–812.

Pizzolato, J. E. (2005). Creating crossroads for self-authorship: Investigating the provocative moment. *Journal of College Student Development, 46*(6), 624–641.

Risman, B. J. (2004). Gender as a social structure: Theory wrestling with activism. *Gender & Society, 18,* 429–450.

Shields, S. (2008). Gender: An intersectionality perspective. *Sex Roles, 59,* 301–311.

Spry, T. (2001). Performing autoethnography: An embodied methodological praxis. *Qualitative Inquiry, 7,* 706–732.

Sullivan, N. (2003). *A critical introduction to queer theory.* NY: New York University Press.

Torres, V. (2003). Influences on ethnic identity development of Latino college students in the first two years of college. *Journal of College Student Development, 44*(4), 532–547.

Torres, V. (2008, May). *The interconnectivity of cognitive, intrapersonal and interpersonal dimensions in recognizing racism.* Paper presented at The Self-authorship Theory Development and Assessment Across the Lifespan International Conference. Riva San Vitale, Switzerland.

Torres, V., & Hernandez, E. (2007). The influence of ethnic identity on self-authorship: A longitudinal study of Latino/a college students. *Journal of College Student Development, 48*(5), 558–573.

14

USING THE SUBJECT-OBJECT INTERVIEW TO PROMOTE AND ASSESS SELF-AUTHORSHIP

Jennifer Garvey Berger

Abstract: This chapter explores the Subject-Object Interview, the measure of Robert Kegan's theory of adult development and one of the primary means of assessing self-authorship. The author focuses on using the interview as an intervention to assist adults in moving toward self-authorship and the dilemmas involved in doing so.

Bryce[1] was a musician and high school science and music teacher when he joined a study I was conducting about his teacher preparation program. As part of the study, he sat down with me for a Subject-Object Interview (SOI), a semi-clinical interview designed to measure his form of mind using the developmental theory of Robert Kegan. I asked Bryce questions that were designed to reach for the edges of his understanding—so that I could have a sense of what he was taking responsibility for, what he saw as inside his own control (e.g., what things he self-authored), and what things he directed more externally. He greatly enjoyed having his thinking pushed and was alert to the new discoveries he was finding as he heard himself struggle with some of the questions. He

My thanks to those readers who read earlier drafts and made this a better piece of work. My readers span three continents (and an island) and five time zones, and all have my gratitude: The editors of this volume, Paul Atkins, Robyn Baker, Michael Berger, Lisa Boes, John Derry, Catherine Fitzgerald, Keith Johnston, Alan Snow, and quite possibly others whose contribution was made in the thick of a deadline and thus not acknowledged as it should have been. It takes more than one head to do this work, and I am honored to have all of your heads keeping company with mine!

[1] All names and some identifying details have been changed to protect the privacy of the research participants who have given generously of their time and thinking.

talked about how the process of the interview was pushing him to see that he was making his decisions based on implicit values and principles that he used constantly but examined rarely. At the end of the interview, he thanked me for the work I had done to help him make these new discoveries, and said he'd have a lot to think about in the future.

****

Jan was a senior executive in a large organization, and for all of her seniority, she struggled with her rage over the actions of some of her employees. She found that some of them did not display the devotion to the organization that she did, and that they flaunted this behavior by doing things like calling their doctors or their nannies during business hours, which Jan found unthinkable. She knew she was in the right on this issue because she had learned very important lessons about loyalty from her first and most important mentor. She had an experienced and well-respected coach who tried without success to help Jan shake this pattern. Jan's coach asked me to administer and report back about a new and unusual use of a developmental measure that would give his client feedback on where she was in her developmental journey and what some potential growth strategies might be. I interviewed Jan and reported that it seemed to me from the interview that she was embedded in a concept of loyalty that was externally derived from a source more than 30 years old. We discussed the possibility of her authoring a new definition of loyalty that was perhaps less bound to particular behaviors, and talked about the multi-faceted path towards self-authorship. While Jan had been coached for three years and had been in therapy for more than ten, having a developmental map laid out before her changed the way she understood herself and her problem.

Jan, her coach, and I began to imagine possibilities for new definitions she might create of loyalty (and other ideals, principles, and values she found she had imported from others rather than authoring for herself). She found that with some support from her coach, she could begin to write—and edit—her own definition of loyalty to be more inclusive and less attached to the outcomes her mentor had valued decades before. Her coach reported two months later that he had never imagined she could change so quickly; somehow, offering her the idea (and the permission) that she could author her own values, plus some support around creating the values she desired, transformed her relationship to herself and the way she made sense of those who worked with her.

In this chapter, I discuss the Subject-Object Interview (SOI; Lahey, Souvaine, Kegan, Goodman, & Felix, 1988), the measure of self-complexity in Robert Kegan's (1982; 1994) theory of adult development. I have been using and teaching about the SOI for more than a dozen years, and my experience with it has not only shaped the way I see development and research, but also the way I understand other people and myself. I explain how it is administered, for what purposes it is used, and what I have learned from my experience with the measure. As we saw with Bryce and Jan, the kinds of questions the SOI asks are not only useful in getting the interviewer some data, but are often experienced as helpful by the interviewees themselves as they face parts of their sense-making that they do not generally face, and they discover disconnections or discontinuities that they normally do not see. Finally, I discuss the implications of what I have learned from this work for supporting self-authorship in general.

Robert Kegan's Theory of Adult Development

The adult developmental theory on which I most rely is Robert Kegan's (1982; 1994) theory of adult development, although my theoretical perspective is informed by other adult developmentalists (e.g., Baxter Magolda, 1992; Baxter Magolda & King, 2004; Cook-Greuter, 2004; Fischer, Yan, & Stewart, 2002; King & Kitchener, 2004; Torbert et al., 2004). Kegan's theory, like those of many of the other adult developmentalists I name, focuses on perspective-taking and a person's capacity for making sense of complexity, ambiguity, and paradox, and thus offers a helpful framework for understanding work in the complex worlds many adults inhabit. Theories like Kegan's show that coping well with the demands of modern life is not just related to any particular set of skills; it is also related to the way individuals make meaning about the world. These ways of making meaning of the world are not inborn, but are developed over time as we increase our capacity to take perspectives, view authority in new ways, and see shades of grey where we once saw only black and white.

I make the most use of Kegan's theory because it offers both descriptions of the different forms of mind and also the process of movement between them. I also value the measure associated with Kegan's theory (the SOI), because it is more than simply a valid and reliable developmental measure; the process of the SOI tends to be enjoyable for the participant and also can, in itself, lead to some important insights, as it did for Bryce and Jan, mentioned previously. The SOI distinguishes the five central "forms of mind"— qualitatively different ways of making meaning—as well as four substages between each form. Research suggests that four of these five major forms of mind are possible in adulthood. Adapting from Kegan (1994), I call these four the self-sovereign mind, the socialized mind, the self-authored mind, and the self-transforming mind.

Those adults who currently see the world through a self-sovereign form of mind are focused primarily on their own perspectives and needs, because they cannot yet take the perspectives of others simultaneously with their own. They cannot get distance from their own thinking or psychology enough to notice patterns in themselves, so they are not able to generate psychological abstractions about themselves or others (when asked to describe who they are, for example, they might give a physical description or talk about their title at work). They are not motivated by abstract causes like loyalty or team spirit because they do not yet have a belief that the good of others is more important than their own success.[2]

Those who currently see the world with a socialized form of mind are able to distance themselves enough from their own perspectives on the world to fully internalize the perspectives of others and thereby value relationships for more than just their own self-interest. However, they may rely strongly on the external perspectives and theories they have come to trust, such that it is hard or impossible for them to generate answers and ideas for themselves without relying on others.

Those with a self-authored form of mind are able to recognize, understand, generate, and evaluate their own standards and values for behavior sufficiently to be differentiated and integrated with respect to those around them. They have an internal set of rules and regulations—a self-governing system—that they use to make their decisions or mediate conflicts.

Finally, those with a self-transforming form of mind—very rarely seen— are able to take a perspective on their self-authored system and understand that their system is—as all systems are—partial. They see the futility of attempting to perfect a self-authored system and instead begin to make sense

---

[2] You can imagine a 10-year old on a soccer field who wants her team to win and thus tries to control the ball and get as many goals as she can, not understanding the system of the team enough to see that because she does not pass to her teammates, the team as a whole is not able to score as many goals as it could if she were trying for fewer goals on her own. This view continues to be held by adults in organizations as well, who can miss that their attempts at success can actually limit the success of the larger group.

of the ways we both construct ourselves and are constructed by our contexts and relationships. They are able to handle multiple roles and layers of complexity with relative ease.

The process of growth as defined by this theory is about moving more and more of what is unseen and unexamined in the way we understand the world—those things to which we are *subject*—to a place where they can be seen and examined—and become *objects* for our inspection, and, if we choose, for our reflective action. Our unquestioned beliefs about the world are held implicitly, and those beliefs shape our experience of the world and the possibilities we perceive. As we begin to question our beliefs and ideas, our inquiry reveals new possibilities and allows us to deal with greater and greater levels of complexity.

The most profound example of a move from subject to object is when gradually, over time, entire meaning-making systems move from being hidden (subject) to being seen (object). This shift means that what was once an unselfconscious lens through which the person viewed the world now becomes something that can be seen and reflected upon. For example, when someone with a socialized form of mind begins to reflect on the way he holds other opinions rather than his own, he comes to see his whole meaning system and can begin to take reflective action to form his own opinions, notwithstanding the opinions of others. When he takes this reflective action of forming his own opinions about things, his socialized form of mind becomes an object for his reflection, and he begins to see the world through a self-authored form of mind. Kegan's theory names four measurable substages between each of the forms of mind I have described.

The Subject-Object Interview

The Subject-Object Interview (SOI) is a measure of complexity of mind that emerges from Kegan's theory of adult development. During the SOI, the interviewer attempts as much as possible to get inside the participant's own experience of the world, particularly her characteristic ways of understanding the world and organizing her experience. In this sense, the interview deals with the most fundamental aspects of the participant's meaning-making, and often exposes for her reflection some of the limits of her meaning-making (as she is asked questions about her sense-making which she has never before considered). The 60–90 minute interview is tape-recorded and transcribed, and a trained and reliable scorer reads it, looking for those things that expose the structure of the interviewee's sense-making (as opposed to a focus on the content of the interview). Content is *what* we think about—the substance of our thinking. Structure is *how* we think about the world—our hidden assumptions about authority, agency, what can be known. Whereas a person at any form of mind might be thinking about a conflict with his boss, the way he makes sense of this conflict—how he sees his own role, how he sees the role of his emotions, the different perspectives he can take—emerges from his particular form of mind, which someone can be trained to analyze. From this analysis, the scorer can reliably determine the form of mind demonstrated in the interview.

The protocol for the SOI requires that a highly trained interviewer probe for how a participant makes sense of what is going on for him. Starting with some key terms that help participants create a brainstorm of current experiences that they can choose to talk about over the course of the interview, the interview continues by following the interests and stories of the participants. The interviewer can follow where the participant leads because the content is not the key focus—it is just the vehicle to get to the structure. The interviewer's job is to listen well and to stick to boundary-mapping questions: What was the most important thing about that? What was hardest for you? What was most at risk? Attempting to score and test hypotheses while simultaneously asking good questions, the interviewer tries to bring enough richness to questions so that the scorer will have much to work with in the transcript. (See Table 14.1 for a brief overview about the interview process.)

The point of this interview is to ask the questions whose answers point to particular forms of mind and not others, and then analyze those responses as the participants offer them. This allows the interviewer to create new hypotheses that lead to more hypothesis-testing questions in themselves.

- What does this person take responsibility for? What does she not?
- What are the central conflicts in her story?
- Whose perspective can she take? Whose perspective is she stuck inside?
- What assumptions about the world shape her view?

TABLE 14.1
SOI Process Overview

What Does the Interviewer Do?	Why Does This Help?
Step 1: Look inside the interviewee's story for key issues: responsibility, conflict, perspective-taking, and assumptions about the world	Each of these issues is likely to be a place where someone has the energy and interest to push her understanding to its edges. These issues are also the places where structure is most apparent.
Step 2: Narrowing the choices.	Every time you begin to ask questions to help you understand someone's form of mind, you should keep an open mind and assume that this person could be self-sovereign, self-transforming, or anywhere in between. After a few questions, though, you will likely have enough data to begin to eliminate certain forms of understanding and explore others.
Step 3: Moving to the edge: most, least, best, worst	Because the forms of mind are cumulative, each person who is self-authored also has some piece of her that is socialized and some piece that is self-sovereign. This means that unless you help her move to the *edge* of her understanding, you cannot know whether the socialized part you are seeing represents her greatest level of complexity.
Step 4: Ask the same question in a new way to go deeper	People tend to answer questions believing that they are being asked for more story. Generally it is the second or third of the moving-to-the-edge kinds of questions that actually moves away from story and into the meaning-making space.

This level of questioning shows the interviewer the limits of the participants' understanding (because no one perspective is unlimited). In addition to showing these limitations to the interviewer, however, over the course of the SOI those limitations can also be quite apparent to the interviewee as well. Consider this participant's response to a question:

> None of these words [of mine] are really capturing it. I just need to spend
> one quiet minute (pause). It's a sense of not having words that can ade-
> quately, can express—and I'm feeling it right now, that it's okay to be dis-
> oriented. It's not necessarily comfortable but it's different from the
> discomfort of something wrong. It's the discomfort that says something is
> disoriented, therefore I lack words.

Here, as in many SOIs, the participant not only bumps up against the edges
of his sense-making, but sees that he has done that in his own experience of
disorientation and not having words. (For more on this entire process, see
Lahey et al., 1988).

Contribution to Self-Authorship

In the past, SOIs were all conducted for research purposes and were not
specifically intended to be helpful, even though they were often experienced
as helpful by the research participants. Many, like Bryce whose story begins
this chapter, find the edges of their own thinking interesting, and like exploring this uncharted territory (for different perspectives on this, see Berger,
2004). Following their own meaning-making all the way to its edges gave
participants a sense of their own limits, a sense of questions they were not
asking or connections they were not making. We have long known that good
questions and good listening would help someone take stock of his life in a
new way (Rogers, 1951), but as I conducted more and more SOIs, I began
to wonder whether helping participants understand their own complexity of
mind could be useful for not just naming adult development but supporting
it. I wondered whether showing people a picture of their own meaning-
making system might open new doors for their development and help them
get unstuck.

The world contains many mysterious things, and once we can actually
see them, we can begin to understand them and then perhaps even to change
them. The X-ray of his clogged arteries was enough to make a friend quit
smoking, exercise regularly, and reduce the fat in his diet, even though he had
known for 20 years that he should do this. I hypothesized that perhaps a picture of a person's meaning-making could be a powerful thing, and if that picture were combined with strategies she might try in order to expand the
edges of her meaning-making, this picture could become a map toward a new

way of seeing the world. Knowing the importance of the adult developmental journey—especially toward self-authorship (Baxter Magolda, 2001)—I wondered whether people would find it easier to forge their own path if they had a kind of permission and guide from this theory. Similarly, I wondered what more I might learn about the development to self-authorship and beyond as I helped people see their own sense-making. To explore these possibilities, I, along with a growing number of colleagues[3], have been using and researching these ideas for the past five years.

Discoveries

I now regularly use the SOI both as a research tool (particularly to develop my understanding about the developmental implications of some process or program) and a tool for promoting growth (particularly to develop someone else's understanding about the possibilities and implications for their own development). I have found that, although those two categories blend into the overall discoveries and learning I have about development in general, in this section I will comment on the discoveries I have made in both these categories.

SOI as a Research Tool   The first time I sat down with a research participant to do an SOI, I worried that the person would be uncomfortable with the depth of my probing, that I would be making a potentially anxious time (being in a research study) even more anxious. I found, though, that the SOI was able to build rapport in a way that even a regular semistructured qualitative interview cannot. Rather than going down a list of questions that I as the researcher cared about, the SOI method meant that I followed the participant down the path that the participant cared the most about. Instead of saying, "Come, follow me toward what I'm interested in discovering," (which is the implicit task for interviewees in most studies), I was saying, "Hey, I'll follow you carefully down any path you choose." This difference meant that we built rapport much more quickly, and people became comfortable and settled into the interview space easily. An SOI begins to feel more like a

---

[3] This group began with Dr. Paul Atkins and Dr. Keith Johnston and now includes many of my partners at Kenning Associates (Carolyn Coughlin, Mark Ledden, and Daryl Ogden), as well as close colleagues like Jane Gray, all of whom have contributed to the thinking in this chapter.

conversation between the participant and himself as the probing deepens, and that experience was helpful for setting us up to explore the other content topics the research was about.[4]

Similarly, because the SOI is so much about the journey of the participant, participants tend to really enjoy the experience. I began to notice a trend at the end of interviews: the interviewees would laughingly suggest that they could come back for another interview like this shortly. In my research, I rarely have funding to give something materially back to the participants to thank them for their investment of time and thought; with an SOI, the interviewees seemed quite pleased with the return on their investment.

It is not just participants who come to love the experience of the SOI, though. I have found that for me as an interviewer, the SOI is an exercise of suspending my judgment or my attempt to be helpful in order to fully understand meaning made by the person sitting across from me. This quest to understand fully—in the absence of wanting to change or correct in some way—not only deepens my theoretical understanding of development, but it often creates a deep kind of affection and resonance with the participant. When I teach about the SOI, I have novice interviewers try out their interviewing skills in a kind of fishbowl interview while the rest of the room observes closely. When any one person in the group finds a way toward the structure of the interviewee's thinking, it is common for the whole group to become electric as a current of deep understanding and regard spreads through the room. People report that the practice helps them develop new listening skills, greater empathy for others, and a deeper form of compassion.

Finally, I found that in a longitudinal study, people often report at the second SOI that the conversation we had at the first SOI changed the way they were thinking about things in their lives and what they noticed in the time after the interview (Berger & Hammerman, 2004). For example, one participant at the second interview mentioned that she had finally left a difficult relationship because, as she talked about it with me, she discovered that it had not been healthy in a long time, but that she had been just averting her mind from the entire question of whether it was the right relationship for her or not. Another participant had realized that she was pursuing goals to

---

[4] Some researchers try to cover content inside the SOI—by having the interview itself focus on the content of their study so that they do not have to do two different interviews. This is a legitimate idea and it also makes the SOI—never an easy proposition—exponentially harder.

gain status without actually thinking about whether she cared about achieving them for her own reasons. At our second interview, she had been spending lots of time in self-examination and thus had a well-considered response to what she was doing and why.

SOI as a Development Tool   It was obviously this combination of experiences as a researcher using the SOI that led me to think that perhaps the SOI would be not just a tool for research but also a tool to help people develop. I have always understood that the SOI is not designed to be a helping interview or a therapeutic intervention. In fact, Lahey et al. (1988), in the *Guide to the Administration and Scoring of the Subject-Object Interview*, remind us:

> We are not trying to *alter* anything, or facilitate a process *for altering* anything about the interviewee. We are not trying to alter thinking, feeling, or behavior; we are not trying to teach, change, help, advise, invite someone to rethink something, to learn the reason for his or her ineffectiveness, to settle their puzzlement, or to try on a new way to frame something. Interviewees often do feel they have learned something from the process, but this is neither our intent nor our agreement to promote. (p 305, emphasis in original)

And yet, I had learned how useful some people found the interview even when utility was clearly not the goal. In fact, I had come to believe that perhaps it was *because* I was not seeking to be helpful—but simply to understand—that people experienced the interview as so unusual. I had also been using adult developmental theories in the background of my work in leadership development programs and leadership coaching. I wondered what it would be like to use the SOI—or something like it—explicitly with clients.

First, I altered the protocol in small but important ways. Rather than trying to determine the highest sustained demonstrated score, as I needed to for research purposes, I decided that the most helpful information for a person to know about himself would be both the *range* of scores he demonstrated over the course of the interview, and what I saw as the *center of gravity* of his sense-making. I also changed my orientation to the structure/content distinction. In this case, as someone trying to help find areas that might be useful developmentally, I decided it was not enough to simply understand the structure; I needed also to understand the way the structure was held by this person and the content areas where I could see some developmental patterns cohering over time. Although structure is still at the forefront of the interview process, paying attention to the content as well means that I find out both about the meaning-making of the person in question and also about the topics and relationships and stories about which the meaning was made. I renamed this interview the GrowthEdge interview to track and highlight the differences between it and an SOI.

Then, with my colleague Paul Atkins, I developed a report that sought to both introduce a client to the theory in general and also to offer a picture of my analysis of his interview. We designed this report to include both generic information about the theory and what it looks like and also a series of excerpts from the interview with our analysis, which helped both bring the theory into reality and also make object the different forms of mind participants were using. Then Paul and I conducted a small action research study to see, in a systematic way, how people responded to this experience (Berger & Atkins, in press). Most found the exercise either somewhat or very helpful. Some, like Jan whose story begins this chapter, found it was the missing piece to a long unsolved puzzle. I found that my initial hypothesis was right: learning about your own sense-making is powerfully developmental.

From our research then, and my practice since, I have learned new things both about the developmental theory I am attempting to use, and also the process of development in general. I have made new discoveries about the dynamics of development and about the motivation for development. I discuss these in the following paragraphs.

Developmental Dynamics Analyzing the interviews differently— looking for ranges and centers of gravity—meant that I began to see developmental patterns that were hidden to me before. Take an interview with Shirley, for example, who saw the world mostly through a self-authored form of mind. Theoretically, and when using an SOI for research purposes, I would try to decide exactly where Shirley was in her thinking. Right around the self-authored space are three related but distinct forms of mind. The mission of a research SOI is to see which one was strongest for Shirley. If Shirley were *nearly*, but not quite, in the self-authored space, she might seem a little too purposeful about protecting her boundaries and about holding tight to who she is and how she makes sense of the world (in order to not fall back into a more socialized space she has just left, where she was made up at least in part by the decisions and ideas of others). If Shirley were *fully* in the self-authored space, the boundaries between her and others would be just a part of the way the world works; they would take no energy to maintain and would not be something she would think or talk much about. If Shirley were moving just *beyond* the self-authored space, she would be discovering that those boundaries are artificially constructed and limiting; her identity would be strong enough for her to let down some of the boundaries between herself and others, and she would begin to talk about the limits of her own way of looking at the world and the need to reincorporate other views and ideas into her own.

Using the GrowthEdge Interview protocol means that instead of choosing between these choices for research purposes, I work to understand the *dynamics* of the way these spaces play against each other. I have found that these three distinct forms of mind are sometimes all present simultaneously, which can catch people in a cycle that is confusing to themselves and others. In this dynamic space around the self-authored form of mind, people can be both pushing to close down their boundaries and also to open them up. Their trailing edges toward the socialized mind can lead them toward defending their boundaries with others and appearing as closed at times to other opinions and perspectives. Their leading edges toward the self-transforming mind can lead them toward loosening their boundaries and appearing as very open. Sometimes they express these distinct ways with different sets of people in their lives (as they are defended at work and opening with friends, for example) but sometimes they express these distinct ways with the same group at different times. In either case, this can be confusing to both the person and also those around him. When I name this as a possible area of conflict for those I work with, I get smiles—sometimes even tears—of relief. Having me spell out and make logical a contradiction this person has been struggling with often opens up a pathway to a sense-making system that feels more coherent—or at least more understandable.

Developmental Motivation and Threat I have never been an unquestioning supporter of development, prodding us all on to develop as much and as far as we can (with prizes for developmental achievements along the way). I am fully aware that a change in sense-making, although a monumental achievement in some respects, comes with a fairly monumental cost. To reach toward a new way of seeing the world means first giving up your old way of seeing the world, understanding that what used to feel complete and fulfilling now feels partial and lacking. This has been highlighted by my conversations with people inside these particular transitional spaces. One very articulate participant, as she considered the move beyond her current understanding (a self-authored form of mind), said:

> It's as if the world was flat and now, peering off the edge, I see that it's round, and I fear that if I step off into the round part, I'll look back and the flat part I know so well will be round too. And I'm afraid that if I turn around, I'll find that there's nothing left that I understand the way I used to know it. It just changes everything—nothing remains the same, and I'll be at the beginning of my knowing.

This reorganization of who she was and everything she knew before is a powerful and terrifying prospect. Also not to be ignored are the real threats to existing relationships when one person grows. Development is not like moving on an escalator, where we all move in the same direction and at the same rate. Development happens in fits and starts, and it happens for some people at one time and others at another time; the odds are slim that you will move at the same rate and pace as important others in your life. This means that development can create big and terrifying changes in not only how we know ourselves but also how we know others and how they come to know us.

Given these major costs of development, it is still my experience that those who are introduced to a developmental trajectory—especially once they see themselves placed into it in this way—tend to want to move forward. This is even true for those who are in a settled self-authored space. On many occasions, I have talked with a person who is making sense in a solidly self-authored way and I have sketched out the major benefits of her self-authored form of mind for her particular leadership role. In the course of my description, I have touched on the self-transforming way of being as a way for her to see what could be next, but I have reiterated that her sense-making is a good fit for her current position, and I cannot offer an argument for any advantage in her growing. Hearing about a potential growth space, however, helps her imagine ways that her sense-making does limit her effectiveness, and most of the fully self-authored leaders to whom I have talked will say something like, *Ah, now that I know there is this next place to grow to, I want to work toward that!* In this way, I can see that even hearing about development in some ways can put your current way of making sense at risk. (Put another way, learning about development can, in itself, be developmental.)

Supporting the Development to Self-Authorship—and Beyond

The work I do is mainly inside organizations, and the people I work with are mostly leaders. From both my research and my practice, I have learned that leadership roles make strong demands on people's sense-making. I have found that these demands call strongly on the individuals inside those roles to be self-authored. Because so much of leadership demands self-authored capacities, those who are socialized (or, much more rarely, self-sovereign) can find real pain in the leadership space. As leaders are called on to create a vision, mediate conflicts, hold the good of both individuals and the organization in their minds simultaneously, those without self-authored capacities can feel insignificant, overwhelmed, and, as Kegan (1994) puts it, in over their heads. Leaders who have not yet consolidated their self-authored capacities can, like Jan whose story begins this chapter, find that no measure of intelligence or hard work can make up for the frustrations of feeling their way of making sense of the world inadequate to the task. To make things worse, these struggling leaders tend not to have a way of making sense of their felt inadequacies, substituting psychological ideas that come more easily—if more harmfully—to mind. They may believe that they are simply insecure, or unimaginative, or not powerful enough. Each of these enduring traits fails to suggest the possibility of moving out from this place and into another place, of growing from a space where you do not know that it is possible to author your life to a space where authoring your life is a common and obvious task. Our common images of development in children—which help us not to despair at the early days when the toddler knows what she wants but cannot express herself—teach us to be patient and thoughtful with those who are growing and know that in time, this stage will be over. Without a corresponding theory of adult development, it is harder to be patient and thoughtful with ourselves.

Similarly, it is harder for organizations to support leaders at different developmental places. Leaders with a socialized form of mind seem to be pushed—sometimes ruthlessly—to grow beyond themselves. Organizations tend to know that they want leaders who act in more self-authored ways, even if they do not have a theory that explains the suite of characteristics that they want[5]. They look for leaders who can name their own direction, separate themselves from the opinions of others, and follow the nuance of the rules instead of just the letter of the law. To get these leaders, organizations will arrange training, hire coaches, and take performance review measures to push people into the self-authored space. A key problem with this is that organizations do not tend to have developmental theories to support their desire to see different behaviors. This means that the solutions they choose are fairly random—a training program here to deal with decision making, a coach to support more executive presence—and the solutions can be as often disheartening as helpful. This is not to say that training programs or coaching in executive presence might not also support the development of the leader in question. These things might do that—or they might not. It is that without a theory of development in place, the organizations often try to fix the symptoms without ever even noticing the root cause of the issue.

It is an irony of leadership that just as organizations do not seem to be able to support and nourish leaders with a socialized mind, they do not seem well placed to nourish and support leaders with a self-transforming mind, either. Instead, the roles seem to stay the same even as the leader himself is growing. In nearly every case, I find that leaders who have begun their journey to the self-transforming mind have also begun their journey out of organizations. They become consultants, volunteer for causes about which they are passionate, try to help from the outside rather than from the inside. Because so many organizations are claiming a desire for leaders to deal more effectively with paradox, complexity, and ambiguity, it would seem that leaders with these self-transforming minds might be a prime resource for the organizations to learn how to retain. Sometimes we need leaders who can

---

[5] This is not to suggest that organizations are uniform in their desires, however. Organizations and individual leaders can also want followers among their staff and middle managers, often looking to socialize staff within a coherent organizational culture. Most confusingly, often organizations want their leaders who are both self-authored in particular ways and also unquestioning followers of particular aspects of organizational culture in other ways. No wonder we're all so confused!

help us to resolve contradictions and at other times we need those who can help us see them and hold them. Great leaders can see these different contexts and make choices about how to act. Often, however, the clamor from commentators and around the management table is for the greater clarity, the clear direction or decisions, the simpler vision that is harder for those with a self-transforming form of mind. One key benefit to a growing understanding of developmental theory could be to make organizations—and individuals—more supportive of leaders with both socialized and self-transforming minds.

Challenges to the Use of the SOI

This chapter does not seek to make a claim that the SOI is the pinnacle of developmental tools or measures. Choosing this as a methodology for a research study or an intervention for your personal development is highly dependent on exactly who you are and what you want to learn. The SOI has several limitations that make it one of the least straightforward of all developmental measures.

First, the SOI is very expensive to use. It requires a highly trained interviewer to collect the data, a highly trained scorer to make sense of a transcription of the interview, and, in those cases where someone is going to get feedback, a highly trained coach and developmentalist to interpret the data. This training begins with a three-day workshop and continues for some people six months or more. The initial weeks sometimes seem designed just let you know what you do not know about meaning-making! The path toward being a reliable interviewer and scorer is fascinating but also enormously difficult and complex.

This means that interviewer skill is a key ingredient in the quality of the data. That is true in most qualitative interviewing situations, but because the SOI does not have a real protocol so much as it has a way of thinking about the questions to be asked, it is even more true in an SOI.

Second, the SOI is a verbal measure that makes use of words on a page rather than either the full-spread of a conversation (with body language, voice tone, etc.). Whereas the interviewer might have access to tone, body language, and other cues, the person who scores the interview (who may or may not be the interviewer, depending on the study design), will have only a transcript to read. This means that the SOI ignores a variety of important meaning cues in its reliance on the spoken word.

Finally, the SOI is a measure of one small slice of what it means to be human—and it only looks at 60 to 90 minutes of that slice. It measures the expressed form of mind of the *interview,* which is often but not always generalizable to the form of mind of the *interviewee.* It matters to always have this as a context for the work you are doing. If there is anything developmental theories help us understand, it is that meaning is made and remade, that making meaning is the prime activity of humanity. We can get closer and closer and closer to understanding one another (and our-selves), but we will never arrive (if you are not convinced of this, see Wilson, 2002). As long as we keep in mind the notion that every theory is a flawed theory, that no theory describes the broad range of human exis-tence, we will be fine. As soon as we forget that we are using a theory and believe that we might have some access to something like The Truth, we have lost our way.

Conclusion

We saw at the beginning of this chapter that Bryce and Jan were each helped in their own way as they caught a glimpse into their own sense-making system and made decisions about what to do with that insight. For the past dozen years, as I have sat with people who have been having these insights, I have been honored to share in many of these sorts of experiences. There are two major lessons for me in this. The first is that being on the edge of our sense-making can be transformative, and a tool like the SOI or the GrowthEdge Interview can support someone to stand at the edge of his sense-making and look out over the uncharted terrain of the future. The second major lesson is that being present with someone at the edge of her sense-making is nearly as powerful and helpful for the interviewer as it is for the participant. By being company for someone at the edge, I am able to both observe her process and also learn from the ways she is similar to and different from others who have been in a similar developmental place. I deepen my theoretical and practical knowledge each time I stand with someone at this edge.

The SOI is still in its early days as a developmental measure: 20 years old in 2008. Using SOI-like interviews as interventions is newer still. In order to deepen our understanding of development, we must keep conduct-ing research studies; in order to make our understanding more complex, we must share those studies with one another. Grasping the fullness of human sense-making and development is a task too great for any of us alone, too complex and multifaceted for any single brain. Our brains—and our hearts—must work together to deepen our understanding of the individual patterns of growth and how to support these patterns, because it is in this understanding that we can find new measures of respect, compassion, and even love for one another.

References

Baxter Magolda, M. B. (1992). *Knowing and reasoning in college: Gender-related patterns in students' intellectual development.* San Francisco: Jossey-Bass.

Baxter Magolda, M. B. (2001). *Making their own way: Narratives for transforming higher education to promote self-development.* Sterling, VA: Stylus.

Baxter Magolda, M. B. & King, P. M. (2004*). Learning partnerships: Theory and models of practice to educate for self-authorship.* Sterling, VA: Stylus.

Berger, J. G. (2004). Dancing on the threshold of meaning: Recognizing and understanding the growing edge. *Journal of Transformative Education 2*: 336–351.

Berger, J. G., & Atkins, P. (in press). Mapping complexity of mind: Using the Subject-Object Interview in coaching. *Coaching: An International Journal of Theory, Research and Practice.*

Berger, J. G. & Hammerman, J. K. (2004). *Understanding teacher change through an adult developmental lens.* Paper presented at the Annual Meeting of the American Educational Research Association Conference, San Diego, CA.

Cook-Greuter, S. R. (2004). Making the case for a developmental perspective. *Industrial and Commercial Training, 36*(6/7), 275.

Fischer, K. W., Yan, Z., & Stewart, J. B. (2002). Adult cognitive development: Dynamics in the development web. In J. Valsiner & K. Connolly (Eds.), *Handbook of developmental psychology* (pp. 491–516). Thousand Oaks, CA: Sage.

Kegan, R. (1982). *The evolving self.* Cambridge, MA: Harvard University Press.

Kegan, R. (1994). *In over our heads: The mental demands of modern life.* Cambridge, MA: Harvard University Press.

King, P. M., & Kitchener, K. S. (2004). Reflective judgment: Theory and research on the development of epistemic assumptions through adulthood. *Educational Psychologist, 39*(1), 5–18.

Lahey, L., Souvaine, E., Kegan, R., Goodman, R., & Felix, S. (1988). *A guide to the Subject-Object Interview: Its administration and interpretation.* Cambridge, MA: Harvard Graduate School of Education.

Rogers, C. R. (1951). *Client-centered therapy: Its current practice, implications, and theory.* Boston: Houghton Mifflin.

Torbert, W., Cook-Greuter, S. R., Fisher, D., Foldy, E., Gauthier, A., Keeley, J. et al. (2004). *Action inquiry: The secret of timely and transforming leadership.* San Francisco: Berrett-Koehler Publishers.

Wilson, Timothy D. (2002). *Strangers to ourselves: discovering the adaptive unconscious.* Cambridge, MA: Belknap Press of Harvard University Press.

PART FOUR

FUTURE DIRECTIONS

Marcia B. Baxter Magolda

Collectively, the authors in this volume have explored: (1) the nuances of self-authorship as a part of the self-evolution process, (2) multicultural perspectives on this concept based on a wide range of research and scholarship, and (3) numerous theoretical and methodological challenges in understanding and assessing self-authorship. In part 4, I synthesize our collective dialogue, highlighting the intersections among the chapter authors' insights about the theoretical and methodological challenges inherent in studying human development across cultures. Chapter 15 also incorporates Robert Kegan's perspectives on these issues, which we gathered through a videoconference prior to the RIVA conference. This synthesis is intended to spark further dialogue and research on the concept of self-authorship.

15

FUTURE DIRECTIONS
Pursuing Theoretical and Methodological Issues in the Evolution of Self-Authorship

Marcia B. Baxter Magolda

Abstract: This chapter synthesizes theoretical and methodological issues identified at the conference and in this volume. Robert Kegan's perspectives, gathered in a video-conference prior to the RIVA conference, are integrated into the discussion to extend the dialogue. Future directions to pursue these issues are woven throughout the chapter.

We structured the working conference *Self-Authorship Theory Development and Assessment Across the Lifespan and Across Cultures* to enable in-depth dialogue among scholars whose work reflected multiple cultural perspectives. This volume is an opportunity to share that dialogue with a wider audience and invite further exploration of the concept of self-authorship. As Boes et al. noted in Chapter 1, the concept of self-authorship that was the impetus for the conference and this book is grounded in the constructivist-developmental tradition. Robert Kegan (1994) coined the term self-authorship to convey a phase in the evolution of meaning-making in which the internal capacity to generate and manage one's beliefs, identity, and social relations emerged. In sketching out his theory of self-evolution, Kegan (1982) brought into conversation two longstanding lines of thought—psychoanalysis and constructive-developmental psychology. In doing so, he attempted to address the tensions between the psychological and the social and between emotion and thought by studying the evolution of meaning-making activity. He portrayed the growth of the mind as a series of organizing principles that integrate emotional, cognitive, intrapersonal, and interpersonal dimensions of development. In this volume we brought together research on these developmental dimensions to inform our understanding of holistic development.

Integrating the psychological and social, Kegan also emphasized the role of contemporary culture in shaping our developmental capacities. His notion that we make meaning in the space between our experiences and our reactions to them (see Chapter 1, this volume) honors the dual influence of culture and personal development in the evolution of meaning-making. The role of culture in the evolution of self-authorship is one of the major theoretical questions explored in this volume.

This chapter offers future directions for theorizing and research based on a synthesis of major theoretical and methodological issues emerging from earlier chapters. Its intent is to continue the spirit of dialogue that Kegan proposed, which was the impetus for and focus of the conference.

Theoretical Questions

The Role of Culture in the Evolution of Self-Authoring

A pressing theoretical question posed in numerous chapters involves the degree to which self-authorship reflects an independent, autonomous stance versus an interdependent, relational stance. Weinstock (Chapter 7) notes that collectivist cultures may give people less epistemic authority than individualist cultures do, thus prompting differences in evolution and endpoints of meaning-making. Similarly, Hofer (Chapter 8) raises the question of whether self-authoring is an agentic concept focused on the individual rather than a communal concept more typical in collectivist cultures. Pizzolato (Chapter 11) explores the notion of the Asian selfway, centered in the collectivist culture, as interdependent and relational in comparison with the Western focus on the autonomous self.

Knowing this issue would be prominent in the conference dialogue, Lisa Boes and I sought Kegan's perspective on the issue in our videoconference prior to the conference.[1] He offered these thoughts:

> In-depth exploration of these ideas leads away from stereotypical notions of
> what self-authorship is about. When I re-read my first book *The Evolving*

---

[1] Because Dr. Kegan was unable to attend our conference, he graciously participated in a two-hour videoconference with Lisa Boes and Marcia Baxter Magolda in April 2008 to share his perspectives. We used that video in the opening session of the conference. His comments in this chapter are drawn from that conversation.

Self, I can see how I conflated issues of style—e.g., "connected" vs. "separated" styles—that come out of feminist psychology; or "introversion" vs. "extraversion"—from Myers Briggs—how I conflated these kinds of distinctions, which might be more of a personality trait, a cross-stage phenomenon that persists over long periods of one's life, with distinctions between epistemological structures. The difference between the Socialized Mind and the Self-Authoring Mind is *not* the same thing as the difference between the connected voice and the separate voice. If I were to critique my own work, you can see the same evolution of theory as you see in the evolution of the individual: increasing differentiation and integration; disentangling things that were fused. If you look at the *Evolving Self,* these more stylistic issues are conflated (e.g., if you are "three-ish" you are more connected, if you are more self-authoring, you're more separate). Feminist psychologies contributed to my and others getting clear that these are two different categories. That means that it is possible to go through all the constructive-developmental stages in a connected way or a separate way. It is possible to have a very connected orientation in self-authoring; it is also possible to have a very bounded, separate orientation in the socializing mind. Even though that kind of boundedness is still going to be authored by the important contexts, relationships or idea communities one is living in. That makes much richer the concept of self-authoring as it shows different ways of being self-authoring.

To explore this notion further, we shared the stories of Jane and Dawn that appear in Chapter 1. We wanted to hear Kegan's thinking on these because Jane's concern focused on sharing her college life and boyfriend with her Asian parents, and Dawn's story involved going against the mainstream by acknowledging her gay sexual orientation. Comparing the two stories, and referring to Dawn's statement that it did not matter that others knew she was gay, Kegan offered:

> Probably, the fact that you might disagree with it not only doesn't matter but it also doesn't necessarily create the threat of disconnection, or the idea that we can't still be connected and close *for having this difference.* Whereas for the first person, Jane, the very fact that I know I am acting in certain ways, having certain beliefs, falling in love with a certain kind of guy who you as my mother would not approve of, already creates a problem where I am living in a kind of guilt, out of "alignment with," out of "good faith with". . . . The nature of our connection is really ruptured whether I let you

in on it or whether I keep it private to myself. That big decision, "Do I tell my parents or not?" actually has no bearing in the sense that, "Do I tell her we're not connected, or do I keep it secret?" In either case, I'm still not connected. Whereas, you get the feeling that for Dawn, that she can hold that view, she can be aware that it may not align with yours, but that doesn't mean that the two of us can't be connected because the nature of the connection isn't predicated on our having the same view. Both young women are very oriented to interpersonal connection, but in very different ways that are arguably a function of their developmental position not their "voice."

This analysis raises the possibility that one could be more closely connected from a self-authoring or fourth-order perspective than from a socialized or third-order perspective. Jane's connection to her parents is ruptured by her new feelings even though she has yet to share them with them. Dawn's connection to others is not ruptured because she does not hold agreement or approval as a criterion for being connected.

Further exploring how people construct experience and meaning-making in a cultural context, Kegan elaborated on the connection between culture and self-authoring:

First we have to grant that culture is powerful; the ways one ought to behave are powerfully communicated through culture. So now your question is: If someone does grow up in this more connection-oriented culture is that a barrier to the evolution to self-authoring? I can imagine situations in which it can create a steeper gradient or a bigger barrier in moving toward self-authoring. I can also imagine contexts in which the orientation to connection is just as strong, but there is still a support to your figuring out what your own way of being connected is. . . . A person did a dissertation here on the Chinese norm of "filial piety". The idea that adult children in their thirties, forties, fifties, sixties, if their parents are still alive, should continue to orbit around the sun of their parents. How might it be possible where that norm is so strongly adhered to for people to become more self-authoring? The dissertation writer only talked with people who practiced the norm of filial piety and he still found lots of self-authoring people who felt they were faithful upholders of the norm. But the way they did it was to protect their parents from their differences, to not "put it in their face," to not tell parents ways in which they departed from beliefs their parents held most dear. They kept the feelings and sensitivities of their parents in mind, but this did not forestall their developing ways of living, believing and acting that run contrary to their parents. Very interesting. Very different from continuing to be shaped by their parents.

We inquired whether this reflected their making conscious choices about how to connect in those relationships based on their heightened sensitivity to how their parents felt. Kegan responded:

> Exactly. I often say to my class—if they get this notion that if you become more self-authoring you'll find relationships less important—that's not what this is about. Let's think about a different distinction. Imagine two people for whom relationships are equally central and predominating in their interests and investments. But with one person, they are entering relationships and following them according to some set of expectations or code that is not of their own creation—either what this person they love, and whom they want to keep loving them, tells them they need to do in order to keep the relationship, or some set of ideas about how relationships should go that they have internalized. In contrast to another person to whom relationships are just as central, but she has authored or created a set of norms and beliefs and notions about how she wants her relationships to go. She selects relationships and makes decisions about whether to take them deeper or whether they are less than she wants them to be *on the basis of her own code* she has developed about relationships. They are both equally connected to the centrality of relationships but in a very different way.

As evident in these comments, Kegan takes the perspective that separation and connection are stylistic dynamics that can be equally prevalent in socialized and self-authoring structures. His discussion of this issue in Chapter 6 of *In Over Our Heads* (1994) includes examples of socializing and self-authoring persons who are both connected and separate.

Zaytoun (Chapter 9) extends the theoretical discussion of individuation and connection by defending and strengthening accounts of the multiplicitous, relational self. Although her agenda is to explore Kegan's fifth order, or the self-transformation that comes from taking self-authorship as object, and its relationship to social consciousness, her linkage of cognitive-structural development with feminist phenomenological approaches, feminist postcolonial approaches, and phenomenological and poststructural philosophical claims raises the possibility that individuation (or autonomy) and connection (or relationship) can be intertwined prior to self-transformation. Advocating continued exploration of the notion of a pattern of differentiation and integration in the evolution of self-consciousness, Zaytoun emphasizes that differentiation means distinguishing ourselves from something with which we were fused in order to reconnect to it in a more complex way. This making of something that was subject into object involves becoming aware of it in order to reflect on it. Zaytoun's explorations of various perspectives on the self raise the possibility that differentiation and integration are distinct from individuation and autonomy. For example, Brison's relational self is simultaneously autonomous and socially dependent. Brison defines autonomy as "relational, or interdependent with others" (Zaytoun, p. 157). Similarly, Anzaldúa's emphasis on negotiating between the inner self and public acts links the self to interrelatedness. These perspectives suggest that autonomy and connection are not mutually exclusive. Zaytoun thus defends "a reflective, inner sense of self or continuity that, although highly interdependent on other beings and its environment, has distinct functions and potentials in the creation of highly functional relationships, communities, and social harmony" (p. 159). Considering autonomy and relationships as intertwined enables viewing self-authorship as deepening the connection to others beyond its form in the socializing mind, as Kegan argued in contrasting Jane and Dawn's narratives. Taking self-authorship as object then further depends on connection to others. Zaytoun's compelling account of these links, which cut across numerous cultural contexts, suggests that the ability to take self-authorship as object heightens the complexity of one's interdependence with others.

These perspectives raise important questions about whether autonomy and connection can be intertwined in the process of differentiation and integration, whether connection and separation are meaning-making structures or stylistic preferences, how self and relationships are constructed in collectivist and individualistic cultures, and how the evolution of meaning-making varies across culture. Because Kegan argued that we develop meaning-making capacities in the context of what culture demands of us, it is quite likely that evolution varies across cultural context. Research specifically focused on these questions would further our understanding of the concept of self-authorship.

Making Culture and Context the Object of Reflection

Numerous chapters raise the question of when it becomes possible for individuals to make culture and other elements of their context the object of reflection. Torres (Chapter 4) reported that Latino/a students in her study began to reflect on negative stereotypes and their interpretation during the crossroads. Being able to consider racism as object allowed them to reject negative stereotypes. Zaytoun's (Chapter 9) discussion of Anzaldúa's *conocimiento* and Kegan's fifth order offers another view of holding one's self, culture, and context as object. Zaytoun argues that doing so yields the "ability to hold self-authorship, self-formation as object, and to hold as subject the contradictions and conflicts within the self and its relationships to others" (p. 160). Kegan's reaction to Jane's story about hesitating to tell her parents about her boyfriend also addresses this issue:

> She says a terrific thing. You can see structural evolution speaking itself when she says, "Ideally, I would want to integrate the two." She says, "When I go home it's hard enough not putting people in cubby holes and being like, so this is my Cambridge life and this is my home life." And then she says, "Ideally, you know, I want to integrate the two." It's almost like she's naming this really wonderful (she probably doesn't experience it at the moment as wonderful, but I mean from a developmentalist's point of view) this sort of wonderful, perfect kind of problem that she recognizes. This is almost a classic problem that tends to precipitate the move toward self-authoring. Using the same way you've been constructing the self, if you move into worlds where the values that are being communicated, the set of affections and loyalties that you bring yourself to are going to be different than those from the reference group that you came, typically your family, then it sort of shows you how this same basic logic—self logic—gets undone by the diversity of [your worlds] . . . just what people kind of hope for from college. But as long as you're moving back and forth between them it starts to become a problem, and that starts to create a disjunction, and it is important to see this is not just about the life-phase of "leaving the family." It's actually about gradually leaving a way of constituting the world—a way of constituting the self—that is now becoming troubled in some way. She is leaving her old self as much as she is leaving her family. She is in the process of building a new relationship to her self, just as much as she is in the process of building a new relationship to her family. For her to raise this

issue that "I want to integrate the two," she's speaking the premises of what developmental theory would suggest. That part of her that wants to "integrate the two" is her developmental leading edge. As that part comes to feel more and more like who she is then these competing worlds of value, will increasingly, so to speak, become object and then they'll become the material the new self uses and shapes, rather than that which shapes the self. This is what it means to be self-authoring.

Jane's recognition of the distinctions between her [college] context and her home culture help her take these as object (e.g., differentiation). This enables her to begin reflecting on them to figure out how to integrate them in a more complex way of operating in the world. She does not need or want to leave her family; rather she is leaving the way of constituting herself that originated in the family culture. The ability to take these as object and rebuild a new way of making meaning requires substantial support, as Kegan describes:

> What are some of the hand-holds, or the supports that are facilitating this new move that she's in the midst of? You can see both a kind of cognitive one and an interpersonal one. The cognitive one might be this idea of social class; it gives you a balcony to stand on so to speak, where you look now on the nature of these expectations in this case, that your parents have. "We sent you off to these Ivy League schools so you'll meet other rich and privileged kids and that's who we want you to marry . . ." or something like this from the parents, to put it crudely. But she now has a position to actually look at her parents' expectations and when she's dwelling completely within them you can see she has these guilt feelings for not fulfilling them or satisfying them. But the category of social class gives her a position to stand apart from these expectations and begin to think about them, interrogate them. That's more the move toward self-authoring. She has a similar kind of hand-hold or kind of support or scaffold that is helping in her friend who is giving her the voice and the permission and making normal this whole circumstance that you will have to someday make decisions that might not completely please your parents and the quote "what every kid goes through." So that's kind of perfect because perhaps she can relate to that in her more third order socializing way, and as she aligns herself with that it enables her to make that kind of move, and "it's an okay thing for me to do so long as I'm thinking about doing it in the context of my relationship with you my good friend, who's saying it's a normal thing for me to do." See even the way she says, "This is a case in point, right?" "Every

kid goes through this?" "You have to decide, right?" She keeps asking the interviewer too, "This is a normal thing for me to be doing, right?" So all of that is supporting that kind of move.

Jane's study of social class helps her take her parents' perspectives as object. Her friend helps her take the notion of disagreeing with her parents as object. Perhaps if she had models of reconstructing the relationship with her parents to include both her and her parents' perspectives, she would be less fearful that being authentic would somehow damage the relationship.

Pizzolato's discussion of Asian selfways (Chapter 11) suggests that, "In Asian cultures selfways send messages of interdependence and the value of relationships" (p. 192–193). A theoretical question worthy of pursuit is the extent to which the internal authority of self-authoring, with its capacity to coordinate external expectations, can be shaped around interdependence and authentic relationships rather than around autonomy. Kegan's earlier comment emphasizes his view that self-authorship is not simply autonomous and in contradiction with relationships, but rather a different way of construing relationships that take both parties' needs into account. The word "self" in self-authorship, as Pizzolato articulates (Chapter 11), complicates interpretation of the balance of autonomy and connection.

Asian selfways also resonate with Zaytoun's description of Kegan's fifth order and Anzaldúa's *conocimiento*, which both emphasize interdependence. Further research to examine how the meaning-making structures beyond socializing blend autonomy and connection would help us understand the degree to which self-authorship as a concept relates to collectivist cultures.

Role of Dissonance, Risk, Support, and Resilience in Development

Constructive-developmental approaches take Piaget's notion of disequilibrium as central to development. Dissonance that calls one's meaning-making structure into question is instrumental in distinguishing ourselves from that which is subject to make it object. Many theories articulate the balance of challenge and support necessary to propel development, arguing that support is crucial in helping people face the challenge of reconstructing new meaning-making structures. Meszaros and Lane's work (Chapter 5) uses the relationship between dissonance, risk, support, and resilience to raise the theoretical question of whether self-authorship is possible in adolescence. Their participants, who were from economically depressed areas and at risk for succeeding in high school, faced risks associated with both race and class. The support they received from parents and staff involved in the intervention program Meszaros and Lane describe helped them build resilience in the face of dissonance and risk. This resilience in turn contributed to the emerging self-authorship that Meszaros and Lane observed. These findings are consistent with Pizzolato's (2003) finding that some high school students who have experienced marginalization exhibit self-authorship upon entering college.

Kegan discussed the concept of dissonance, risk and resilience with us as we explored Dawn's story about coming to accept her sexual orientation (see Chapter 1):

> The other [question] in this is, "Where do these things come from?" Here you have another classic source of not just the dislodging that begins to move people out of the socialized mind but a classic situation that can be a support to coming over to the other side of this bridge and being more self-authoring. That is the experience of feeling oneself as out of the norm or that the story of your own life is no longer fitting the dominant narrative that's been presented to you in your culture. This can be a function of feeling oneself a part of some other group that is outside the mainstream. This could be in the context of ethnicity, sexual orientation, it could be one's social class. . . . Of course you can move toward self-authoring without feeling yourself a part of some group that is out of the mainstream. I don't mean that's the only way to make the move, and it can be a burden, of course, initially, to feel oneself, often through no choice of one's own, discovering the difference in one's ethnicity or sexual orientation or politics or religion or whatever it might be, one's body shape. . . . So from the third order, that can be very painful. But especially if there is a community of support, this is where identity politics and the value of ideological communities is—that can move one from feeling bad, wrong, less than, as you take a perspective on yourself from the dominant culture to finding a community of peers who value it.

These perspectives suggest that working through dissonance and risk to build resilience necessitates a network or community of supportive others, a notion that relates with Torres' (Chapter 4) Latino/a students who avoided dissonance because of lack of support, and thus stagnated in their growth. The need for a supportive community resonates with my longitudinal participants' accounts of learning partnerships that promoted their development toward self-authorship (Baxter Magolda, 2004; 2009). These perspectives also raise the good possibility that self-authoring comes from productive experience with risk rather than age. Building resilience via support from others also provides another potential link between autonomy and connection.

Pizzolato (Chapter 11) raises another aspect of the role of dissonance in promoting development. She synthesizes research that reveals that the experience of dissonance varies by culture. What constitutes dissonance varies depending on the way people make sense of themselves. For example, Asian American students felt less dissonance in being asked to make a choice that was not ideal for themselves compared with European American students. Pizzolato's insights remind us that cultural messages and the way they shape construction of the self and relationships mediate the factors that influence development.

Role of Dimensions in Development

The role of culture is also interwoven in considering how multiple developmental dimensions intertwine. One of our guiding questions at the conference was: What can be gained in refining our understanding of the evolution of self-authorship by exploring the interweaving of the three dimensions across multiple ages and cultures? Meszaros and Lane's chapter suggests an intersection among the three in adolescence as adolescents encountered dissonance (cognitive) and built resilience (intrapersonal) through support (interpersonal) to move toward self-authorship. Weinstock's (Chapter 7) observation of epistemology in Jewish and Bedouin adolescents raises the possibility that the epistemological dimension is highly influenced by culture, or the interpersonal dimension. Hofer (Chapter 8) extended this cultural role in epistemology to college students. I shared narratives (Chapter 2) about how the epistemological, intrapersonal, and interpersonal dimensions were interwoven in my longitudinal participants' experiences. For the most part, they had a dimension that was prevalent in their experience and they often used it as a lens through which to approach the other dimensions. King (Chapter 10) explores a wide range of developmental literature to raise questions about whether dimensions are equal partners in the evolution of meaning-making or whether the cognitive dimension is the strong partner. Pizzolato (Chapter 11) synthesizes numerous research findings to conceptualize how the dimensions are tightly intertwined across the evolution of meaning-making. She argues that self-authorship is the "ability to consciously control the three dimensions" (p. 200). Collectively, this work raises important questions that warrant further research, including clarification of the varying perspectives on whether cognitive or epistemological labels are best for that dimension.[2]

Our conversation with Kegan also spoke to the interrelationship of dimensions. In exploring Dawn's story about bringing herself to relationships and the struggles she encountered, he offered this commentary:

> So two ways to be thinking about becoming more fully self-authoring: One way is that I am pretty fully self-authoring in some arenas of my living— say, work—and I have put some of these other arenas on hold because to maintain my self-authoring self in those is a higher art, a more complicated demand such as intimacy or reconnecting with one's parents as the adult one has become. Some people may develop self-authoring capacity and never reconstruct relationships with their parents. In some sense you can say they are fully self-authoring but they have limited the range of their living, or they could be more self-authoring if they could bring it to another arena. This is a little like the "decalage" idea in Piaget's theory—there is some arena in which it is most easy for you to get the new structure together, then out of the comfort of that you risk applying it to other arenas—bringing along sides of yourself that haven't yet fully been reclaimed at the new, more complex order of consciousness.
>
> Another way you can think of becoming more fully self-authoring is the process of gradually exercising one's new structure from a more tentative to a more solid way of being, across all the arenas of one's living. For example there may be a time when I have to use my self-authoring capacity largely to remain self-authoring. I use it to be on my guard for those situations where I might be likely to cave in again. That's what 4(3) in the scoring system is all about. Yes the leading structure is the self-authoring structure but there is still enough of the three-ish structure around that you have to use your self-authoring structure to hold that off. There might be a little of each going on in this last excerpt. It is an indication of her becoming more self-authoring both because she can bring herself to intimate relationships and sees a way she can stay self-authoring while opening herself up to this scary, exciting possibility, and that she is able to see a way she can throw herself

---

[2] Multiple interpretations of how best to label the dimension regarding how we come to know exist throughout this book. See Chapters 1, 10, and 11 for specific explanations of the varied use of these terms.

into this, but not in a way that leaves her feeling that she is totally bereft of the capacity to observe what is going on. On each of those counts, that could be a move toward greater self-authoring. When you get into the realm of intimacy it has a lot of abandon as an aspect of it, when you get into the realm of coming to a new relationship to a serious illness and beginning to really question how much one can control, and this whole notion of going with the flow, that raises the issue of whether we are seeing something beyond self-authoring.

These comments suggest that developmental transformation may occur in a particular dimension before it occurs in another. Torres (Chapter 4) noted that her participants never "progressed more than one phase in one dimension without positive development in the other dimensions" (p. 82), leading her to concur with the synergistic relationship among the dimensions Kegan described.

Connections Among Self-Authorship and Related Concepts

Numerous chapters link the concept of self-authorship to related concepts in a wide range of literatures. Many focus on the cognitive or epistemological dimension as a pillar of self-authorship. For example, Hamer and van Rossum (Chapter 3) explore self-authorship from the vantage point of their 25-year study of Dutch students' learning conceptions, and offer their perspective on how learning and teaching conceptions relate to numerous epistemological and self-authorship theories. King (Chapter 10) links self-authorship to Reflective Judgment, Hofer (Chapter 8) draws in epistemic beliefs, Weinstock (Chapter 7) integrates Kuhn's epistemological theory, and Brownlee and colleagues (Chapter 6) focus on personal epistemology as it relates to self-authorship. These chapters contain rich connections to broader literatures that raise questions about how development might proceed if the remaining dimensions were explicitly integrated.

Other chapters introduce multiple perspectives on the self, relating to both the intrapersonal and interpersonal dimensions of development. In Chapter 9, Zaytoun explores phenomenological, postcolonial, and feminist perspectives on the self. In doing so she draws connections between autonomy and connection, and highlights contradictions in how these various perspectives view the concept of self. Pizzolato (Chapter 11) incorporates multicultural perspectives of the self, particularly from research on Asian American students, in relation to cultural context. Zaytoun (Chapter 9) and Hamer and van Rossum (Chapter 3) address movement beyond self-authorship using other literature bases to explore what forms this might take. These chapters illustrate the value of exploring related concepts for a broader understanding of self-authorship. Future research incorporating more of these perspectives would shed light on many of the theoretical questions raised in this volume.

Methodological Questions

Pursuing the theoretical questions raised in this volume is complicated by the methodological challenges in assessing a construct as complex as self-evolution. As Creamer (Chapter 12) notes, many scholars have addressed "the difficulty in assessing underlying meaning-making structures that are used across contexts and that distinguish between stages of reasoning that are recognized or articulated from those that are actually employed" (p. 221). Creamer and colleagues constructed a quantitative measure of the three dimensions of self-authorship to explore the relationship between reasoning and action in career decision making. Pizzolato has also constructed a quantitative measure (2007) but as she points out (Chapter 11), finding items that clearly distinguish self-authorship characteristics is extremely difficult. The fact that existing measures are constructed on the existing perspectives of self-authorship further complicates the question of whether cultural difference is adequately accounted for in these measures. Despite these complications, work toward creating valid yet less time- and expertise-intensive measures of self-authorship would go a long way in pursuing theoretical questions and assessing self-authorship in practice.

Pizzolato (Chapter 11) suggests that accounting for culture in qualitative approaches requires "devis[ing] interview questions that elicit participant discussion of dissonance from diverse origins" (p. 202). Acknowledging that what interviewers ask affects the responses interviewees offer, she advises careful attention to even open-ended questions. She also encourages careful follow-up questions to solicit the meaning of cultural phrases as well as coding processes that emphasize the emergence of new patterns from the data. Although qualitative methods typically approach interviewing as an open-ended process, paying particular attention to enabling multiple cultural possibilities to emerge in the data and its interpretation are crucial.

Jones (Chapter 13) takes up the issue of enabling multiple cultural possibilities via an autoethnographic approach to the study of self-authorship. Drawing on poststructural and queer theoretical approaches and using the theoretical lens of intersectionality, Jones explores the utility of autoethnography, "a unique methodological approach that utilizes narrative writing to illuminate both the individual lived experience and the larger sociocultural conditions in which these stories are nested" (p. 224). She offers a compelling argument that the complexities of identity and self-authorship require a methodology that elicits them. Her description of autoethnography as a blend of looking outward at one's social and cultural experience and looking inward at the self moving through these experiences resonates with Anzaldúa's negotiation of inner self and public acts. Jones offers a thorough analysis of the benefits and challenges of linking personal experience and sociocultural analysis and highlights new questions that arise in that process. As Jones points out, "self-authorship, like other complex phenomena, benefits from examination using multiple interpretive lenses" (p. 241). The contrast between Creamer's quantitative measure and Jones' autoethnographic approach are stark; yet both clearly contribute to exploring the theoretical questions surrounding self-evolution.

Constructive-developmental approaches to assessing self-authorship have focused on in-depth interviewing (see Baxter Magolda & King, 2007 for a summary of these approaches). Kegan and colleagues' Subject-Object Interview (Lahey, Souvaine, Kegan, Goodman, & Felix, 1988) is summarized in Berger's chapter (14) as she explores the question of how to use the interview as an intervention to promote self-authorship. Because the Subject-Object Interview (SOI) prompts the interviewee to choose the content of the conversation and explores how the person experiences that content, it engages the interviewee in a reflective exercise. Berger reports that as the interviewer explores to find the edges of the interviewee's thinking, the interviewee stands to discover new insights. Finding that participants enjoyed this interview and could gain insights from it, Berger modified the SOI to the GrowthEdge Interview in order to help participants understand the complexities of their use of multiple ways of making meaning. Thus her modified approach offers yet another way to address the individual in context and the complexities of self-evolution. Sharing her interpretation of her interviewees' sense-making with them offers them an opportunity to reflect on it and consider how to respond, bringing researcher and participant into a new relationship. Similar to Kegan's story (see Chapter 1) about his client who tended to absorb other's feelings, simply presenting another way of looking at one's own meaning-making sometimes dislodges what was subject and allows the person to reflect on it.

Researchers in the Wabash National Study of Liberal Arts Education (www.liberalarts.wabash.edu/nationalstudy) found a similar effect using their informal conversational interview. Students in the pilot study returned, asking to interview again the following year, because they found the conversation so helpful. As a result, the team constructed a reflective conversation guide on the basis of the Wabash interview (Baxter Magolda & King, 2008). I have reported this same phenomenon in my longitudinal study in which participants suggest that these reflective conversations help them make sense of their experience in new ways.

Berger's distinction between using measures for research and promoting development is useful as we consider the challenges of intensive qualitative approaches for research and their simultaneous value in practice. Qualitative approaches—whether constructive-developmental or autoethnographic—require considerable training and expertise to interpret effectively. Yet many educators are in positions to promote development without this extensive training. Using variations of these interviews to engage people in reflective conversations, as long as educators give the task of making sense of it all to the person doing the reflecting, can help people develop. Whether this takes the form of reflective journals or personal conversations, asking probing questions to enable the person to explore the edges of their own thinking can be productive even if the educator is not an expert in interpreting the reflections. Kegan and Lahey (2000) offer a good example of a reflective exercise in their book *How We Talk Can Change the Way We Work*. They offer a four-column map exercise to guide readers to consider concerns in their lives, reflect on the commitments that underlie the concerns, and the values and commitments that keep readers entrenched in current ways of operating. The map then guides readers to identify assumptions inherent in these commitments and devise plans to test them. Readers are free to engage the exercise as they choose and can benefit from exploring their development without extensive training in developmental theory. Similarly, *Authoring Your Life: Developing an Internal Voice to Navigate Life's Challenges* (Baxter Magolda, 2009) is addressed to adults in their twenties and thirties as a reflective journey to promote their development and the development of those around them.

Future Directions

Many of the contributors to this volume have outlined future theoretical and methodological research needed to further our understanding of self-evolution in general and self-authorship in particular. This chapter highlights some of the key issues as they relate to the role of culture in self-evolution and the complexities of understanding this multifaceted concept across age, experience, and culture. As Jones suggested, we must continue working on all fronts to generate effective measures from which to analyze these concepts, keeping in mind that broadening the concepts beyond our current imaginations is important. Studying the intersections of various perspectives, as many authors have done here, illustrates that ideas we have framed as mutually exclusive may not be so. Exploring the nuances of self-evolution and self-authorship in depth, as we did at the conference and through this volume, enables getting underneath the surface to see these complexities and interpret them in more nuanced ways.

We hope this volume invites you into the continuing dialogue about the nature of self-authorship and its relationship to our functioning more effectively in our world.

References

Baxter Magolda, M. B. (2004). Learning Partnerships Model: A framework for promoting self-authorship. In M. B. Baxter Magolda & P. M. King (Eds.), *Learning partnerships: Theory and models of practice to educate for self-authorship* (pp. 37–62). Sterling, VA: Stylus.

Baxter Magolda, M. B. (2009). *Authoring your life: Developing an internal voice to navigate life's challenges.* Sterling, VA: Stylus.

Baxter Magolda, M. B., & King, P. M. (2007). Interview strategies for assessing self-authorship: Constructing conversations to assess meaning making. *Journal of College Student Development, 48*(5), 491–508.

Baxter Magolda, M. B., & King, P. M. (2008). Toward reflective conversations: An advising approach that promotes self-authorship. *Peer Review 10*(1), 8–11.

Kegan, R. (1982). *The evolving self: Problem and process in human development.* Cambridge, MA: Harvard University Press.

Kegan, R. (1994). *In over our heads: The mental demands of modern life.* Cambridge, MA: Harvard University Press.

Kegan, R., & Lahey, L. L. (2000). *How the way we talk can change the way we work: Seven languages for transformation.* San Francisco: Jossey-Bass.

Lahey, L. L., Souvaine, E., Kegan, R., Goodman, R., & Felix, S. (1988). *A guide to the Subject-Object Interview: Its administration and interpretation*: Available from: Subject-Object Research Group, 201 Nichols House, HGSE, Cambridge, MA 02138.

Pizzolato, J. E. (2003). Developing self-authorship: Exploring the experiences of high-risk college students. *Journal of College Student Development, 44*(6), 797–812.

Pizzolato, J. E. (2007). Assessing self-authorship. In P. S. Meszaros (Ed.), *Self-Authorship: Advancing students' intellectual growth, New Directions for Teaching and Learning* (Vol. 109, pp. 31–42). San Francisco: Jossey-Bass.

Questionnaire Items Used to Measure the Dimensions of Self-Authorship, by Phase

PHASE (Item #)	INTRAPERSONAL DIMENSION
External Formulas	1. My primary role in making an educational decision . . . is to acquire as much information as possible.
	2. My primary role in making an educational decision . . . is to seek direction from informed experts.
Crossroads	4. My primary role in making an educational decision . . . is to consider my own views.
Self-Authorship	3. My primary role in making an educational decision . . . is to make a decision considering all the available information and my own views.

PHASE (Item #)	INTERPERSONAL DIMENSIONS
External Formulas	13. The most important role of an effective career counselor or advisor is to be an expert on a variety of career options.
	14. The most important role of an effective career counselor or advisor is to provide guidance about a choice that is appropriate to me.
Crossroads	8. If a teacher or advisor recommended a career in a field that I have never considered before, I would explain my point of view.
	15. The most important role of an effective career counselor or advisor is to help students think through multiple options.
Self-Authorship	6. If a teacher or advisor recommended a career in a field that I have never heard of before, I would try to understand their point of view and figure out an option that best fits my needs and interests.

16. In my opinion, the most important role of an effective counselor or advisor is to provide students information that will help them to make a decision on their own.

PHASE (Item #)	EPISTEMOLOGICAL DIMENSION

External Formulas

9. To make a good career choice about a career, I think that facts are the strongest basis for a good decision.

11. To make a good career choice about a career, I think that experts are in the best position to advise me about a good choice.

Crossroads

10. To make a good career choice about a career, I think that it is largely a matter of personal opinion.

22. When people have different interpretations of a book, I think that some books are just that way. It is possible for all interpretations to be correct.

Self-Authorship

12. To make a good choice about a career, it is not a matter of facts or judgment, but a match between my values, interests, and skills and those of a job.

24. When people have different interpretations of a book, I think that multiple interpretations are possible, but some are closer to the truth than others.

26. Experts are divided on some scientific issues, such as the causes of global warming. In a situation like this, I would have to look at the evidence and come to my own conclusion.

27. Experts are divided on some scientific issues, such as the causes of global warming. In a situation like this, I think it is best to accept the uncertainty and try to understand the principal arguments behind the different points of view.

CONTRIBUTORS

Marcia B. Baxter Magolda is distinguished professor of educational leadership at Miami University of Ohio. She is author or co-editor of eight books, three of which are based on her 22-year longitudinal study of self-authorship, and over 50 articles and chapters on the evolution of self-authorship and pedagogy to promote self-authorship. She is a co-principal investigator in the Wabash National Study of Liberal Arts Education. She has received numerous awards including the Association for the Study of Higher Education Research Achievement Award in 2007.

Jennifer Garvey Berger is chief researcher and manager of organisational learning at the New Zealand Council for Educational Research and a partner in the leadership development consultancy Kenning Associates. Before moving to New Zealand, Jennifer was an associate professor in the Graduate School of Education's Initiatives in Educational Transformation (IET) Program at George Mason University. Her research in both countries focuses on understanding the ways adults learn and grow over time and on giving voice to that journey. In her writing and her teaching, Jennifer explores the workplace as one of the major centers of learning for adults, and she uses her work to help adults think about their work and their workplaces in ways that help them gain new perspectives and capacities to make positive changes in their classrooms and offices. Jennifer's current work centers around the Subject-Object Interview, a measure of Robert Kegan's theory of adult development, which she has taught to researchers and practitioners from North America, Europe, Asia, Australia, and New Zealand.

Donna Berthelson is a senior lecturer in educational and developmental psychology in the School of Early Childhood at Queensland University of Technology. In addition to her work with Brownlee, she is involved in longitudinal research on family and school influences on children's development.

Lisa Boes is a Research Officer at the Derek Bok Center for Teaching and Learning, working with graduate students to improve their teaching and helping design assessments of student learning. As the resident dean of Pforzheimer House at Harvard College, she has an opportunity to explore her interest in the college student development and the connection between classroom pedagogies and purposefully designed out-of class learning experiences.

Gillian Boulton-Lewis, professor emeritus, is an adjunct professor in the School of Design at the Queensland University of Technology. Her research interests are in learning and its implications for education across the lifespan. Her recent research involvement is focused on moral development in early childhood and sustainable learning communities for seniors.

Joanne Brownlee is a senior lecturer in the School of Early Childhood at Queensland University of Technology in Brisbane, Australia. Her research investigates early childhood professionals' personal epistemology and the impact of such beliefs on early childhood practice. She is extending her research to child care center directors and how leadership styles are impacted by epistemological beliefs.

Jennifer Buckley works in the National Survey of Student Engagement center at Indiana University. She worked for nine years in the Residence Life area at UNLV, where they revised their division based on the Learning Partnerships Model.

Elizabeth G. Creamer is professor of educational research and evaluation in the School of Education at Virginia Tech. She is co-principal investigator of the Women and Information Technology project funded by the National Science Foundation, principal investigator of a grant to investigate climate in undergraduate engineering programs, and director of research and assessment for VTAdvance, another project funded by the National Science Foundation. She also teaches courses in qualitative research. She is the author or co-author of three books and 45 refereed journal articles and scholarly book chapters.

Rebecca Hamer is research coordinator for Platform Science and Technology in the Netherlands. Formerly a RAND Europe senior policy analyst, she has extensive experience as a researcher and has published in a variety of areas, including education, health, and transport. She is well versed in quantitative and qualitative methodology and in combining methods from various disciplines, encouraging innovative approaches in the Platform's research agenda. Currently she is concluding her joint doctoral thesis (co-authored with Erik Jan van Rossum) linking European research on learning and teaching conceptions to the developmental epistemological tradition represented by Baxter Magolda and Kegan.

Barbara Hofer is an associate professor at Middlebury College specializing in educational, developmental, and cultural psychology. Her research focuses on the development of personal epistemology and how it interacts with learning strategies, motivation, cognition, and academic performance. She has also worked on cross-national studies of academic achievement and schooling, and is interested in the interrelationship of mind and culture.

Susan Robb Jones is an associate professor in counseling and personnel services at the University of Maryland. Much of her research and publications have been in the areas of identity development, meaning-making, and community service participation.

Patricia M. King is a professor of higher education in the School of Education at the University of Michigan. Her teaching and research focus on learning and development among late adolescents and adults, including college students. She has written two books and published more than 50 articles, and is currently principal investigator of the University of Michigan team of the National Study of Liberal Arts Education sponsored by the Center of Inquiry in the Liberal Arts at Wabash College.

Crystal Duncan Lane is a doctoral student in human development and graduate research assistant in the Center for Information Technology Impacts on Children, Youth, and Families within the College of Liberal Arts and Human Sciences at Virginia Tech. She earned a bachelors degree in human development and psychology from Virginia Tech, and a masters degree in marriage and family therapy from East Carolina University, where she also completed a post-master's fellowship in interdisciplinary rural health at the Brody School of Medicine. Crystal has been a Certified Family Life Educator (CFLE) with the National Council on Family Relations since 2001.

Peggy S. Meszaros is the William E. Lavery professor of human development and director of the Center for Information Technology Impacts on Children, Youth, and Families at Virginia Tech. She is principal investigator on a National Science Foundation grant using self-authorship and the learning partnership model, has extensive teaching, research, and administrative experience, including middle school and high school teaching of science, and has been a faculty member and administrator for 28 years at private and public higher education research institutions. She has published over 80 scholarly articles and book chapters and edited a recent New Directions monograph on self-authorship.

Jane Elizabeth Pizzolato is assistant professor of higher education and organizational change at the University of California, Los Angeles. An educational psychologist by training, her research focuses on examining cultural influences on self-authorship and epistemological development, particularly as they relate to academic achievement during the high school and early college years.

Vasti Torres is associate professor of higher education and student affairs administration in the School of Education at Indiana University. She teaches courses in student affairs administration, student development theory, and research in higher education. Her research focuses on how the ethnic identity of Latino students influences their college experience. She was the principle investigator for a multi-year grant investigating the choice to stay in college for Latino students. She is active in several student affairs and higher education associations. During 2007–2008, she served as the first Latina president of a national student affairs association, ACPA. Dr. Torres holds a Ph.D. in counseling and student affairs administration from the University of Georgia.

Erik Jan van Rossum teaches qualitative methodology at Twente University in the Netherlands. His interest in epistemology and students' conceptions of learning in higher education began in 1980, and he has authored over 30 articles on conceptions of learning and teaching. Currently he is concluding a joint doctoral thesis (co-authored with Rebecca Hamer) in which he reconciles the European school of thought of phenomenography and learning conceptions with major U.S.-based epistemological approaches and Kegan's concept of self-authorship. He plans to pursue qualitative research on conceptions of wisdom and higher orders of consciousness.

Michael Weinstock is a lecturer in the Department of Education at Ben-Gurion University of the Negev, Beer-Sheva, Israel. His research focuses on folk epistemology, epistemology in the disciplines, and various aspects of argument, such as argument skills, the use of evidence and explanation in argument, and the identification of informal reasoning fallacies.

Kelli Zaytoun is director of women's studies and associate professor of English at Wright State University in Dayton, Ohio. Her recent scholarship links identity and cultural issues to philosophical and psychological approaches to self-concept, cognition, and social consciousness. She is the author of multiple essays on development.

green
press
INITIATIVE

Also available from Stylus

Journal Keeping
How to Use Reflective Writing for Learning, Teaching, Professional
Insight and Positive Change
Dannelle Stevens and Joanne E. Cooper

"A superb tool for educators who want to be reflective practitioners, and help their students become reflective learners. I hope this fine book will be widely read and used."

—*Parker J. Palmer*
(author of *The Courage to Teach, Let Your Life Speak,*
and *A Hidden Wholeness*)

"This book describes a practical strategy for promoting learning and thinking, artfully grounded in adult development and learning theory. They offer multiple possibilities for readers to use journaling for personal growth, fostering their own and others' learning, and managing professional life."

—*Marcia B. Baxter Magolda*

Learning Partnerships
Theory and Models of Practice to Educate for Self-Authorship
Edited by Marcia B. Baxter Magolda and Patricia M. King

"Those interested in strengthening the ties between theory and practice and between faculty and student affairs can find inspiration here. Those committed to developing the co-curriculum to promote self-authorship will have a better sense of how to do that from this book. With this volume, Baxter Magolda and King continue to make significant contributions."

—*Journal of College Student Development*

Making Their Own Way
Narratives for Transforming Higher Education to Promote
Self-Development
Marcia B. Baxter Magolda

"...provides long-awaited answers to critical questions regarding how college impacts students' lives. Through an accomplished interview technique, the author provides us with an inside tour of the lives and minds of hundreds of college graduates. The longitudinal design allows us to comprehend more fully the lifelong impact of higher education. The author weaves these stories into a highly usable framework for educational improvement."

—*AAHE Bulletin*

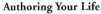

Authoring Your Life

Developing an Internal Voice to Navigate Life's Challenges

Marcia B. Baxter Magolda

Foreword by Sharon Daloz Parks

"No one has carried the concept of 'self-authorship' forward more richly, or with greater use for the reader, than Marcia Baxter Magolda. Anyone interested in supporting their own, or others', adult development will benefit enormously from this book."

—*Robert Kegan*,
Meehan Professor of Adult Learning, Harvard University,
and co-author of *Immunity to Change*

"Offers a timely, crucial map of possibilities for helping ourselves and others to grow and to meet the implicit and explicit demands of post-modern life. By sharing real life experiences from courageous adults, and how they made sense of and navigated their way through them, she illuminates the internal landscape of personal growth as a developmental process. This book, informed by constructive-developmental theory, will enable us to nurture adult development."

—*Ellie Drago-Severson*,
Associate Professor of Education Leadership, Teachers College, Columbia University,
and author of *Helping Teachers Learn*, and *Leading Adult Learning*

"The stories take you inside the stress of the kinds of real dilemmas and dramas that are similar to your own, and can serve as a flashlight—illumining your own path as they shine light on familiar feelings and boost your courage. This book matters for all of us."

—*Sharon Daloz Parks*,
author of *Big Questions, Worthy Dreams:
Mentoring Young Adults in Their Search for Meaning, Purpose and Faith*,
and *Leadership Can Be Taught: A Bold Approach for a Complex World*

For scholars, this book includes the latest articulation of the author's theory of self-authorship. It is also suitable as a first-year experience / freshman seminar text.

22883 Quicksilver Drive
Sterling, VA 20166-2102

Subscribe to our e-mail alerts: www.Styluspub.com